# China Currents
# 2021 Special Edition

# China Currents
# 2021 Special Edition

*Penelope B. Prime and James R. Schiffman, Editors*

*China Research Center, Atlanta, Georgia*
*www.chinacenter.net*

*Sponsored by the School of History and Sociology*
*and the Ivan Allen College of Liberal Arts*
*at the Georgia Institute of Technology*

*Cover design: Vanessa F. Garver*

For electronic browsing and ordering of this, and other China Research Center titles, visit www.chinacenter.net

For more information, please contact:
China Research Center
Atlanta, Georgia
info@chinacenter.net

*China Currents: 2021 Special Edition*
Penelope B. Prime and James R. Schiffman, Editors

ISBN: 978-0-9826415-8-3

Published in the United States by China Research Center

Design and Production: Carbon Press, Inc.
Manufactured in the United States of America

First Edition

# Contents

## *Special Issue: Vol. 19, No. 2, 2020: COVID-19*

## *Special Issue: Vol. 18, No. 1, 2019: The CCP 19th Party Congress*

## *Politics and International Relations*

# Preface

Economic reform and development in China and China's rising role in global affairs are reshaping the global system in the 21st century and fueling an unprecedented social transition within China itself. China Currents is a forum for thoughtful, concise articles analyzing society in contemporary China, published by the China Research Center at ChinaCurrents.com. This printed Special Edition includes selections organized by topics from issues Vol.17, No.1 (2018) through Vol.19, No.1 (2020).

The Center would like to gratefully acknowledge financial support from our institutional sponsor, the School of History and Sociology of the Ivan Allen College of Liberal Arts at the Georgia Institute of Technology. Beginning in 2017, the Center is based at Georgia Tech and is directed by Dr. Hanchao Lu, Professor of History.

We would also like to thank East West Manufacturing and Project Success, Inc. for their support as Gold sponsors. Our dedicated editorial team includes Dan Williams, Stephen Herschler, Clifton Pannell, Shu-chin Wu, and Lisa Guthrie. The views expressed in these articles are those of the authors.

Founded in 2001, the China Research Center is dedicated to promoting understanding of greater China based on research and experience and to working collaboratively on events and projects with the public and private sectors. The Center draws much if its expertise from educational and service institutions around the southeast U.S., including Agnes Scott College, The Carter Center, Dalton State

University, Emory University, Georgia College & State University, Georgia Institute of Technology, Georgia State University, Kennesaw State University, Mercer University, Oglethorpe University and the University of Georgia. The Center is also a founding member of the International Consortium for China Studies based at the National School of Development, Peking University.

The associates of the Center believe that favorable U.S.-China relations are crucial for promoting economic development in the U.S. and greater China and peace in the region. One of the foundations of favorable relations is mutual understanding based on knowledge and open communication. The associates specialize in the study of a wide variety of aspects of Chinese society, including language, culture, history, politics, economics, business, society, international relations, demographics, geography, and the environment. The Center's goal is to make knowledge and expertise available to a wide variety of constituents within and beyond our academic communities, as well as to enhance our academic work via cross-disciplinary and cross-institutional collaboration.

*Penelope B. Prime, Ph.D.*
*James R. Schiffman, Ph.D.*
*October 2020*

## Decoupling between the U.S. and China May be as Disruptive as COVID-19

*Yawei Liu*
*Vol. 19, No.2*
*2019*

In an interview with Fox Business News on May 14, U.S. President Donald Trump said, "There are many things we could do (to China). We could cut off the whole relationship." He went on to say, "Now, if you did, what would happen? You'd save $500 billion if you cut off the whole relationship." When asked about Chinese President Xi Jinping, Trump said he has "a very good relationship" but "right now I just don't want to speak to him." Since coming to office in 2017, President Trump has done more than all the presidents since Jimmy Carter combined to damage U.S.-China relations. Unpredictable as he has been, President Trump has never before publicly entertained the idea of cutting off the whole relationship with China. The president's supporters often say that Mr. Trump should be taken seriously but not literally. But even if talk of severing the relationship is Trumpian hyperbole, there is no doubt that a growing consensus has emerged – not just in the White House – that a tougher line toward China must be taken. Therefore, it is instructive to examine what might happen if the largest economy in the world cuts itself off from the second largest economy.

What would the world confront if China quits collaborating with other leading nations in responding to pandemics like COVID-19, climate change, and nuclear proliferation? The West could afford to isolate China for 30 years from 1949 to 1978 when it was militarily weak, ideologically xenophobic, and economically irrelevant. As powerful as China is now, cutting it off from the U.S. and pushing it out of the global community would be troubling if not dangerous. The question is what has driven the administration to publicly talk about taking this drastic measure?

## Where the bilateral relationship is now?

The relationship between the U.S. and China was at a historic low due to trade, high tech, and other issues when COVID-19 broke out in Wuhan, China, in late 2019 and early 2020. It might have been a great opportunity for Beijing and Washington to switch gears and find new ground to cooperate.

Unfortunately, leaders in both nations failed to seize the moment. The notorious "decouplers" close to the White House – represented by Peter Navarro, a trade adviser to Trump, and Michael Pillsbury, a China watcher favored by Trump – saw the outbreak as a golden opportunity to increase the pace of disconnecting with China. Other administration officials chimed in. Secretary of Commerce Wilbur Ross declared it would create momentum for the U.S. manufacturing sector to bring jobs from China back to the U.S. Secretary of State Mike Pompeo used a domestic and international lecture tour to castigate China for attacking American democracy, stealing American intellectual property, using debt to entrap developing countries, and applying coercive diplomacy to its neighbors. The State Department began to treat Chinese media outlets in the U.S. as hostile entities and later sharply reduced the number of their employees in the country.

When Wuhan locked down, the U.S. offered no official moral or material support. On the contrary, it sent a high-caliber delegation to Germany to lobby allies and others at the Munich Security Conference against using Huawei technologies or products. The U.S. Navy continued to conduct freedom of navigation patrols in the South China Sea. The USS McCampbell (DDG 85), a guided-missile destroyer, passed through the Taiwan Strait on March 25, something an American ship has not done since the Cross-Strait crisis in 1996 before Taiwan's first direct presidential election. A Wall Street Journal op-ed entitled "China, the Real Sick Man of Asia" seemed to crystalize the American reaction to China's suffering and touched a raw nerve in China's national psyche. Even worse, on March 26 President Trump signed the TAIPEI Act into law, the third act passed by Congress since 2017 that was designed to change the status quo in the Cross-Strait relations.

China has responded tit for tat to the perceived American slight and humiliation. It lashed out at the U.S. for being one of the first nations to ban Chinese citizens from entering the country. It expelled several Wall Street Journal reporters after the aforementioned op-ed was published. It then sent other American reporters packing. It refused a proposed shipment of personal protective equipment organized by the USAID in early March when the COVID-19 situation came under control in Wuhan. The Chinese ambassador to the U.S. began to complain that the political virus was as destructive as the coronavirus. In mid-March, when the outbreak began to spread in the U.S. and the American death toll began rising, Zhao Lijian, China's newly appointed Foreign Ministry spokesman, declared an information war on the U.S. via Twitter. He wondered whether the U.S. military brought the virus to Wuhan during the World Military Games in October 2019 and demanded that the U.S. identify its own patient zero.

In response to Zhao's provocative tweets, U.S. leaders began to use either "Chinese virus" or "Wuhan virus" when referring to COVID-19. Secretary Pompeo's insistence on using the term made it impossible for the G-7 Summit to issue a communique after an online consultation. Bilateral insults escalated until President Donald Trump and President Xi Jinping talked over the phone on March 26. A temporary truce was violated toward the end of April when President Trump decided to withhold payment to the World Health Organization (WHO) because of its alleged China-centric behavior.

Soon after, the administration began to talk about holding China accountable for the disastrous spread of COVID-19 in America and elsewhere. U.S. intelligence agencies were ordered to seek evidence about whether the virus came out of a lab in Wuhan. Members of Congress accused China of concealing the outbreak and hoarding PPE. American allies have joined the chorus. Lawsuits against China were filed in the U.S. and ways to punish China became a daily discussion point during the White House coronavirus task force briefings. A GOP campaign strategy paper was leaked, revealing advice to all GOP candidates to blame China for America's lack of effective response to COVID-19. More recently, Kevin McCarthy, Republican leader in the House of Representatives, formed a China task force with a mission to investigate China's malign global activities. The Democrats in the House backed out of the task force because, in the words of Speaker Nancy Pelosi, the GOP's fanatic effort to tie China to the failure of the administration to contain the virus effectively was an "interesting diversion." Pelosi said Democrats would not provide justification for such scapegoating.

Then, a second truce appeared to be on the horizon. On May 4, Deputy National Security Adviser Matthew Pottinger told participants at a forum on U.S.-China relations held virtually at the University of Virginia that the U.S. would not seek punitive measures against China during the COVID-19 crisis. Interestingly his wife, Yen Pottinger, a virologist who used to work at the CDC on AIDS and TB, spoke at the same conference on the prospect of U.S.-China cooperation during the pandemic. Three days later, China's top trade negotiator, Vice Premier Liu He, had a conference call with U.S. Trade Representative Robert Ligthizer and Treasury Secretary Steven Mnuchin. Both sides pledged to honor the first phase trade agreement hammered out earlier and emphasized the importance of U.S.-China cooperation during the pandemic. The positive turn in early May seemed to have collapsed by the middle of the month when China signaled that Beijing could scrap the trade deal due to America's senseless pursuit of reparations from China for COVID-19 deaths and when Trump threatened to cut off all relations with China.

Forty-one years after the normalization of relations between the U.S. and China, one of the most consequential anchors for global peace and prosperity is now facing the prospect of a grand decoupling. If allowed to continue unchecked, the world will likely face a grave period of political uncertainty, economic disruption, and security vulnerability unseen in recent history. Although Chinese leaders have never openly challenged American supremacy and have always called for a win-win relationship with the U.S., Chinese media's narrow focus on American failures in responding to the pandemic and sharp attacks on the American attempts to hold China accountable for the global spread of the coronavirus have presented a dastardly picture of the U.S. At the same time, ordinary Americans, who usually do not pay much attention to Chinese affairs, have been exposed to the vicious criticism of China. This mutual antagonism can only serve to drive the two nations further apart.

## Could the U.S. and China still cooperate during the pandemic?

It is never too late for the two most consequential powers on earth to cooperate during the pandemic. In fact, the epic endeavor to contain the virus will face much more difficult prospects if the U.S. and China refuse to work together. Leaders in both countries during their phone calls have expressed their willingness to cooperate in fighting COVID-19. But what happens daily seems to indicate that mutual distrust is so deep that neither side is ready to enter into an effective partnership.

According to the Chinese Foreign Ministry, from March 1 to May 5, China supplied the U.S. with 6.6 billion masks, 344 million surgical gloves, 44 million protective garments, 6.75 million goggles, and 7,500 ventilators. Yet, the U.S. keeps talking about reducing the American dependence on China for pharmaceutical products and PPE, and allege PPE made in China are shoddy in quality. American officials constantly accuse the Chinese government of concealing the outbreak, but no one has publicly acknowledged that, as the New York Times reported, Dr. George Gao, director of the Chinese CDC called Dr. Robert Redfield, his counterpart in the U.S. CDC, during the New Year break and alerted him to the outbreak in Wuhan. In fact, by late February, according to the Chinese Foreign Ministry, there were more than 30 such communications from China to the U.S. But months into the crisis, it seems that no one in either capital is focusing on a crucial need: that the U.S. and China must work together during this pandemic to return to any semblance of normalcy. How could the U.S and China coordinate, cooperate and collaborate in containing the virus?

First, official communication could be ramped up. China was ahead of every country in dealing with this brutal and pernicious virus. It has a lot of experience to share with the U.S. in treatment, methodology, drug application, and reopening. Professional staff from U.S. CDC and Chinese CDC are believed to be holding regular meetings on the outbreak and containment. NGOs, university entities, and research institutions in both countries have been conducting regular, small-scale online information sharing sessions. But there is no official organization of any of these activities. During the Obama Administration, there were close to 100 mechanisms of dialogue between agencies of the two governments. At this critical time when bilateral cooperation is most needed, communication at the top level of the country and central government agencies is reduced to a couple of phone calls. There is almost zero inter-governmental consultation between the U.S. and China. This is a shame and should be corrected.

Second, considering where African, Latin American, and other developing regions are in their fight against COVID-19, it is crucial for the U.S. and China to work together to provide leadership, expertise, and assistance. No country will be safe if any other country has failed to contain the virus. As Ethiopian Prime Minister Abiy Ahmed noted in an op-ed in the Financial Times on March 25, "Momentary victory by a rich country in controlling the virus at a national level, coupled with travel bans and border closures, may give a semblance of accomplishment. But we all know this is a stopgap. Only global victory can bring this pandemic to an end." No global victory could be declared if the U.S. and China refuse to enter into a partnership to work with developing countries to stop the virus. The two countries cooperated closely in stopping Ebola in West Africa in 2014-2016 and they need to do this again. In Africa exiting models for coordinating assistance around disease prevention show promise as models for U.S.-China coordination around COVID-19. U.S. PEPFAR (President Emergency Plan for AIDS Relief) was instrumental in building African health capacity and infrastructure to fight against HIV/AIDS and other diseases, while Chinese medical teams have provided medical assistance and support in almost all African nations. The ongoing efforts of the African CDC—through support by the U.S, China, and other countries—has allowed member states to continue preparing for this new threat. Closer U.S.-China cooperation in Africa could turn the possible weakest link in the global defense against COVID-19 into a much stronger line of containment.

Third, both countries should and must work together in testing, producing, and eventually distributing a coronavirus vaccine. The virus will stop mankind from working and living normally absent an effective vaccine that is available to everyone in the world. The U.S., China, and other developed countries have engaged in a race to produce a viable vaccine, but as of now, there is no active cooperation between China and the West. China must be criticized for not providing a live virus sample to the U.S in the early stages of the outbreak, but blaming

China for trying to steal Western secrets related to the vaccine without any hard evidence will simply prevent indispensable multilateral cooperation. Vaccines are not computer chips, and all involved need to pool their knowledge and share information. The U.S and China must take the lead in coordinating this scientific race against the constantly mutating virus.

**Where will the Sino-American relationship be after the pandemic?**

U.S.-China decoupling is not a matter of if but a question of how serious it is and where it is happening. According to the U.S.-China Investment Report released by the National Committee on U.S.-China Relations and the Rhodium group on May 9, Chinese FDI to the U.S. in 2019 was almost zero. An order from U.S. Department of Commerce on May 15 bars any company in the world that uses American machinery and software from supplying Huawei. Four U.S. senators wrote to President Trump and asked him to suspend a program that enables international students to stay in the U.S. for up to two years after graduation. The largest body of international students in the U.S. comes from China. The U.S. has stipulated that visas for Chinese media workers will be restricted to 90 days. Measures aimed at decoupling are taken daily by the Trump Administration.

This may be why Chinese Foreign Ministry spokesman Zhao Lijian expressed no surprise and showed no sign of nervousness when asked to comment on President Trump's May 14 declaration that he is considering cutting off the relationship with China. Zhao's response was: "A steady and growing China-U.S. relationship serves the fundamental interests of the two peoples and is conducive to world peace and stability. At present, China and the U.S. should strengthen cooperation to prevail over the pandemic at an early date, and focus on saving lives, and resuming economic development and production. This, of course, calls for the U.S. and China working together towards the same goal."

Compared to what official Chinese media outlets have heaped on Secretary of State Mike Pompeo and adviser Matthew Pottinger, this response is shockingly tame but also utterly terrifying. The China Institutes of Contemporary International Relations, a think tank affiliated with China's Ministry of State Security, recently issued a report indicating that the U.S.-China relationship is at its lowest point since 1989 and that armed confrontation is not inconceivable. Hu Xijin, the outspoken editor in chief of the Global Times, has called the Chinese government to expand its nuclear arsenal arguing, "We are facing an increasingly irrational U.S., which only believes in strength." Wang Haiyun, a retired major general, demanded the Chinese government dig out and punish "those traitors who have been bought out by the United States and do its bidding." Others argue there is no need to react to the lunacy of the American administration. China simply needs to prepare for the worst. According to this line of thinking, the U.S. is deciding to decouple when it has the least in its toolbox. Time will be on China's side. Cui Tiankai, the longest serving Chinese ambassador to the U.S., recently told a reporter that he does not care if the bilateral relationship does not return to where it was before the pandemic. He only cares about looking forward to a better and brighter framework of U.S.-China interaction. One Peking University professor told this author, "Not too long from now, there will be a raging debate in the U.S. on who has lost China, similar to the same debate that was launched in 1949."

American aggressiveness and recklessness in decoupling and China's response, characterized by a sense of resignation, seemingly well-planned preparedness and determination at playing the long game, all point to a bleaker prospect for the bilateral relationship. Businesses, academic and research institutions, NGOs, and ordinary people on both sides of the ocean should fasten their seat belts and be ready for a bumpy ride in the coming months, if not years. The bilateral breakup may be as disruptive as COVID-19.

## How will U.S.-China rivalry change the landscape of global well-being?

Neither China nor the U.S. has fared well in its response to the pandemic. China's initial effort to stifle the doctors and conceal the outbreak has proven costly and counterproductive. It is wrong and misleading to assume China will replace the U.S. and become dominant in world affairs. The U.S., after being alerted by China at least three weeks before the virus invaded the homeland, was ill-prepared and has been ineffective in containment, even months after declaring a national emergency. The mediocre, if not incompetent, performance of the U.S. government has disappointed and will continue to disillusion people from all over the world – people who used to believe in America's supreme national will to respond to crises big and small, enviable resources, and dominating advances in biomedical research. As a result, the debate on which system of governance is more effective in alleviating national suffering and protecting people's lives will continue inside and outside the two countries. But whatever edge China has gained in effectively containing the virus in a relatively short period of time has been compromised by its refusal to acknowledge initial deficiencies and to allow international experts to investigate the origins of the virus in Wuhan.

The ramifications for the U.S. and China are serious. Countries around the world will be asking two essential questions: First, can China be trusted, given how it mishandled the outbreak initially? Second, can the U.S. be relied upon, considering how it has bungled the fight to contain the virus? China's reluctance to make all information related to the virus available to the world and its own people makes it difficult for other countries to have confidence in it. The lackluster American response and its unilateralism in making decisions that will impact the world make other countries doubt its commitment to international responsibility in addressing future challenges. These uncertainties could lead to an era of shaky alliances and new partnerships. It is possible that the EU or another existing or newly created power bloc could seize global leadership.

The international system will face unprecedented challenges as long as the U.S. and China engage in zero-sum rivalry. The U.S. and other Western countries are determined to investigate whether WHO was involved in any "wrongdoing" in alerting the world about the outbreak in China in a timely and unbiased manner. If hard evidence emerges that points to China exercising undue influence on WHO for self-serving purposes, one potential consequence could be an exodus of the U.S. and its followers from the organization. Would a parallel but competitive WHO be created? Would WHO's parent organization, the U.N., face the same challenge? Secretary Pompeo recently said that the U.S. may never return to the WHO. The U.S. has already withdrawn from UNESCO and the U.N. Human Rights Commission.

The possibility of China setting up a new international order bent on serving its own interests is remote. It will either leave the international system or stay put and call for reforms. The unity of the U.S.-led international system, if it still exists after the pandemic, may lead to two possible outcomes. First, as a new kid on the block, China could become a more mature and responsible stakeholder in the international community. But if China is again infected by the victimization mentality, it could decide to shut down its long-running reform and opening up. The second outcome, which is not impossible, would be bad for China, for the U.S., and for the world. It would make the international system more vulnerable and responses to global challenges chaotic, sporadic, and ineffectual.

In conclusion, the post-pandemic world likely will be an era of deep uncertainty characterized by an escalating rivalry between the U.S. and China. A Sino-U.S. economic and financial disconnection could lead to another arms race and a disastrous global economic downturn. Challenges to the international order and institutions would be more severe as both Beijing and Washington ramp up pressure. Countries, particularly developing ones, would be forced to choose sides, leading to possible realignment of the international community unseen since the end of the Cold War. Finally, as U.S. and China both attempt to restore reputations tainted by their responses to the pandemic, numerous new power centers could emerge to either stabilize the situation and restore sanity to the management of international affairs or create even more uncertainty and disruption.

---

*Dr. Yawei Liu is the Director of the China Program at The Carter Center in Atlanta, Georgia, and Associate Director of the China Research Center.*

*Special Issue: Vol.19, No.2, 2020: COVID-19*

# Chinese Economy amid COVID-19 Pandemic:
# Prospects and Policies

*Xuepeng Liu*
*Vol. 19, No.2*
*2020*

The COVID-19 pandemic has done more than cause the Chinese economy to contract. It also raised the real possibility of China decoupling economically from other parts of the world and dealt a blow to the China model of development. But there are steps China can take to ease if not prevent the worst effects of the coronavirus emergency.

According to the National Bureau of Statistics of China, Chinese GDP in the first quarter of 2020 declined by 6.8 percent from a year ago as the country battled coronavirus through large-scale shutdowns and quarantines to limit human interactions. This is the first time China has reported a negative growth rate in the first quarter since 1992 – the first year China started to report quarterly GDP data. Manufacture production and fixed investment fell 10.2 percent and 16.1 percent respectively in the first quarter from a year ago. In services sectors, wholesale and retail sales fell 17.8 percent, while online sales of physical goods rose 5.9 percent because people bought more online during the lockdowns. The hardest hit is in the hotel and restaurant sector with a 35.3 percent decline. The consumer price index (CPI) increased by 4.9 percent in the first quarter.

The growth forecast for China and the world economy varies. The IMF projects an average five percent growth rate in the next two years (1.2 percent in 2020 and 9.2 percent in 2021), compared to a -3 percent growth globally in 2020.[1] The World Bank is more optimistic, projecting a 5.9 percent, 5.8 percent, and 5.7 percent rate respectively in 2020, 2021, and 2022 for China but a 2.5 percent growth rate for the whole world in 2020.[2] Given the importance of China as a manufacturing center in the world and its continued growth momentum, most estimates predict a faster growth in China than in the rest of the world in the near future.

Nevertheless, this pandemic has already posed a tremendous challenge to China and will continue to be so over a long time. Three key factors stand out. First, China faces different challenges in the short run as compared with the long run but is more comfortable with handing the immediate crisis than more difficult but needed structural changes. Second, China's economy will be hurt by potential decoupling from the global markets. And third, China's experience of pandemic control does not suggest that China's system at this point is a viable alternative to the Western democracies and market systems.

The recovery in the second quarter of 2020 will continue to face strong headwind. In the first quarter, production has always been a bit slower during the Chinese New Year holiday, so the effects of the lockdowns on production were muted relative to the effects on demand. In addition, despite the cancellation of some orders, many firms still had some previous orders to fulfill during the first quarter of 2020. The effect of the lack of new orders, especially international orders, will become more obvious starting from the second quarter, except for medical products. Therefore, the downturn in the economy during the rest of 2020 will likely continue. However, China has successfully joined global value chains in many industries and the rest of the world is highly dependent on China's supply of parts and components, as well as many assembled final products. So, it is unlikely for the rest of the world to decouple with China immediately. In the short term, the Chinese economy will continue to supply the world as a global factory and will likely to do better than the rest of the world.

In the long term, however, China will face more uncertainties depending on the severity of the COVID-19 pandemic. If the rest of the world enters a severe recession, this will hurt the Chinese economy which depends heavily on international markets. Even worse, if the rest of the world forms an alliance against China, attempting to decouple from China by diversifying their global value chains, this will be painful for the Chinese economy. Decoupling is very unlikely if only one country like the U.S. takes actions by erecting trade barriers or withdrawing investment from China because such an attempt will eventually fail if all of the companies in other countries, such as Germany, Japan, and Korea, can take advantage of the cheaper labor in China and compete against American firms globally. However, if major Western economies can jointly take collective actions against China, this will hurt China even if such actions are somewhat against economic principles and the trend of globalization. Even though every country will suffer in the short run, policy makers in the western countries may be able to justify such a decoupling from a dynamic perspective for long run gains at the cost of some short run losses to social welfare. The Chinese government should prepare for the worst scenario and handle this global crisis properly to avoid this.

Unless an effective vaccine is found, the COVID-19 will likely stay for a while. Countries may have to prepare to work around this virus. For China in particular as the most populous country, employment is a national priority. With the sharp declining demand domestically and internationally, it is no longer practical to maintain the previously set GDP growth goals. To ensure an economic recovery and avoid mass unemployment, however, a decent economic growth rate is still needed. To achieve these goals, a set of comprehensive and coherent policies should be in place.

In the short run, a country cannot resume all jobs immediately while the risk of contagion still exists. More effective policy to help those hit hard by the pandemic is probably fiscal stimulus such as direct money transfers to citizens or wage subsidies to firms. At the same time, proper measures should be taken to ensure safety when reopening the economy and extreme caution should be used to prevent systematic risks that may arise during the time with slow growth. This is especially important to China where people and policy makers have become accustomed to fast growth for decades. These risks include but are not limited to financial risks, public, corporate or individual debt crises, inflation, and political uncertainty. In the short run, the Keynesian type of counter-cycle policies can help to address this crisis.

However, these kinds of against-wind policies will not be a proper choice in the long run. Instead, China should continue to push forward structural changes and institutional reforms. Continued efforts should be made to deepen economic and political reform, which has lagged since Xi Jinping took power. On employment, China needs to pay special attention to rural migrant workers who usually travel long distances from home for work and were hit the hardest during the pandemic. A certain set of safety nets should be established to protect their jobs and health. Otherwise, this public health crisis can turn easily into a widespread social and economic crisis. Given the close ties of the Chinese economy with the world market, China should embrace candid and open-minded policies to rebuild the trust of the rest of the world. A large part of such trust has been lost in the recent several years, and especially so during this pandemic of COVID-19. The constitutional change to a lifetime presidency, increasing reliance on state-owned enterprises, tighter control of the government under Xi Jinping, and widespread nationalism are the true enemies of China.

Finally, what are the implications of this pandemic for the so-called "China model," which features a heavy hand from government? China took swift actions to lock down cities and quickly controlled the spread of the virus, which contrasts sharply to what happened in the rest of the world, especially the Western world with market economies and democratic political regimes. Many people hail the success of the China approach and some claim its overall superiority over Western systems. This is unfortunately a misperception and may have serious consequences.

The control of contagious disease is a classic example of an "externality" in economics and is often used to explain "market failures." Because the benefit of contagious disease control to an individual is far smaller than the benefit to the whole society, an individual tends to take less than optimal caution and measures to control its spread. In this case, government can help by forcing people to take vaccines, wear masks, or even tolerate locked downed cities. China's regime with a strong central government and previous experience with the SARS is well-suited to address these kinds of crises. The same logic works for other types of market failures, including but not limited to public good provision and other types of activities with externalities such as high-speed trains. It is not surprising to see China's success in these areas and indeed the Western world should learn from China to redesign policies to ensure quicker and more effective responses to these market failures or crises.

However, we cannot simply generalize it to all other areas where market and individual decisions should take control. Many decisions in society involve trade-offs, and no regime is perfect in all aspects. China's regime does have advantages in some areas over Western democracies, but the inadequate response to this pandemic in the Western countries alone is certainly not sufficient to justify its overall inferiority to China's regime.[3] Such an awareness can help China to deepen the reforms and handle international conflicts. For instance, although the more centralized regime of China does give some advantages to Chinese firms when competing against companies in the Western world, this is not sustainable as shown by the current trade war between the U.S. and China. To fully integrate into the world economy, China will have to embrace more market reforms and institutional changes to ease the tension with the Western market economies, rather than commanding even more control over the economy and society as the current regime under Xi Jinping is doing. China's economic miracle over the last several decades did not occur because there was more and more control from the government, but rather because of less and less control over time.

### Notes

1    *https://www.imf.org/en/Publications/WEO*

2    *https://www.worldbank.org/en/publication/global-economic-prospects*

3    *Besides the lack of central government directives, there are many other cultural, political and economic reasons to explain the relatively slow responses to the COVID-19 pandemic in the Western world. The Western world has its own problems to address. This is beyond the scope of this article, which focuses on China.*

*Dr. Xuepeng Liu is Professor of Economics, Kennesaw State University and an Associate of the China Research Center.*

*Special Issue: Vol.19, No.2, 2020: COVID-19*

# COVID-19 and Changes to the Global Supply Chain: Some Observations from China

*Björn Wahlström*
*Vol. 19, No.2*
*2020*

## Introduction

COVID-19 has proven to be a great disruptor. First it caused the national shutdown of China as factory after factory turned the lights off, sending Western firms scrambling for goods of all kinds. Next the disruption spread globally, causing a shutdown of consumer spending in the West, and sowing confusion on all sides of the supply chain.

As China factories resume operations, the risks to the global supply chain and opportunities for reducing those risks have become clear.

## Sourcing

The first phase of COVID-19 served as a wake-up call for Western firms that were overly dependent on China. As province after province and industry after industry shut down, it became clear that many Western firms could not manufacture their products without China, at least not in the quantities required. Supply sources that could easily be moved to other countries had mostly already relocated. Garments and consumer electronics were in this category. Supply chain directors faced the challenge of finding alternative suppliers of critical parts overnight, in the midst of a growing global health crisis. We saw clients trying to relocate assembly lines to places like Vietnam or Thailand, only to discover that factories in Southeast Asia also depended on parts from China. Indeed, factories in that region are mostly owned by Chinese entities.

Most companies were ultimately unable to move production, other than for small parts, at such short notice. The lesson for supply chain directors is to build in contingency planning for critical parts during calmer times. Many Western firms are now lining up other manufacturing countries for their products and components. Some are even bringing manufacturing back home, and Japan has announced a $2.2 billion expenditure on companies relocating out of China.[1] Companies with security-related products are first in line, including face mask manufacturers and potentially also other medical components.

## Quality

Another issue in the wake of COVID-19 is the lack of knowledge and control over the Chinese supply chain. As the crisis subsided in China and manufacturers were starting back up, we found that many factories were using alternate sub-suppliers for parts, often without informing their clients of the changes, and indeed without themselves understanding that they were changing specifications. On paper, replacement parts looked the same, but quality varied from the originals and indeed also varied within batches. The problem was compounded at this stage by the travel restrictions from the outside, as auditors were unable to visit factories themselves.

A further challenge for organizations of all sizes in many industries involves standardizing operations and processes. This is accomplished through initial alignment with international standards and then asking independent auditors to evaluate compliance and issue certifications. Yet, because operations continue after receipt of certifications, compliance often starts to slip – sometimes inviting high risks.

In these cases, we recommend a tried and true "trust but verify" method of due diligence to avoid losses and conflicts. It shouldn't be difficult to determine which of the certified processes maintained by a partner company is most important to your organization. Due diligence then can be a one-time assessment and applied continually through process oversight. It is best not to wait for slipups because those could be costly financially, operationally, and from a reputation perspective. The same goes for quality control in the supply chain. The more complicated and high-value your product is, the more scrutiny you should apply. This is especially necessary when third-party manufacturers are returning to normal production volumes after widespread shutdowns. This "return" will likely entail a lot of scrambling and cutting corners.

## Fraud

In the wake of COVID-19, the frequency of fraud and scams has gone up dramatically. The hook has mostly involved exploiting the general uncertainty in China.

Consider for example the so-called "CEO email" scam. This is when a finance person in an organization receives an email allegedly from their company's senior executive with urgent instructions to immediately transfer funds to an outside party to help complete a commercial deal.

Scammers in these cases rely on the lack of redundant controls (secondary approvers) over the release of funds to outside parties. We have seen multiple cases of companies losing significant sums of money without much hope for recovery. It is prudent, therefore, to look at the fine details of financial management and redundant approval processes of the organization with which you plan to (or already) do business. Several governments recently issued guidance to businesses in an effort to strengthen internal controls and avoid such scams. However, application is inconsistent, and losses continue. The fix is easy, but verification is necessary.

The current situation unfortunately means an increased risk of fraud: from price gouging and online scams to deliberate and unjustified interruption of agreed payments or delivery of supplies. One of the new vulnerabilities stems from remote work arrangements for millions of people supporting supply chains. As teams and individual employees remain physically separated, isolated decision-making and degradation of compliance with existing policies and procedures should be expected.

### Lessons

Make sure each manufacturer you're relying on is aware of your concerns, and that concerns are forwarded downstream. Ask to see material bills and material samples. Don't assume that suppliers are putting extra scrutiny on materials. Ask for estimated delivery times of key materials, and make sure you are aware of which regions your key materials are shipped from so you can try to verify independently how likely issues are to arise with a certain vendor. Please also make sure to direct questions not only to English-speaking representatives but also to top management of your vendors and suppliers in their native languages because that helps build trust and enhances collaboration in solving problems.

### Notes

1    *https://www.forbes.com/sites/kenrapoza/2020/04/10/kudlow-pay-the-moving-costs-of-american-companies-leaving-china/#64ed263f13c6*

---

*Björn Wahlström is the Managing Director of Current Consulting Group, a risk and supply chain consultancy headquartered in Hong Kong and active in China.*

*Special Issue: Vol.19, No.2, 2020: COVID-19*

## Public Health in China: Bull's Nose Ring or Tail?

*Zhuo (Adam) Chen*
*Vol. 19, No.2*
*2020*

Like a bull in a china shop, COVID-19 has shattered lives and wrecked economies worldwide. With millions of people in lockdowns, quarantines, or other forms of restrictions on mobility because of the ongoing COVID-19 pandemic, questions abound. Was the pandemic preventable? Who should be held responsible for the outbreak? How are we going to prevent the next pandemic? What was the source of the virus? It would take several doctoral dissertations to respond to all these questions in a manner that is not too cursory. I will, therefore, focus this essay on China's public health systems, including its evolution over time, its handling of the outbreak, and key lessons learned.

### China's Public Health Systems
*Public Health in Ancient China*

It is debatable whether ancient China and other early civilizations had a systematic way of dealing with public health issues. However, ancient Chinese did discover primitive forms of strategies used today for infectious disease containment, including vaccination, quarantine, and prevention (IOM, 2007). The origin of vaccination can be traced back to the practice of variolation (smearing of a skin tear of someone with smallpox to confer immunity) in 17th century China (The Immunisation Advisory Centre, 2016). Isolation and quarantine of leprosy patients had been conducted in China, with the first house for leprosy patients in China built in 1518 in Fujian. Early forms of community hygiene had been used in large populations centers in ancient China, including the clearing of sewage (Chinese Academy of Science, 2003).

Culture is also relevant to public health. It is widely known that traditional Chinese medicine has emphasized the importance of prevention. At times, China's social norms had improved the balance of nutrition and reduced the likelihood of epidemic gastrointestinal infections. Anecdotes suggested that Chinese laborers building the transcontinental railways in the U.S. were less likely to suffer from malnutrition and diarrhea because their diet included a mix of vegetables and meats, and they consumed little alcohol (PBS, Not dated).

### Dawn of Western Medicine and Public Health in China

The last century of the Qing Dynasty (1636–1912) witnessed the introduction of Western medicine. Peter Parker (伯驾1804–1888), a Yale-trained missionary and physician, founded the first-ever Western-style hospital in China, the Ophthalmic Hospital in Canton, on November 4, 1835 (Wikipedia, 2020a). The hospital later became the Second Affiliated Hospital of Sun Yat-sen University. In 1844, Dr. Divie Bethune McCartee (麦嘉缔) established the first successful Presbyterian Church (USA) mission station in mainland China in Ningbo, where he practiced medicine (Wikipedia, 2020b). The introduction of Western medicine accelerated in the last decade of the Qing Dynasty. In 1906, several religious groups banded together to establish Peking Union Medical College (PUMC) Hospital,[1] which from 1916 was supported by the China Medical Board. In 1910, missionaries from the UK, Canada, and the U.S. founded the West China Union University Medical College, and in 1914, Xiangya Medical College was founded by the Hunan Yuqun Society and the Yale-China Association (雅礼学会).

With the growing acceptance of Western medicine, the idea of modern public health gradually gained a foothold. In 1905, the Qing court established a police department with its very own hygiene unit (Du, 2014), marking the start of modern public health practices. Supported by the China Medical Board, PUMC created China's first academic department of public health, and actively promoted public health practice. PUMC collaborated with the Capital Police Department to create an Institute of Public Health on May 29, 1925. A major task of the institute was the training of public health nurses. In 1929, the Peking Municipal Government created possibly the first department of health by Chinese authorities. The pioneers of public health practices forged ahead while lamenting the lack of authority and funding. In 1934, health organizations in Peking started annual campaigns of vaccination against smallpox, cholera, diphtheria, scarlet fever, and typhus (Du, 2014). The war with Japan and the Chinese civil war ensued, hampering further development of public health. However, Chiang Kai Shek, leader of the Republic of China, promoted his signature New Life Movement during wartime. Hygiene was one of the pillars of the movement, sparking one of the earliest modern health education campaigns in China (Dirlik, 1975).

*Public Health in the People's Republic of China*

With Chiang's retreat to Taiwan and the establishment of the People's Republic of China in 1949, the role of the private sector in providing health care in China has subdued. China's then Ministry of Health, a responsible body for overseeing health care services and running of the country's health care network, soon began transforming private hospitals into public ones, including the PUMC Hospital. By the late 1960s, government-funded and -run hospitals fully took over health care services in China. In rural areas, barefoot doctors (赤脚医生) took responsibility for public health. They were considered a new cadre of community-level health workers that brought basic curative care, health education, and a continuous public health approach to large swaths of the rural population in China. Barefoot doctors managed a village-level cooperative medical scheme, which some considered a successful model in improving primary care in rural settings (Blumenthal & Hsiao, 2015).

Public health was a high priority for the nascent government of the People's Republic. Between 1950 and 1952, more than 512 million of China's then roughly 600 million people were vaccinated against smallpox. When the last patient recovered in 1961, smallpox was eradicated in China, 16 years before global eradication (Wang, 2019). Of note is that China declared the elimination of sexually transmitted diseases (STDs) by 1964 with the efforts spearheaded by George Hatem (马海德), a Maronite American who was the first foreigner naturalized as a Chinese citizen in the People's Republic. Dr. Hatem also served as a physician for Mao Zedong in Yan'an (Porter, 1997). Unfortunately, STDs reappeared in the 1980s with the liberalization of commerce and mobility and correspondent changes in social customs and sexual behaviors.

Indeed, as an unexpected consequence of China's economic liberalization and the privatization of agriculture, the rural health system started to collapse in the late 1970s and early 1980s. Recent efforts have been made to re-establish a system of "village doctors," who have again assumed responsibilities of public health.

China's primary health agency had been reorganized several times. The Ministry of Health (1949-2013) merged with the Family Planning Commission to form the National Health and Family Planning Commission (2013-2018), a not-so-subtle hint of the change in the long-standing "one-child" policy. The Commission took the much-shortened name of the National Health Commission in 2018.

China's health care reforms are relevant to public health as well. Several insurance and safety networks had been established for urban and rural residents, including a rural cooperative medical scheme and basic medical insurance for urban residents. These insurance schemes were merged (三保合一) and managed under the various levels of health care security agencies. One goal of the 2009 health care reform was to provide essential public health services to vulnerable populations.

**China's Lead Public Health Agency: The Chinese Center for Disease Control and Prevention**

The Chinese Center for Disease Control and Prevention (China CDC) became the principal national-level public health agency, but disease prevention in the People's Republic dates back to the Epidemic Prevention Stations (EPS) of the 1950s. In 1953, China modeled its health system on the Soviet Union's and established EPSs to contain and eliminate infectious diseases. By 1957, more than two-thirds of China's roughly 2,050 counties had an EPS. They vaccinated the population, with laudable achievements such as elimination of smallpox in 1960 and, to some extent, STDs by 1964 (Wang, 2019).

On December 23, 1983, then Ministry of Health created the China Center for Preventive Medicine, subsequently renamed the Chinese Academy of Preventive Medicine on January 19, 1986 (China CDC, 2018). In 2002, the Academy merged with several other institutes, including the Institute of Occupational Health and Institute for Health Education and formed the China CDC on January 23, 2002. (China CDC, 2012). As its name suggests, the China CDC considered the U.S. Centers for Disease Control and Prevention (U.S. CDC) a model for public health practice. The honor of the first provincial CDC in China earlier went to the Shanghai CDC, which was established in November 1998.

China CDC's mission is "to create a safe and healthy environment, maintain social stability, ensure national security, and promote the health of people through prevention and control of disease, injury, and disability." Under the auspices of China's National Health Commission, China CDC takes leadership in disease prevention and control and provides technical guidance and support for China's public health community. Shortly after China CDC's creation, it took on the task of dealing with the 2002-2003 outbreak of the Severe Acute Respiratory Syndrome (SARS).

China ramped up investments in infectious disease control after the SARS outbreak. To address the need for enhanced disease surveillance systems identified after the SARS outbreak, China launched a nationwide system in 2004 that is capable of reporting infectious disease and emerging public health events via the internet. By 2013 the system had more than 70,000 reporting units, including CDCs at different levels and incorporating most of the medical providers in China.

During the 2009 round of health care reform in China, there were proposals to enable China's CDC systems to take on the basic public health services. However, as the China CDC has been primarily a science and technical support agency, the plan did not materialize.

*China CDC vs. U.S. CDC*

COVID-19 has prompted numerous assessments of the public health systems across the world, including a comparison of the CDCs in China and the U.S. The following compares the two agencies in terms of workforce, budget, authority, and coordination with regional health authorities.

The China CDC is limited in terms of workforce with a total of 2,120 Full-time equivalents (FTEs) in 2016, compared with the 11,195 FTEs for its counterpart in the U.S., a figure that does not include several thousand of contractors (Frieden, 2020).[2] The Public Health Foundation put the U.S. government public health workforce at 403,323 in 2011, with county/city and state-level public health workers totaling 287,267 (University of Michigan/Center of Excellence in Public Health Workforce Studies, 2012). Meanwhile, statistics from the 2017 China Health Statistics Yearbook reported national, provincial, prefectural, and county CDC employees in China at about 193,000 FTEs.

Second, the U.S. CDC's budget dwarfs that of the China CDC. In 2019, The U.S. CDC had a budget of $11 billion, while the total budget of the National Health Commission (which includes China CDC and many other units) in 2019 was just over $3 billion.3

Third, the U.S. CDC is a federal agency with a legal mandate to quarantine patients who may pose risks to public health across national or state borders. The China CDC serves as one of the supporting technical institutes but the legal mandate to quarantine patients resides in governments at the county level or higher. Successful efforts in epidemic detection and control require the strong leadership of the national public health institute.

Fourth, China CDC does not have authority over provincial, prefectural, and county-level CDCs, as many observers have assumed. Being a supporting agency of the central government, China CDC provides technical guidance to local CDCs. A local CDC, however, usually reports to the local health commission, which has the final say on operations, including financing and personnel. The China CDC merely works with local health commissions and local CDCs when outbreaks occur. As China CDC does not have strong influence in funding or personnel decisions, its recommendations may be brushed off, and it may not be provided with full information.

This comparison probably is made at an inconvenient time because the U.S. CDC faced sharp criticisms for its handling of the COVID-19 pandemic (Abutaleb, Dawsey, Nakashima, & Greg, 2020). CDC's failure to produce an adequate test for COVID-19 was a black mark against the agency. An unintended implication is that more financial and human resources are not associated with better outcomes. However, I argue that the mediocre performance of the U.S. CDC this time resulted from a combination of misfortunes, political interference, and possibly lack of political influence. As one of the most renowned public health agencies, the U.S. CDC remains a model for public health agencies worldwide. I relegate an in-depth examination of the performance of the U.S. DC in containing COVID-19 to future analysis.

## COVID-19 and China's Public Health System

As of May 26, 2020, there were 5,304,772 cases worldwide of COVID-19 and 342,029 deaths (WHO, 2020). Recent estimates put R0, the number of people a contagious COVID-19 patient might infect if no intervention is involved, at 5.7 (Li et al., 2020; Sanche et al., 2020; Xu et al., 2020). Note that the number is an estimate, and the true R0 is unknown, possibly not to be known. However, the estimated R0 does indicate that COVID-19 is highly contagious. Transmission by asymptomatic or presymptomatic people and an incubation period ranging from two to 14 days pose a serious challenge to public health communities (Bai et al., 2020).

China's public health system faced initial vehement criticism for its presumed delay in detecting and communicating information about early cases of COVID-19. Early warning signs emerged in late December of 2019, but it took days for the China CDC to be informed. It was around this time that Dr. Wenliang Li, a doctor with the Central Hospital of Wuhan, posted an online message warning about the outbreak. A few days later, he was reprimanded by Wuhan authorities and forced to confess to making false statements. After Dr. Li died of COVID-19 he was hailed as a national hero.

It wasn't until early January that central authorities disclosed information about the virus to the world, prompting more allegations, strongly denied by Beijing, that the central government had withheld vital information. In fact, it's unclear what the central authorities knew about the coronavirus in late December and the first part of January.

But it is clear that other factors influenced the uproar over the reporting delay. First, after reading a paper published in the New England Journal of Medicine (Li et al., 2020) in late January, a popular blogger accused the authors, most of them China CDC scientists, of purposely delaying the reporting of their findings about the virus. It later turned out that the blogger had made a gross misinterpretation of the timeline that was retrospectively dated. Although the blogger retracted his post, the notion that China CDC delayed the reporting quickly spread. Second, many have been frustrated by the fact that the outbreak was not reported sooner via the direct report system. However, a delay in reporting early COVID-19 cases in the system indicates issues in enforcing reporting protocols. Dr. Sheng Hua, a prominent economist, later revealed that the director-general of China CDC learned of the outbreak through his social network instead of the reporting system, and a national-level investigation was quickly set up afterward.[4] This incident points to an issue that has long pestered China (or any large country with powerful regional governments) – how the central government leads and coordinates with regional authorities.

The public also questioned China CDC's management of risk communication during the epidemic, demanding timely reporting and transparency. To be fair, China CDC technically is not a government agency and does not have the authority to publish information related to outbreaks. Besides, China CDC may not be fully capable to function in health communication – the Center for Health Education was separated from China CDC after a short-lived marriage. An integrated approach emphasizing coordination between different agencies would better serve the public.

Nonetheless, China CDC has played a critical role in containing the COVID-19 outbreak in China. Along with other provincial and local CDCs, they have put field staff in Hubei province to conduct epidemiological investigations and contact tracing (The Novel Coronavirus Pneumonia Emergency Response Epidemiology Team, 2020). They have contributed to the understanding of the epidemiological features of COVID-19 (Li et al., 2020) and promptly advocated for international collaboration to contain the pandemic (Abutaleb et al., 2020).

We need to note that the China CDC comprises only a part of China's public health system. To achieve its objectives, China CDC coordinates with provincial and local CDCs, as well as public health functions embedded in the health care systems, including hospitals and community health centers. At the height of the outbreak in Hubei, more than 40,000 health care providers from other provinces converged on Hubei province to offer much-needed assistance to the local health care systems. The contribution of all the parties to containing the COVID-19 outbreak should not be forgotten.

It is worth recalling the earlier section on the history of China's public health efforts. The major approaches that China's public health system used to contain COVID-19 continue to include old methods such as social distancing, quarantine, and sanitation. Social distancing and other measures to reduce mobility are effective in the containment of COVID-19 (Prem et al., 2020). Meanwhile, although Chinese scientists are making progress in developing vaccines for COVID-19, the take-up rate of flu vaccine in China has been poor, which may have led to hospital-acquired infections during the flu season. The lack of coverage of flu vaccination is partially attributed to the separation between the health care systems and public health. In China, the payers – various levels of the health care security administrations – are not allowed to cover flu vaccination, which is budgeted in the basic public health services provided by community health centers.

## Looking Forward

Dr. Jeffrey Koplan, former director of U.S. CDC, and Dr. Yu Wang, former director of China CDC, together published an analysis 10 years after the 2002-2003 SARS outbreak. They highlighted the need for enhanced disease and symptom surveillance systems, effective infection control, and a central focus of public health for coordination and leadership with delegated responsibility and authority, among other things (Koplan, Butler-Jones, Tsang, & Yu, 2013). Seven years later, the call still stands true for China, and probably for the U.S. and the rest of the world as well. The COVID-19 pandemic further highlights the need for concerted multi-sectoral efforts (Chen, Cao, & Yang, 2020). The following offer food for thought and possible topics for more in-depth discussions on China's public health system.

1.   Strengthening the leadership of public health agencies deserves attention. Elevating the status of Chinese CDCs would help to facilitate timely communication and decision-making. Clarifying the legal authority of Chinese CDCs would be useful (Li et al., 2020).

2.   Provincial and local public health systems, as essential components of the national public health system, need to be sustained. In addition to the China CDC, China's provincial and local CDCs have also suffered workforce shortages (Wang et al., 2019). Capacity building at the regional and local levels is critical for successful epidemic control.

3.   China's public health system needs to coordinate between different levels of CDCs and collaborate with local hospitals. A world-class direct reporting system is fantastic, but it will function properly only with adequate training and a close working relationship with the staff members of health care providers.

4.   To prevent transmission of infectious diseases, early identification of cases and their close contacts are crucial. Because asymptomatic and presymptomatic COVID-19 patients are both contagious, it is vital to identify close contacts of COVID-19 patients and to implement effective self-isolation and quarantine guidelines. Massive efforts in contact tracing have paid off in containing the epidemic in the Chinese City of Ningbo (Chen et al., 2020).

5.   China's public health system needs to recruit and retain talent. Current wage levels for the workers in China's CDC systems are not comparable to those with equivalent qualifications in health care, fueling a recent exodus of people from the CDC system. It is not too late to examine the pay scale of the CDC workforce nationwide and assess alternative mechanisms of recruiting and retaining talent.

6.   Improving risk communication is critical. Health communication is a burgeoning field that involves multidisciplinary collaboration among behavioral science, communication, and public health. China's public

health system needs to build up its capacity in health communication, not just for the prevention and control of infectious diseases but also for chronic diseases.

## Concluding Remarks

Policymakers have competing priorities. Resources and attention are often directed to projects that show quick and certain returns at the price of reduced investment in public health. COVID-19 proves such a tactic to be risky and provides an opportunity to reflect and revise our approaches. In times of uncertainty, prevention and preparedness is key to avoiding a future redux of the COVID-19 pandemic. We must strengthen public health institutions by providing sufficient financial and human resources and conferring them concrete and implementable authorities. We also need to improve collaboration between central and regional authorities, and most importantly, trust the expertise of public health workers.

If a bull is near a china shop, it is better to lead it by holding its nose ring. Failing to prevent or detect an epidemic is the same as grabbing the bull's tail – imagine what might happen to the china shop.

*Acknowledgments and Disclaimer*

*The author acknowledges Ms. Yeran (Cynthia) Deng for excellent research assistance. I learned about the enlightening metaphor of bull's nose ring vs. tail from Professor Zuofeng Zhang, who attributed the metaphor to Professor Guangwen Cao. I thank Professors Penny Prime and Hanchao Lu for the invitation to present this material at the China Research Center seminar series and to submit it to this journal. The thorough editing of Drs. Betty Feng and James Schiffman is much appreciated. Any remaining errors are undoubtedly and totally my own.*

## Notes

1   *Alternative sources put the establishment of the Hospital in 1921, which may correspond to reorganizing of the hospital.*
2   *https://www.cdc.gov/budget/documents/fy2020/fy-2020-cdc-congressional-justification.pdf*

## References

Abutaleb, Y., Dawsey, J., Nakashima, E., & Greg, M. (2020). *The U.S. was beset by denial and dysfunction as the coronavirus raged. Washington Post.* Retrieved from https://www.washingtonpost.com/national-security/2020/04/04/coronavirus-government-dysfunction/

Bai, Y., Yao, L., Wei, T., Tian, F., Jin, D. Y., Chen, L., & Wang, M. (2020). Presumed Asymptomatic Carrier Transmission of COVID-19. *JAMA.* doi:10.1001/jama.2020.2565

Blumenthal, D., & Hsiao, W. (2015). Lessons from the East–China's rapidly evolving health care system. *N Engl J Med, 372*(14), 1281-1285. doi:10.1056/NEJMp1410425

Chinese Academy of Science. (2003). *Epidemics and prevention in ancient China (*中国古代的流行病及其防范*).*

Chen, Y., Wang, A., Yi, B., Ding, K., Wang, H., Wang, J., . . . Xu, G. (2020). The epidemiological characteristics of infection in close contacts of COVID-19 in Ningbo city. *Chinese Journal of*

*Epidemiology, 41(0), 0-0. doi:http://dx.doi.org/10.3760/cma.j.cn112338-20200304-00251*

Chen, Z., Cao, C., & Yang, G. (2020). *Coordinated Multi-Sectoral Efforts Needed to Address the COVID-19 Pandemic: Lessons From China and the United States. Global Health Research and Policy, 5. doi:10.1186/s41256-020-00150-7*

China CDC. (2012). *New Chapter for China's Public Health. Retrieved from http://www.chinacdc.cn/ztxm/jksn/snzj/201202/t20120207_57053.html*

China CDC. (2018). 陈春明同志生平 *(Obituary: Madam Chunming Chen). Retrieved from http://www.chinacdc.cn/jlm/yw/201805/t20180519_172420.html*

Dirlik, A. (1975). *The Ideological Foundations of the New Life Movement: A Study in Counterrevolution | The Journal of Asian Studies | Cambridge Core. The Journal of Asian Studies, 34(4), 945-980. doi:doi:10.2307/2054509*

Du, L. (杜丽红). (2014). 近代北京公共卫生制度变迁过程探析*(1905-1937).* 社会学研究*, 29(6), 1-23.*

Frieden, T. (2020). *A Strong Public Health System: Essential for Health and Economic Progress. China CDC Weekly, 2(8), 128-130.*

IOM. (2007). *Strategies for Disease Containment. In Ethical and Legal Considerations in Mitigating Pandemic Disease: National Academies Press (US).*

Koplan, J. P., Butler-Jones, D., Tsang, T., & Yu, W. (2013). *Public Health Lessons from Severe Acute Respiratory Syndrome a Decade Later. In Emerg Infect Dis (Vol. 19, pp. 861-863).*

Li, L., Wang, H., Liang, X., Bi, Z., Ren, J., Wang, L. (李立明, 汪华, 梁晓峰, 毕振强, 任军, & 王岚). (2020). 关于疾病预防控制体系现代化建设的思考与建议（*Recommendation on the modernization of disease control and prevention*）. 中华流行病学杂志*, 41(4), 453-460.*

Li, Q., Guan, X., Wu, P., Wang, X., Zhou, L., Tong, Y., . . . Feng, Z. (2020). *Early Transmission Dynamics in Wuhan, China, of Novel Coronavirus-Infected Pneumonia. N Engl J Med. doi:10.1056/NEJMoa2001316*

PBS. (Not dated). *Workers of the Central and Union Pacific Railroad | American Experience | PBS. Retrieved from https://www.pbs.org/wgbh/americanexperience/features/tcrr-workers-central-union-pacific-railroad/*

Porter, E. A. (1997). *The People's Doctor: George Hatem and China's Revolution: University of Hawaii Press.*

Prem, K., Liu, Y., Russell, T., Kucharski, A., Eggo, R., Davies, N., . . . Klepac, P. (2020). *The Effect of Control Strategies to Reduce Social Mixing on Outcomes of the COVID-19 Epidemic in Wuhan, China: A Modelling Study. The Lancet. Public health, 5(5). doi:10.1016/S2468-2667(20)30073-6*

Sanche, S., Lin, Y. T., Xu, C., Romero-Severson, E., Hengartner, N., & Ke, R. (2020). *High Contagiousness and Rapid Spread of Severe Acute Respiratory Syndrome Coronavirus 2. Emerg Infect Dis, 26(7). doi:10.3201/eid2607.200282*

The Immunisation Advisory Centre (2016, 2016-09-22). *A brief history of vaccination. Retrieved from https://www.immune.org.nz/vaccines/vaccine-development/brief-history-vaccination*

The Novel Coronavirus Pneumonia Emergency Response Epidemiology Team (2020). *The Epidemiological Characteristics of an Outbreak of 2019 Novel Coronavirus Diseases (COVID-19) — China. China CDC Weekly, 2(8), 113-122.*

University of Michigan/Center of Excellence in Public Health Workforce Studies. (2012). *Strategies for Enumerating the U.S. Governmental Public Health Workforce. Retrieved from Washington, DC: http://www.phf.org/resourcestools/Documents/Enumerating_the_Public_Health_Workforce_Final_Report_2012.pdf*

Wang, G. (王贵强). (2019). 永不停歇的疫战：中国传染病防治70年. *Retrieved from http://www.nhc.gov.cn/xcs/wsjksy/201909/a923a05f768640808ca3853b662c5a2a.shtml*

Wang, K., Mao, A., Meng, Y., Yang, Y., Dong, P., Qiu, W. (王坤, 毛阿燕, 孟月莉, 杨玉洁, 董佩, & 邱五七). (2019). 我国公共卫生体系建设发展历程、现状、问题与策略 *(Development history, current situation, problems, and strategies of public health system construction in China)*. 中国公共卫生*, 35(7), 801-805.*

WHO. (2020). *Coronavirus disease (COVID-2019) situation reports. Retrieved from https://www.who.int/emergencies/diseases/novel-coronavirus-2019/situation-reports*

Wikipedia. (2020a, May 5, 2020). *Peter Parker (physician). Retrieved from https://en.wikipedia.*

org/wiki/Peter_Parker_(physician)

Wikipedia. (2020b, April 4, 2020). *Divie Bethune McCartee. Retrieved from https://en.wikipedia. org/wiki/Divie_Bethune_McCartee*

Xu, Z., Shi, L., Wang, Y., Zhang, J., Huang, L., Zhang, C., . . . Wang, F. S. (2020). *Pathological findings of COVID-19 associated with acute respiratory distress syndrome. Lancet Respir Med.* doi:10.1016/s2213-2600(20)30076-x

*Dr. Zhuo (Adam) Chen is Associate Professor, Department of Health Policy and Management, University of Georgia; Li Dak Sum Chair Professor in Health Economics, University of Nottingham, Ningbo China; and an Associate of the China Research Center.*

*Special Issue: Vol.19, No.2, 2020: COVID-19*

# The Chang-Lan Fellowships:
## Reflections on the Value of Experiential Learning

*Michael Wenderoth*
*Vol. 20, No.2*
*2020*

Two years ago, I flew back to a small town in Minnesota, the unlikely place that sparked my interest in China more than two decades ago. I went to see friends and former professors and learn about the progress of the Chang-Lan Fellowships, which my mother and I established there almost 25 years ago to foster a better understanding of China through experiential learning.

On that trip, the trade war was kicking in. Presidents Trump and Xi had many of us, accustomed to years of deepening ties and growing prosperity, extremely concerned about deteriorating relations. And as I write, the global pandemic, far from bringing us together, appears to be pushing the U.S. and China even further apart.

I'm deeply worried. Just when we need more personal connections, more constructive dialogue and a more nuanced understanding of China – which I discovered the experiential focus of the Chang-Lan Fellowships fosters extremely well – we are dangerously close to a new era, in which borders and minds might be closing down those important activities.

My observations on the Chang-Lan Fellowships began with my questioning whether experiential learning was even relevant today, given dramatic changes in technology, globalization, and financial pressure on colleges. But reaching out to the more than 60 fellowship alumni made me realize experiential learning still has a powerful role. In fact, I'm even more convinced that we should be doing everything possible – particularly in our current crisis – to ensure experiential learning not only survives but expands.

## A brief history of the Chang-Lan Fellowships

In 1996, my late mother, Judy Chang Wenderoth, and I set up the Chang-Lan Endowed Fund at Carleton College, in memory of her parents and my grandparents, Drs. Sing-Chen Chang (张信诚) and Chien-Wei Lan (蓝乾蔚), who came to the U.S. in the 1940s. The Fund supports independent undergraduate student fellowships and has two key requirements: projects must be experiential in nature (versus formal academic study), and Fellows must share their experience with the larger community upon return.

We wanted more Americans to better understand China, which we believed would become increasingly central in the world. But we were worried about the race to specialize in our studies and work, so we wanted the fellowships to encourage curiosity and exploration outside of one's major, drawing students who never had thought much about China.

My mother, an architect, believed learning often came from doing and exploring, not solely through traditional academic study. So, we hoped the fellowships would generate personal contact with Chinese, which might lead to memorable stories, fresh perspectives, and closer relationships.

Past fellowships have included David Riedel's retracing and re-sketching of the 1934 Barbour expedition of the Yangtze (2002); David Jinkins' journey to understand changing worker culture in Manchuria through bathhouses and noodle shops (2003); Nicki Catchpole and Molly Patterson's examination of the transformation of teahouses (2004); and Pierce McDonnell's exploration of how China understands and presents its maritime history (2018).

Past Fellows have shared their experiences publicly at Carleton, and today can reach an even wider audience through the internet. For example, Pierce McDonnell's presentation at the San Francisco Maritime Museum; Erik Lagerquist and Nyla Worker's website to share solar insights; and Christian Heuchert and Alan Zheng's recorded discussion on tourism in pastoral Gansu communities.

## Conversations with Past Fellows: Benefits of Experiential Learning

Stepping back on campus, I was struck by change. One hundred students, about five percent of Carleton's student body, is mainland Chinese, versus zero percent when I graduated. History, which I studied, has plummeted in popularity, replaced near the top with computer science, the closest to a pre-professional major you can get at a liberal arts college. Tuition and fees have skyrocketed ($65,000 a year today, versus $17,000 in 1990). And, of course, the campus is wired with technology: resources around the world are available with a few keystrokes.

When you've got Chinese voices on campus, and you can WeChat video with Sichuan villagers from tiny Northfield, Minnesota, do you really need to send students to China? When there's immense pressure to land internships to secure well-paying jobs to justify tuition, is there still a place for off-the-resume exploration?

Reaching out to alumni who received fellowships as early as 2001, I came away with a much better understanding of how experiential learning addresses these questions:

*1) Experiential fellowships foster independence and confidence.*

How easy it is to forget what it was like to be 20. Fellows said they grew immensely from designing their projects and executing them themselves, abroad.

Kyle Schiller, who explored Buddhism by visiting temples across China with Adam Rutkowski in 2017, said he matured quickly having to travel on his own. His fellowship spurred further desire to contrast China with Japan, where he went the following year. An engineer at Airbnb, Schiller credits the fellowship with giving him confidence to pursue diverse interests in learning, innovation, and improving global health. Rutkowski worked on energy sustainability at Otherlab, liquid thermodynamics at SpaceX, and will soon start a PhD at Princeton.

In 2001, Sarah Karbeling traveled with Akiko Nakano down the Yangtze to understand the human impact of the Three Gorges Dam. A high school physics teacher in Iowa, she said that summer gave her a strong sense of independence. That's something I heard from many women, who received more than half the Chang-Lan Fellowships, and from science majors, who often have brutal major requirements that afford little time to go abroad.

David Riedel, who re-sketched sections of the Yangtze, credits his fellowship with helping him see where art could lead him. The Chang-Lan boosted his application to Yale's School of Architecture, which led to a career with Kohn Pedersen Fox in Shanghai. Now he is cofounder of AI SpaceFactory in New York, which develops advanced construction technologies for space exploration.

With parents and our educational system "snowplowing" the way for today's youth, it's easy to forget that most learning comes from forging out on your own, going in new directions, and making mistakes. Fellows emphasized how their independent, in-person exploration of China accelerated that process.

*2) Experiential fellowships widen our perspectives, challenging what we've read and been fed.*

Remember your first trip to China? All Fellows grew up with the internet but stressed the importance of seeing China with their own eyes.

"We're living in an echo chamber, with the internet reinforcing our beliefs, with much of it misleading information," Anthony Wong told me. "So, I tell younger people today that it's more important than ever to go out and see for yourself."

Wong, a banker and now regulator at the Hong Kong Securities and Exchange Commission, received a fellowship in 2005 to explore Chinese identity, contrasting overseas Chinese communities (he is from Malaysia) with his distant relatives in Fujian.

Karbeling, the high school physics teacher, admits that she doesn't do much related to China these days. But those conversations with displaced villagers helped her reconcile what she read at home and saw in the news, a human element she can even bring into discussion about physics.

Pierce McDonnell, a math and history major, combined his passions in shipping and history by working at the Shanghai Maritime Museum. He didn't just explore the archives and exhibitions but also worked alongside museum staff and hosted Chinese visitors. That provided multiple perspectives on China's maritime history, gave him a lifelong contact with the director there, and deepened his interest in the travels of Zheng He.

Sharing their experiences upon return forces Fellows to make sense of their experience, both in their own minds and to people back home. Using multimedia, story, and analogies to connect with their audiences, all said they saw their home country in a new light. Many grappled with differences between what they experienced and what they had read, studied, or assumed. This year will be particularly interesting, as the college awarded fellowships to two mainland students, a first.

3) *Experiential fellowships lead to jobs, foster long-term success.*

"Success" is dependent on how you define it. But contrary to turning them into wandering poets, Chang-Lan Fellows said the experience aided them professionally.

Nicki Catchpole had to postpone her fellowship due to the SARS outbreak in 2003. She said her conversations in Sichuan over tea made her more adept at conducting research and helped her land her first job upon graduation. That eventually took her back to Asia, and now has her analyzing business technology in New York.

"The open nature of the fellowship… there's nothing like it," she said. "Figuring how to create structure to make sense of something and deal with obstacles that arose was invaluable."

David Jinkins said he was madly curious about how China's economic shift was affecting worker culture in northeast China. Though his focus today has shifted from China, the fellowship took him to Taiwan for a master's and Penn State University for a doctorate. Now he is in Denmark, where he serves as associate professor of economics, specializing in international trade.

Jessica Lilu Chen fell in love with the stories of Muslim minorities on her fellowship. That started a journey to a PhD in religious studies at Stanford University, the recent publication of her book on Islamic history in early modern China, and her current work as a hospice chaplain in California.

The fellowships helped many stand out in job interviews and has served them in the longer arc of their careers. But most recalled how tough it was to convey to recruiters how the experience could be applied to their first jobs. That's not surprising since top executives cite soft skills (adaptability, assimilating information, communication, creativity) as critical, but they generally don't do the entry-level hiring. There's also increasing evidence that those same soft skills, not the quantitative ones, may be more valuable in a world of increased automation, and that generalists with wider-ranging experience, not narrow specialists, produce more cutting edge scholarship and innovations, given their ability to make disparate connections.

**Expanding Experiential Learning**

There's a price to funding students and providing the critical support to make experiential learning work well. Patience, in short supply these days, is also needed to allow exploration to take its course. So, student fellowships like the Chang-Lan may not be possible at all institutions, nor be right for every student.

But there are many ways to integrate experiential learning into courses, study abroad programs, and independent study and work. At IE Business School, for example, I teach a course on business in China. One course I deliver entirely on campus; the other includes a weeklong immersion in Shanghai.

With the course on campus, I have drawn inspiration from Chang-Lan Fellows. For example, we conduct live WeChat video conversations with diverse experts in China; I integrate rich video, interactive articles, and simulations into coursework; and students deliver exercises and projects that pair them with mentors across China.

These changes have deepened student understanding of China, but I still can't find a substitute for taking them there and sending them on their own explorations. When a student suddenly finds her internet sites blocked, she learns to navigate and live the experience, and then reflect on the broader implications. I see minds opening in our blogs, discussions on the bus, and group chats (we use WeChat, another way to enable the lived experience). Executives are no different: they can read a McKinsey report or hear my lecture, but until we buy a beer at a corner shop using WeChat pay, the vast implications of a mobile ecosystem usually escape them.

Those who go to China and explore seem to have deeper empathy and perspective than they had before their trips. The most valuable part is watching them grapple with contradictions between what they read or thought and what they see and experience, such as the trade-offs between convenience and personal privacy, between more individual rights and top-down rule.

When they've spent their time in China well, they become humbler, and I find they are less prone to demonize – or overhype – China. We could definitely use more of that these days.

There's of course a balance between in person, experiential learning and time in the classroom. Fellows and the students I take to China need background on China's history, political economy, culture, and language. But I find giving them too much information stifles refreshing questions that even seasoned experts overlook or have become too jaded to ask. And as a professor, there are benefits for me: seeing China through their eyes challenges my own views, particularly the constructs I've formed over the years.

When the pandemic ends, I hope we can safely mix more in person, and not retreat behind our walls into our online echo chambers. For those seeking to heighten the experiential in their organizations, I attribute the modest success of the Chang-Lan Fellowships to four sources:

- Dedicated professors who see themselves as mentors. Carleton has been nationally recognized for leading the way in undergraduate teaching, which comes down to people. The number one reason Chang-Lan Fellows apply is because a professor encourages them. Riedel, who sketched the Yangtze, said the late Professor Roy Grow not only pointed out the opportunity but also challenged him to use it to explore his interest in art. You can't have a journey of a thousand miles without that initial step (and yes, sometimes a loving push helps).

- Strong fellowship support. Professors are under heavy pressure and are not always accessible. That's where strong, professional staff steps in. Carleton is lucky to have Marynel Ryan Van Zee, PhD, Director of the Office of Student Fellowships. She handles all internal and external fellowship opportunities, serving as adviser and coach to guide student applications so they are set up for success.

- Adjusting (or experimenting) as necessary. We faced a Catch-22 at Carleton: we wanted more students without China backgrounds or Mandarin skills to apply, but that group wasn't thinking about China, and often were the least prepared to take advantage of an independent summer in country. To address the challenge, we opened half the fund to support summer internships. While adhering to the Fund's core aims, internships enable students with less China background to experience the country. For most, the summer sparks greater appreciation and gets a good percentage of them to consider applying for the more independent fellowships.

- Re-examining what "experiential" means. Do you have to be physically in China to experience China? It may in fact be wiser to explore some sensitive topics from outside the country. With lockdowns in place worldwide, the five Chang-Lan Fellows awarded for 2020 are re-examining this topic, proposing creative approaches. Changlan Wang (no relation) may be able to conduct her research into emotional response online. Marianne Gunnarsson, who will examine doctor-patient conversations, has already deferred to the winter.

I don't have a quantitative measure on the impact of the fellowships, but Fellows I spoke to had thoughtful views on current events and had plenty of examples of how their experience enhanced their life trajectories. Even if few of them continue to work in China, one alum said it best, "Doesn't matter. Pretty much everything anyone does today has some connection to China. Americans are doing ourselves a big disservice if we don't understand what's happening there."

Are the experiential Chang-Lan Fellowships playing their part to enhance U.S-China relations? My answer, to use an expression I picked up from my time in Minnesota, is a resounding "You Bet." I hope we consider how to dramatically increase the experiential learning of China for more Americans. The future of U.S-China relations greatly depends on it.

*Notes*

*Quotes have been condensed or edited for clarity. The author takes sole responsibility for any discrepancies in transcription or interpretation.*

吃水的人，不忘挖井的人 *(Those who drink water, should not forget who dug the well)：Michael would like to express his gratitude to key Carleton staff and faculty who have made the Chang-Lan Fellowships successful over the past two decades: Chris Solso, Dean Liz Ciner, Marynel Ryan Van Zee; to Professor Penny Prime and the late Professor Roy Grow, for co-designing his first experiential experience in China in 1992, a program decades ahead of its time; to Professor Prime for providing advice, years later, on ways to design his courses and immersions on China at IE Business School; to the 60+ Carleton Chang-Lan Fellowship alumni who shared their stories and who have gone into leadership positions around the world; and to his mother, the late Judy Chung-Yung Chang Wenderoth, and his grandparents, Drs. Sing-Chen Chang, and Chien-Wei Lan, from whose well he continues to drink.*

*Michael C. Wenderoth is an Executive Coach and a professor at IE Business School in Madrid, Spain.*

## Special Issue: Introduction

*Stephen Herschler*
*Vol. 18, No.1*
*2019*

One of the benefits of being a member of the China Research Center is ready access to colleagues possessing wide-ranging expertise on Chinese affairs. Five years have passed since I last drew upon these resources in a China Currents special edition examining policy trends under the new Chairmanship of Xi Jinping post 18th Party Congress. (See Vol.14, No.2, 2014). In introducing those essays, I boldly proclaimed Xi to be "no cypher."

In retrospect I sounded like the master of understatement. Truth is, I'm no China swami. Indeed, the past five years have been as humbling for me as they have been fascinating. I did not anticipate five years later, after the 19thParty Congress, that:

- I would join hundreds of millions of people in studying "Xi Jinping Thought."
- The Party, with Xi Jinping as its nucleus, would work determinedly toward infusing key aspects of this Thought, not just conceptually but organizationally into every facet of state-society relations in China.
- Xi Jinping Thought would contain as a conceptual hub a "China Dream" formulated to counter the American Dream, complementing a "China Model" formulated to counter international neo-liberal models of development.
- A constitutional two-term limit to the presidency would be brushed aside, enabling Xi to rule until, well, whenever.

I would not have predicted the global ambitions of the Belt and Road Initiative. Closer to home, I would not have predicted Donald Trump's candidacy, much less how his election would inflame U.S.-China relations, be it through a trade war or resurgent Cold War rhetoric in Washington.

In brief, my five-year plan would have failed.

To rectify that going forward, I have diligently studied the Chairman's words at the 19thParty Congress, words that set forth China's goals not for the next five years, nor for the next 15 years, but all the way to the nation's "great rejuvenation" by 2049, not coincidentally the centenary of the PRC's founding (see Vol.17, No.1, 2018.)

Still, with such major domestic and international developments impacting governance, I feel somewhat like the proverbial blind man and the elephant – or rather, the blind man and the dragon.

Fortunately, six China Research Center members who contributed their expert insights five years ago were willing and able to come to my aid again, including a Center alumna. Many of the essays put recent policy developments in perspective relative to their previous analyses, thereby highlighting continuity and change in Party governance in a wide range of policy arenas, including administration, Party discipline, economics, media, the environment, and U.S.-China relations. The timeliness of the analysis encompasses developments through the first half of 2019.

Baogang Guo's opening essay on administrative reform foreshadows governance trends apparent in many of the other essays. He examines a 2018 comprehensive institutional reform, one of unparalleled scope and scale in the post-Mao era, that aims to reassert unequivocally Party dominance over governance through creation, reorganization, and consolidation, creating a melded Party-state apparatus through which central organs can exert increased control.

Xuepeng Liu's essay examining "Market vs. State" in the domestic economy finds an ongoing advance of the state with a commensurate retreat of the private while, on the international front outlines the force dynamics and flashpoints of the Sino-U.S. trade war as well as activity on the related battlefronts of investment and technology.

Andrew Wedeman's update on the anti-corruption campaign shows it still to be a defining trait of Party control of the Party-state apparatus, suggesting that the removal of "tigers, wolves, and flies" serves not just to take out prospective challenges to Xi's power but aims to ensure the regime's long-term survival.

Hongmei Li's essay on Party-state governance of media focuses on the increasingly comprehensive control over social media domestically through the examples of WhatsApp, WeChat, blogs, and a commensurate wide-ranging international initiative to exercise soft power through state-sponsored initiatives ranging from corporations and Confucius centers to state media blitzes promoting the global Belt and Road Initiative.

Eri Saikawa's update on initiatives to reduce air pollution reveals that while prodigious policy measures taken in the past five years have measurably improved air quality, the question remains whether the government will be willing to temper growth and adequately address all factors impacting air quality.

Director of the Carter Center China Program Liu Yawei fittingly concludes this edition with an interview on U.S.-China relations under Xi and Trump in a range of areas, including North Korea, trade, as well as research and education. He counters any facile "clash of civilizations" frame, arguing that both sides stand to benefit far more from cooperation than from conflict.

Overall, the essays highlight a Party-state intent on achieving an ever-firmer grasp domestically while nurturing an ever-greater influence internationally – all part of the Party's self-proclaimed historic mission of making China great again.

An ambitious plan – but will it work?

Again, I'm no China swami, but I will hazard an educated guess that the Party's recent abolition of term limits means there's a good shot that, five years hence, I will have another opportunity to reach out to China Research Center colleagues for their fresh insights and expert evaluations of Xi's dragon ride.

In the meantime, I'll keep in mind the analysis proffered some 2,000 years ago by another scholar of Chinese governance, one with his own particular feel for dragons, Han Feizi:

The beast called the dragon can be tamed and trained to the point where you may ride on its back. But on the underside of its throat it has scales a foot in diameter that curl back from the body, and anyone who chances to brush against them is sure to die. The ruler of men too has his bristling scales. Only if a speaker can avoid brushing against them will he have any hope for success.

---

*Dr. Stephen B. Herschler is Professor of Politics at Oglethorpe University and an Associate of the China Research Center.*

# Revitalizing the Chinese Party-State: Institutional Reform in the Xi Era

*Baogang Guo*
*Vol. 18, No. 1*
*2019*

Since the publication of my review of Chinese administrative reform in China Currents five years ago, significant changes have happened in China's governance system. Most notable is the debut of a new round of comprehensive institutional reform in 2018.

One assessment says the reform is based on "scientific design" and is no less than "an institutional revolution."[1] State Councilor Wong Yong explained the reform plan at 3rd Plenary Session of the 13th National People's Congress (NPC) in 2018. He said the reform will, among many other things, optimize the functions of the party and the state agencies, which includes consolidating existing government departments and agencies, and improving the efficiency and effectiveness of the overall state decision-making process.[2]

Prior to this round of reform, China tried many institutional reforms. But none was as comprehensive as this latest one. The reform plan not only includes a reorganization of the administrative governance system, but it also makes important changes in CCP's central party organizations, the committee system of the NPC and the Chinese People's Consultation Conference (CPCC), some CCP-controlled national interest groups and social organizations, and most significantly, the military. It appears the reform is intended mainly to revitalize the aging party-state system. Consequently, it has reversed the trends of political reform aimed at separating the party from the state.[3]

Several recent central and local pilot experiments, such as the "Fuyang Model" and "Shunde Model," can help us understand the direction of the latest reform.[4]

The "Fuyang Model" started in Fuyang city in Zhejiang province in 2007. It focuses on establishing multi-departmental coordinating committees to make key decisions. The "Shunde Model," originated in the Shunde District of Foshan city in Guangdong province in 2010. It concentrates on consolidating party and government departments that have similar functions. The decade-long piecemeal changes in consolidating administrative responsibilities and forming "super-ministries" also paved the way for the latest institutional facelift.

As early as 2015, the CCP initiated a feasibility study on the new nationwide institutional reform. By July 2017, preparation was accelerated under a directive from Xi Jinping. A plan was quickly drafted and circulated among top CCP party and government leaders as well as leaders in other "democratic" parties.[5] After making some important revisions based on feedback from these top political elites, the 19thCCP Central Committee approved a plan on deepening reform of party and state institutions in its 3rdPlenary Session held February 26-28, 2018.[6] Unlike many previous experiments, which were mostly local and carried out piecemeal and bottom-up, this round of reform emphasized strong central leadership and top-down implementation. This recentralization of reform leadership is the key element of Xi's institutional reform.

## Strengthen the Party Leadership

According to the plan released by the CCP in March 2018, the CCP central leadership committee structure was overhauled. A Central Comprehensively Deepening Reforms Commission, Central Committee for Comprehensive Law-based Governance, Central Cyberspace Affairs Commission, Central Financial and Economic Committee, and Central Foreign Affairs Work Committee were established. These new commissions or committees were formerly central leading groups. The upgrade gives these institutions more prominence and power. The members of each committee usually consist of the heads of the related party and state organs. Therefore, the goal of these committees is to strengthen not only the party's central coordinating role but also inter-department cooperation and policy consistency. In addition, a central leading group for education and a working committee for central and state organs were established. Some existing leading groups such as the Central Leading Group for Maintaining Stability were abolished.

One of the highlights of the institutional reform is the creation of the new and powerful National Supervisory Commission (NSC). The NSC functions as the highest anti-corruption apparatus in China. It is tasked with working with CCP's Central Discipline and Inspection Committee (CDIC) to monitor all government employees who exercise state powers. This includes not just high-ranking officials and civil servants but also managerial employees of the state-sponsored civic organizations, state-owned managerial employees, teachers, researchers, and doctors who work in public institutions. Its legal status is equivalent to the State Council, the Supreme Court, and the Supreme People's Procuratorate. The former National Anti-Corruption Bureau, the Office Against Dereliction of Duty, and the anti-corruption department of the Procuratorate were merged into this new powerful institution. A new Supervision Law was quickly drafted and adopted by the NPC in 2018, which establishes the legal authority of this new body. The NSC was given a broad range of powers, including asset-freezing, searching, and detainment. Many were concerned about the lack of checks and balances against individuals who work for this new institution, which directly oversees all other public employees.[7] In response, the NSC promised to create a set of internal monitoring systems. A quickly adopted amendment to the Constitution authorized the NPC as the supervisory body over the work of the NSC.

## From Separation of the Party and State to Division of Labor

The consolidation of several major administrative agencies with CCP's internal party organizations comes as the biggest surprise to many China observers. In previous decades, the CCP explored a way to separate the party from the state. This reform has apparently been abandoned under the Xi administration. The new approach seems to draw on experience with the "Shunde Model" and geared party-state relations toward a division of labor instead of a separation of powers. Its goal is to institutionalize the party's leadership in elite recruitment, propaganda, united front, and military affairs.

The consolidation of several key state administrative entities with party organs strengthens the party-state rather than dismantling it. This move has led to widespread disappointment among liberal scholars and Western China watchers. Under this change, the Party Publicity Department acquired the State Administration of Press, Publication, Radio, Film, and Television (SAPPRFT). In the past, the Publicity Department always played an important role in censoring media content. The consolidation gives this party organ absolute control over official propaganda, ideological work, speech, publication, films, and communication media. It also manages the content and screening of websites, social media, and publishing houses. The department is only subject to the guidance of the Central Guidance Commission on Building Spiritual Civilization.

Another major consolidation of party organs with state agencies involves the Department of United Front (DUF). The National Religious Affairs Administration (NRAA) and the Overseas Chinese Affairs Office (OCAO) of the State Council now become a part of the DUF. The cabinet-level department of the State Ethnic Affairs Commission (SEAC) is also officially merged with the DUF.

**Revamping the State Council**

To continue the decade-long administrative reform undertaken during the Hu Jintao Era, the latest institutional reform plan also calls for the restructuring of many government departments and agencies within the State Council. The goal is to streamline administrative powers, simplify administrative review and approval processes, and rationalize administrative responsibilities.

Under the institutional reform plan of the State Council, which was approved by the NPC last year, the number of ministries is reduced by eight. The State Council now has 26 ministries or offices. Several cabinet-level super-ministries are created, and a couple of more brand-new ministries are established. The new Ministry of Natural Resources (MNR) takes over eight new functions from other ministries or agencies. The MNR, which replaces the Ministry of Environmental Protection (MEP), takes over seven functions from other ministries or agencies and broadens its scope and power. The China National Tourism Administration (CNTA) is now a part of the Ministry of Culture and Tourism (MCT). Other new agencies created include China International Development Cooperation Agency (CIDCA), the National Health and Social Security Bureau (NHSSB), and State Immigration Administration (SIA).

Two new cabinet-level ministries are created. One is the Ministry of Veteran Affairs (MVA). The other is the Ministry of Emergency Management (MEM). China has about 39 million registered veterans.[8] Reports of veteran protests in recent years suggested some serious issues with the settlement, compensation, and preferential treatment these veterans received. The creation of the new MVA is a timely response to these issues. The new "super ministry" MEM will take on disaster management powers and resources that were previously spread over 13 other ministerial departments, thus becoming the single government institution in charge of emergency response, similar to Federal Emergency Management Agency (FEMA) in the U.S. or the Ministry of Emergency Situations (MES) in Russia.[9]

**New Economic Regulatory Institutions**

Creating a system of market regulatory agencies has become a challenging task. The new reform establishes several economic-related regulatory institutions. A State Market Regulatory Administration (SMRA) takes over responsibilities previously held by the State Administration for Industry and Commerce (SAIC), General Administration of Quality Supervision, Inspection and Quarantine (AQSIQ), Certification and Accreditation Administration (CAC), Standardization Administration of China (SAC), and China Food and Drug Administration (CFDA).[10] Consequently, the SAIC, the AQSIQ, and the CFDA will cease to exist. The SMRA is given very broad responsibilities, including comprehensive market supervision and administration, unified registration of market entitles, organization and guidance of market-related law enforcement, including anti-monopoly enforcement, and product and food quality and safety.11 A China Banking and Insurance Regulatory Commission (CBIRC) is created to consolidate two powerful yet inefficient banking and insurance regulators, namely, the China Banking Regulatory Commission (CBRC) and China Insurance Regulatory Commission (CIRC).

Several specialized teams will be created to strengthen China's administrative law enforcement related to economic activities. The teams will specialize in market supervision, ecological and environmental protection, cultural markets, traffic and transportation, and agriculture.

## Plan Implementation

Despite the magnitude and scope of these changes, central authorities required these unprecedented institutional reorganizations to be completed in 12 months. All institutional changes and personnel reassignments at the central and provincial level of governments were completed by the end of 2018, and the restructuring and reform of local city and county governments were completed by the end of March 2019. Officials say the NPC revised more than 40 laws to keep up with these drastic institutional changes. At the national level, the reform has affected almost two million people and more than 80 institutions. It represents a total reduction of 18 ministerial-level department and agencies and 107 internal offices within 39 ministerial- level departments and agencies. At the county and city level, institutional reduction in percentage terms comes to 5.26% and 7.23% respectively.12 Although the refinement and readjustment of these institutions' responsibilities, internal offices and departments, and staffing are ongoing, the new administrative system has become operational.

It is interesting to note that although provincial institution setups are supposed to match that of the central government, the provincial governments were given certain discretion. The number of provincial institutions no longer must match that of the central government. Most provincial governments have only 60 or fewer institutions. Some even created specialized offices to suit their own needs. Shanghai's reform plan eliminates 15 bureaus or offices. Guangdong province still has the stand-alone Bureau of Radio and Television; it has not been merged with the provincial Party's Publicity Department. Hainan province has only 55 party and government institutions, of which only 43 correspond to the institutions at the central government level. The other 12 offices are offices unique to Hainan. 13

Many government-affiliated social institutions, such as research institutes, hospitals, etc., will be gradually detached from the government. In Liaoning province, the existing 27,514 public institutions have been consolidated into 2,366 units, a 90% reduction that affects more than 400,000 people. The other 1,174 for-profit public institutions have been converted into state-owned enterprise groups.14

Many offices and functions will be consolidated. According to the plan adopted by Sichuan provincial government, each county will establish an Administrative Examination and Approval Authority (or Center) and Bureau of County Management and Law Enforcement. The party and government departments with a similar function will be consolidated into one office.15 Many counties now only keep about 19 county-level administrative departments.

## Conclusions

It is too early to assess the effectiveness of these comprehensive institutional reforms and their impact on the administrative governance system. But some trends can be observed clearly. First, as a result of institutional reform, the role of the CCP in government institutions has been strengthened. With the latest call for restoring CCP's all-around leadership, all major decisions at all institutional levels will have to be approved by party committees in the related departments and agencies, even though the party committees will not be involved in day-to-day public administration and law enforcement. A more coherent leadership core may lead to an improvement of governance efficiency, but it may also hinder the implementation of a system of rule by law. A direct party rule is traditionally more prone to the influence of the rule of men, especially "strong men."

Second, political centralization has given the national government more control over provincial and local governments. The central leadership core headed by Xi Jinping has acquired unprecedented political power through the new reforms. One possible negative impact will be a significant reduction in local governance and policy innovations. According to China's own account, the prolonged anticorruption campaign and the strengthening of the cadre of oversight have already had a chilling effect on the willingness of local officials to take risks in experimenting with new policy initiatives. Morale is low among many Chinese officials.16

Finally, despite the political recentralization, economic liberalization will continue. Administrative simplification, delegation, and deregulation will continue to be promoted. China vows to further improve the business environment. According to Premier Li Keqiang, China "will cut the time it takes for opening a business in China by another half, and we will reduce the time required for reviewing a project application by another half."17 The irony of the "China model" – namely, economic liberalization without political liberalization – will continue.

For the foreseeable future, the Chinese government will continue to focus on perfecting the new governance system and resolving many new issues associated with merger, acquisition, transfer, and reassignment of administrative authorities. The effort is likely to take years. Only time will tell whether this round of institutional reform will achieve its intended goals.

## Notes

1   Liu He, Institutional Reform for Better Governance," *China Daily*, March 15, 2018.

2   Wang Yong, "Explanation on the State Council's institutional reform program," report to 1st Plenary Session of the 13th NPC, *Xinhua News Agency*, Beijing, March 13, 2018.

3   Matthias Stepan and Sabine Muscat, "In Xi's China, the party morphs into the state," https:// www.merics.org/en/blog/xis-china-party-morphs-state, accessed June 18, 2019.

4   Wang Miao, "The Fuyang and Shunde Models for super-ministry reform at county level," *China Reform Daily(in Chinese)*, http://www.crd.net.cn/2010-10/29/content_5146056_3. htm, accessed Feb. 18, 2019.

5   Xi Jinping, "Statement on the final draft of the Decision to Deepen the Reform of the Party and State Institutions and the Implementation Plan," available from http://news.sina.com. cn/o/2018-04-11/doc-ifyzeyqa5508761.shtml, accessed March 18, 2019.

6   "Plan for Deepening the Institutional Reform of the Party and State", *Xinhua News Agency*, http://www.xinhuanet.com/politics/2018-03/04/c_1122485476.htm, accessed Feb. 18, 2019.

7   Zhou Wei and Li Zheng, "China adopted National Supervision Law to legalize the practice of "shuang gui" (temporary detention), *BBC*, https://www.bbc.com/zhongwen/simp/chinese-news-43451802, accessed Feb. 18, 2019.

8   Huo Xiaoguang, et al., "Break the waves and set sail again – The Party Central Committee with Comrade Xi Jinping as the core promotes the reform of the party and state institutions," *Xinhua News Agency*, July 6, 2019, http://www.xinhuanet.com/politics/2019-07/06/c_1124718574.htm, accessed July 7, 2019

9   Cao Yue, "A turning point in China's disaster preparedness?" https://www.chinadialogue.net/article/show/single/en/10768-A-turning-point-in-China-s-disaster-preparedness-

## References

1.   Liu He, Institutional Reform for Better Governance," *China Daily*, March 15, 2018.

2.   Wang Yong, "Explanation on the State Council's institutional reform program," report to 1st Plenary Session of the 13th NPC, *Xinhua News Agency*, Beijing, March 13, 2018.

3.   Matthias Stepan and Sabine Muscat, "In Xi's China, the party morphs into the state," https:// www.merics.org/en/blog/xis-china-party-morphs-state, accessed June 18, 2019.

4.   Wang Miao, "The Fuyang and Shunde Models for super-ministry reform at county level," *China Reform Daily(in Chinese)*, http://www.crd.net.cn/2010-10/29/content_5146056_3. htm, accessed Feb. 18, 2019.

5.   Xi Jinping, "Statement on the final draft of the Decision to Deepen the Reform of the Party and State Institutions and the Implementation Plan," available from http://news.sina.com. cn/o/2018-04-11/doc-ifyzeyqa5508761.shtml, accessed March 18, 2019.

6.   "Plan for Deepening the Institutional Reform of the Party and State", *Xinhua News Agency*, http://www.xinhuanet.com/politics/2018-03/04/c_1122485476.htm, accessed Feb. 18, 2019.

7.   Zhou Wei and Li Zheng, "China adopted National Supervision Law to legalize the practice of "shuang gui" (temporary detention), *BBC*, https://www.bbc.com/zhongwen/simp/chinese-news-43451802, accessed Feb. 18, 2019.

8.   Huo Xiaoguang, et al., "Break the waves and set sail again – The Party Central Committee with Comrade Xi Jinping as the core promotes the reform of the party and state institutions," *Xinhua News Agency*, July 6, 2019, http://www.xinhuanet.com/politics/2019-07/06/c_1124718574.htm, accessed July 7, 2019

9.   Cao Yue, "A turning point in China's disaster preparedness?" https://www.chinadialogue.net/article/show/single/en/10768-A-turning-point-in-China-s-disaster-preparedness-

10.   Katherine Wang, Mimi Yang & David Zhang, "China's new State Administration for Market Regulation: what to know and what to expect," https://www.ropesgray.com

11.   State Council, PRC, "Provisions on the Jurisdictions, Departments, and Staffing of the State Administration for Market Regulation," translation provided by https://gain.fas.usda.gov.

12.   Hou Xiaoguang, et al, op cit.

13. First Finance, "Many provincial institutional reform plans were approved," https://www.yicai.com/news/100039295.html, accessed Feb. 18, 2019.

14. Hou Xiaoguang, op cit.

15. http://www.sohu.com/a/275845968_100160824, accessed Feb. 18, 2019

16. Xinhua News Agency, "Three prescriptions for officials who don't perform their duties," http://www.xinhuanet.com//politics/2015-04/08/c_127663639.htm, accessed March 31, 2019.

17. Xinhua News Agency, "Premier Li: China vows to further improve the business environment." http://english.gov.cn/premier/news/2018/03/20/content_281476083768480.htm, accessed March 23, 2019.

---

*Dr. Baogang Guo is Professor of political science at Dalton State College and an Associate of the China Research Center.*

# A Crushing Tide Rolling to a Sweeping Victory: Xi Jinping's Battle with Corruption after Six Years of Struggle

*Andrew Wedeman*
*Vol. 18, No.1*
*2019*

In late 2012, early 2013, newly selected Chinese Communist Party (CCP) General Secretary Xi Jinping ordered an intensification of the regime's ongoing attack on corruption. Party investigators and the Procuratorate would, he declared, not only "swat at flies" (the rank and file), but would also "hunt big tigers" (senior officials), including those in the innermost circles of power. At the 19thParty Congress in October 2017 and then again in January 2019 at the 2ndPlenum of the 19thCentral Discipline Inspection Commission (CDIC), the party's internal watchdog, Xi claimed that the "crushing blows" dealt by crackdown had won a "sweeping victory" and that the party was now consolidating its success in China's long war with corruption.[1] The victory was not, he warned at the 3rdPlenum of the 19thCentral Discipline Inspection Commission 14 months later in January 2019, complete, and he called for the struggle to continue with unabated vigor.[2]

Rhetorical claims notwithstanding, key questions remain about Xi's protracted assault on corruption. What triggered the crackdown? Was the crackdown actually a political witch hunt disguised as an anti-corruption crackdown? What has the crackdown achieved and has it actually reduced corruption?

## Origins of the Crackdown

After the adoption of economic reforms in the 1980s and the beginning of the post-Mao economic boom, corruption also took off, with sums of money changing hands steadily expanding and mounting evidence that corruption was not a street/grassroots level problem but one that increasingly infected the middle levels of the party-state bureaucracy. Faced with rising corruption, the party responded with a series of drives against the rank-and-file "flies" in the 1980s and then a drive against corruption at the county and department levels in 1993. Over the next two decades, the party's "war on corruption" ground on year-in and year-out. In the process, several major scandals, including the arrest of Beijing Party Secretary and Politburo member Chen Xitong in 1995 and Shanghai Party Secretary and Politburo members Chen Liangyu (no relation to Chen Xitong) in 2006, shook the party.

During 2011-2012, a series of new scandals likely revealed to the party leadership that corruption at the top was perhaps not a matter of "a few bad apples." In March 2011, the CDIC announced that Liu Zhijun, the Minister for Railways, was under investigation. Liu was at the heart of a web of corruption that had been feeding off the massive investments being made in the construction of China's rapidly expanding high-speed rail system. Liu, according to rumors, had gotten so brazen that he claimed he was going to buy a seat on the Politburo. Later that year, General Liu Yuan, the son of Liu Shaoqi, the former Chairman of the People's Republic of China (PRC), accused Lieutenant General Gu Junshan, Deputy Director of the People's Liberation Army's General Logistics Department, of raking off huge sums from the sale of use rights to military-controlled property and using part of the money to pay off senior military officers.[3]

More dramatically, in February 2012, Wang Lijun, the former Director of the Chongqing Public Security Bureau, fled to Chengdu, the capital of neighboring Sichuan province, to seek political asylum in the U.S. consulate. According to news reports, Wang had fled Chongqing after he had clashed Bo Xilai, the city's party secretary. After a falling out, Bo demoted Wang to head the city's Environment Bureau. Wang countered by telling Bo that he had evidence that Bo's wife, Gu Kailai, had murdered an English businessman named Neil Heywood after the two had a falling out over bribe money that Heywood had been helping Gu launder. Bo struck Wang who then fled the city fearing for his life. After the State Department declined his request for asylum, Wang called friends in Beijing to dispatch agents from the Ministry for State Security to guide Wang past Chongqing police, who had surrounded the consulate, and to escort him onto a flight to Beijing.

In combination, the Liu, Gu, and Bo cases likely suggested to Xi and other senior leaders that three decades of battling corruption at the middle and rank and file levels had not prevented corruption from spreading upward into the core of the party-state leadership. The Bo case must have been particularly disturbing because Bo was a member of China's red aristocracy. Bo's father, Bo Yibo, was a first generation revolutionary and one of the eight most senior members of Deng

Xiaoping's reformist coalition. Bo himself had been a high-profile proponent of a Maoist revival that include the "singing of red songs" and a populist social welfare program aimed at China's lower classes.

It appears, therefore, that as he prepared to take over as paramount leader, Xi Jinping confronted evidence of extensive corruption at the very top of the party-state power hierarchy. Although such corruption posed an obvious threat to the party's grip on power, it also presented Xi with a Janus-faced opportunity to strengthen his own grasp on the reins of power. On the one hand, a bold assault on corruption writ large gave him the chance to position himself as the new upright leader sweeping out rotten, self-serving, money-grubbing officials who had betrayed the people. At the same time, an attack on corruption also gave Xi a justification for going after powerful officials who might have wished to hem him in and render him a weak leader, one who would be little more than the nominal first among equals within the Politburo Standing Committee. Purging – cleansing – the party as a whole, in other words, served not only the goal of attacking corruption at all levels within the party-state, it also afforded Xi an avenue to consolidate his own political interests. As such, the issue is not whether Xi's drive against corruption was a political witch hunt or an apolitical anti-corruption cleanup, because it sought to achieve multiple goals concurrently. Rather the key to understanding Xi's crackdown is how it was targeted.

**The Tiger Hunt**

The 1982, 1986, and 1989 crackdowns had primarily targeted the so-called flies – the rank and file. In 1993, the leadership shifted the focus to the middle levels of the party-state hierarchy, focusing on leading officials and cadres at the county, departmental, prefectural, and bureau levels. The crackdown launched in 2012-2013, resulted in dramatic increases in the number of investigations by conjoined party Discipline Inspection Commission and the state Ministry for Supervision, with the number of disciplinary cases investigated rising from 155,000 in 2011 and 172,000 in 2012 to 226,000 in 2014 and 330,000 in 2015. In 2017, the number of cases increased to 527,000. In 2018, the Supervisory Commission conducted 638,000 investigations, a four-fold increase compared to 2011. The total number of criminal indictments filed by the Procuratorate increased much more modestly, rising from 44,000 in 2011 to a peak of 55,000 in 2014, a 25 percent increase. Thereafter, the number of individuals indicted on corruption-related charges fell, dropping to 46,000 in 2017, 1,000 fewer than in 2012. The number of corruption-related cases tried by the courts more than doubled from 27,000 in 2011 to 56,000 in 2017.

The modest overall increases in the number of criminal indictments and trials, almost all of which would result in convictions, masked dramatic increases in the attack on high-level corruption. Whereas the number of indictments for rank and file officials increased from 44,453 in 2012 to a peak of 50,444 in 2014, the number of indictments for senior officials at the county-department levels rose from 2,396 in 2012 to a peak of 4,568 in 2015, an 80 percent increase. The number of senior officials at the prefectural-bureau level increased more than four-fold from 179 in 2012 to a peak of 769 in 2015. The number of senior officials at the provincial-ministerial levels increased over eight-fold from just five in 2012 to 41 in 2015. As a result, whereas the crackdown may have led to a surge in disciplinary investigations but not criminal indictments of ordinary officials, it resulted in a surge in criminal prosecutions of senior officials.

The attack on high-level corruption was, in fact, what sets Xi's crackdown apart from previous anti-corruption drives. Whereas press reports document a total of 30 cases involving officials at or above the vice-ministerial and vice-gubernatorial levels between 2000 and 2011, between 2012 and March 2019, 204 senior officials – which the Chinese press calls "tigers" – were charged with corruption-related offenses.[4] During those same time periods, whereas one military officer (Admiral Wang Shouye) was convicted of corruption prior to 2012, since then 78 officers holding ranks of major general and above have either been charged with corruption or were reportedly sidelined after allegations of corruption were leveled against them. Although the number of civilian tigers "bagged" peaked at 41 in 2014, thereafter the number of senior civilian officials charged with corruption has remained considerably higher than compared to the period prior to the current crackdown. The announcement that nine senior officials have been charged with corruption during the first month of 2019 suggests that the tiger hunt is not over. The attack on corruption in the senior ranks of the military, by contrast, appears to have been limited to the period 2012-2015.

In sum, the available data suggest that the crackdown on violations of disciplinary regulations and official extravagance begun when Xi Jinping assumed power in the fall of 2012 continues unabated as of early 2019. Criminal prosecutions of state officials and party cadres, however, peaked in 2015 and as of the end of 2017, the last year for which data on indictments by the Procuratorate and trials by the People's Courts were available. At the time of this writing, it appeared that the overall intensity of the crackdown was beginning to wind down, with the exception of the attack on corruption within the most senior ranks of the party-state apparatus, where investigators and prosecutors continue to "bag" new "tigers."

Over the past several years, Xi's investigators have in fact taken down a considerable number of big tigers. Between January 2018 and June 2019, 38 senior officials including 13 holding the rank of vice-governor, 10 vice chairs of either a provincial people's congress or provincial people's political consultative conference, five vice ministers, five managers of major state-owned companies, two mayor of major cities, one provincial party secretary, the former chair of the Xinjiang regional government, and one deputy provincial party secretary have been charged with corruption. Most notable among those charged were Zhao Zhengyong, Party Secretary of Shaanxi; Lai Xiaomin, Chair of China Huarong Asset Management; Meng Hongwei, a former Vice Minister for Public Security and the President of Interpol. Zhao was at the center of a new "Shaanxi Earthquake" that cut a wide swath through the Shaanxi provincial apparatus. Lai is suspected of having improperly loaned major sums to many of the high-flying tycoons who have been cut down during the crackdown. Meng, finally, was recalled from his post as the first Chinese to head Interpol and charged with accepting Y14,000,000 in bribes. Meng pleaded guilty. The tiger hunt thus shows few signs of coming to an end.

### A Crushing Tide?

As a drive against corruption, it seems likely that Xi's crackdown has yielded positive results. At a minimum, it has culled large numbers of corrupt officials and has likely cowed other corrupt officials, leading them to stop accepting bribes and stealing public monies, at least so long as the "heat is on" and they fear getting caught and punished. If these officials begin to sense that the crackdown has run its course and the things are "getting back to normal," they may begin to once again discount the risk of getting caught and revert to their corrupt ways. By the same token, amid the sound and fury of the crackdown other officials who have not resorted to corruption may be scared off and keep their hands clean. But they too could turn corrupt if they sense they can get away with taking bribes and stealing public monies because "everybody else is doing the same thing." Thus, if the crackdown has in fact reduced corruption, it is hard to determine whether the reduction will prove permanent or whether future upsurges in corruption will necessitate future crackdowns.

If the focus of Xi's crackdown was high-level corruption, was the primary purpose of the campaign actually a political purge of his rivals, as has been frequently asserted? Absent hard evidence of Xi's intent, the only way to determine whether the real goal was to curb corruption or gain political advantage would be to focus on whom the crackdown targeted.

Network analysis of the tigers and those linked to them reveals two central figures: former Politburo Standing Committee member Zhou Yongkang and former Director of the Central Committee's General Office Ling Jihua. Zhou had served in a variety of senior posts, including Vice Minister for Petroleum, General Manager of the China National Petroleum Corporation, Secretary of the Sichuan Provincial Party Committee, Minister for State Land and Resources, Minister for Public Security, and Secretary of the Central Committee's Politics and Law Commission. Ling was widely considered former General Secretary Hu Jintao's right-hand man. Zhou was due to retire from his official posts at the 17thParty Congress. Ling, on the other hand, was expected to be elected to the Politburo at the congress and become Hu's eyes and ears after Hu retired.

In theory, Zhou and Ling might have been the leaders of factions opposed to Xi Jinping. Ling had the backing, it was argued, of the powerful "Youth League" faction which had risen to prominence under Hu, who had been secretary of the league in the 1980s. Zhou was said to be a protégé of former General Secretary Jiang Zemin. Zhou was also said to have backed Bo Xilai in his bid for a seat on the Politburo Standing Committee. The assumption that Hu and Jiang opposed Xi seems questionable, however, because Xi must have received their endorsements when he was selected to become general secretary.

If Zhou and Ling were potential rivals, by the time of the 17thParty Congress both had been weakened. The arrest of Bo robbed Zhou of his entrée into the inner circle of power. Ling, on the other hand was politically crippled when his son Ling Gu plowed a $700,000 Ferrari into a Beijing bridge abutment during the early hours of March 8, 2012, killing himself and serious injuring two women passengers. An attempt to cover up the accident failed and reports about the crash and Ling Gu's death spread rapidly on the internet. Ling was quietly moved aside. At the 17thParty Congress he was not elected to the Politburo and was named to Director of the Central Committee's United Front Department.

Zhou was removed from his post as Secretary of the Politics and Law Committee in May 2012 and was put under investigation in July 2013 after extensive discussions among the current leadership in consultation with former general secretaries Jiang and Hu. While Zhou remained in limbo, party investigators began rounding up his former subordinates and colleagues. Ling was put under investigation in December 2014, after his brother Ling Zhengce, a senior official in Shanxi province, had been arrested and charged with corruption in June 2014. Zhou, his wife Jia Xiaoye, and his son Zhou Bin were convicted of accepting bribes. Zhou received a life sentence. Other members of Zhou's family were also charged with corruption. Ling and his wife Gu Liping were convicted of accepting bribes. Ling received a 12-year prison sentence.

Whether Zhou and Ling were political threats to Xi is not clear. For the most part, Zhou's "faction" consisted of his former secretaries and subordinates. Ling, on the other hand, was charged with accepting bribes from a variety of provincial leaders in return for arranging their promotions. It is thus not clear if either Zhou or Ling headed political factions or were simply tied into networks of self-serving officials bound together in pursuit of illicit plunder. Regardless of whether Zhou or Ling were true political enemies, their arrests certainly afforded Xi the opportunity to take down a wide range of central and provincial leaders and replace them with his allies and loyalists.

The attack on corruption in the military was equally ambiguous. It appears that the arrest of Lieutenant General Gu Junshan exposed General Guo Boxiong and General Xu Caihou, both of whom were vice chairs of the Central Military Commission, the party-cum-state body that controls China military. Guo and Xu had been collecting large bribes from officers seeking promotions and transfers. Both retired in November 2012. Xu was terminally ill at the time of his arrest and died before his court martial. Guo was sentenced to life in prison. Although Guo had held field commands in the past, he had been a headquarters staff officer since 1999. Xu had spent most of his career as a political commissar and as part of the General Political Department staff. It thus is not clear that Guo and Xu were part of an anti-Xi bloc in the army or even possibly part of a coup plot.

The fall of Politburo member and Party Secretary of Chongqing Sun Zhengcai also does not appear to have stemmed from fears that Sun had become a political threat to Xi. Sun has been described as a protégé of former Premier Wen Jiabao and had been a subordinate of former Politburo member Jia Qingling. His membership in the Politburo was not necessarily evidence of that he was a "force" with the party. Sun likely got a seat on the Politburo because he was party secretary of Chongqing, a provincial-level city that appears to command a seat on the Politburo because of economic importance. Some had suggested that Sun might get elected to the Politburo Standing Committee at the 19thParty Congress and that because of his age (54 in 2017) he might be a potential successor to Xi at the 20thParty Congress in 2022. But aside from his age, there seems to have been little evidence that Sun was a major political player.[5]

Ultimately, the main purpose of Xi's crackdown seems to have been to attack serious corruption among the party, state, and military leadership. As argued earlier, by the time Xi assumed the office of general secretary, there was strong evidence of serious high-level corruption. Moreover, there was public pressure for action against corruption. Public opinion polls conducted by Pew Research between, for example, showed that whereas 78 percent of those surveyed said corrupt officials were a moderately big or very big problem in 2008, fully 90 percent of those surveyed in 2014 held those views.

## Conclusion

As of mid-2019, it is not clear that Xi's attack on corruption has produced a "crushing tide" or a "sweeping victory." The crackdown certainly produced a surge in the number of party members and state officials investigated by the Discipline Inspection Commission and later the Supervisory Commission. In total between 2013 and 2018, the Supervisory Commission investigated 2.3 million party members, about three percent of the total membership. Upward of 300,000 individuals have been indicted for corruption-related offenses.[6] Most of those indicted were convicted and sentenced to prison. Almost 280 individuals holding ranks at or above the level of vice-minister and general had been investigated for corruption.

Despite these numbers, it is unclear whether Xi's crackdown will make a difference in the long-term. In the immediate term the crackdown has likely taken out enough corrupt officials to make a difference. It is also likely that the crackdown has scared off some and driven others to stop taking bribes. But the crackdown has also reportedly led to a degree of bureaucratic paralysis because officials fear being accused of corruption. The popularity of the crackdown is also difficult to gauge. In its early days, the crackdown was clearly very popular. Citizens who sought to expose official corruption using social media, however, quickly found out themselves facing restrictions and penalties. The party thus made clear that the crackdown was a party affair and the public's role would be strictly limited to that of a passive audience. Many ordinary citizens have also grown cynical about corruption. They see officialdom has inherently corrupt and believe that those who get caught and punished as merely the "unlucky" and "unloved," the poor saps who lacked the friends in high enough places to protect them.

The lack of decisive victory is perhaps not surprising. The party has been fighting corruption for decades and its war on corruption is by necessity a protracted war. Corruption, moreover, is ultimately not controlled by crackdowns and arrests. Real victory comes from changing official ethics and codes of conduct. Anti-corruption crackdowns are thus actually a response to the prior failure of a regime's anti-corruption program. Although further analysis is needed, the evidence produced by Xi's 2012-2019 anti-corruption crackdown suggests that corruption worsened significantly in the years before he was named general secretary. Xi, in other words, has been fighting against the failure of his predecessors to take effective action to control corruption.

### Notes

1    Xi Jinping, "Secure a Decisive Victory in Building a Moderately Prosperous Society in All Respects and Strive for the Great Success of Socialism with Chinese Characteristics for a New Era," October 18, 2017, available at http://www.chinadaily.com.cn/china/19thcpcnationalcongress/2017-11/04/content_34115212.htmand "Xi calls for fundamental improvement of CPC political ecosystem," Xinhua, 1/11/2018, available at http://www.xinhuanet.com/english/2018-01/11/c_136888965.htm.

2    "CCDI adopts communique at plenary session," China Daily, 1/13/2019, available at http://global.chinadaily.com.cn/a/201901/13/WS5c3b1b31a3106c65c34e41c3.html.

3    Liu Shaoqi died in 1969 after suffering repeated beatings by Red Guards.

4    Counts of the number of tigers bagged and the number of provincial/ministerial officials indicted different because some of the tigers remain under investigation by the Supervisory Commission and have not been remanded to the Procuratorate for a criminal investigation.

5   *Prior to his posting to Chongqing, Sun had served as Party Secretary of Jilin province and Minister for Agriculture, neither of which is a particularly powerful position.*

6   *Herein I am assuming that the number of indictment will be approximately the same in 2018 as they were in 2017.*

---

*Dr. Andrew Wedeman is Professor of Political Science at Georgia State University and an Associate of the China Research Center.*

# Market vs. Government in Managing the Chinese Economy: Domestic and International Challenges Under Xi Jinping

*Xuepeng Liu*
*Vol. 18, No.1*
*2019*

This essay is a reflection on what I wrote five years ago on the Decisions of the 11th Party Congress' 3rd Plenum of China's Communist Party in 2013 (Liu, 2014). In the original essay, I pointed out that the dominant role played by state ownership stated in the Decisions somewhat contradicts the decisive role of the market in the same Decisions. My concern at that time was on the direction of change regarding the roles of market versus government in the economy. This seems to be an appropriate time to evaluate what has happened during the past five years under President Xi Jinping and what to expect in the future.

Overall, the trend of changes under Xi seems troubling both domestically and internationally. At home, Xi is now president for life after a constitutional change approved by the Communist Party. On the economy, the government has intentionally and unintentionally been pursuing policies that strengthened the state-owned sectors. In the following, I will discuss primarily the following two issues: (1) state versus market in the Chinese economy under Xi with a special focus on China's industrial policies; and (2) the ongoing trade war between the U.S. and China.

### State versus Market in the Economy under Xi and China's Industrial Policies

Over the last several decades, the relative role of state-owned sectors has been declining. Based on the data from the National Bureau of Statistics of China, Lardy (2014) shows that the share of state-owned sectors in industrial output dropped from 78 percent in 1978 to only 26 percent in 2011. He also shows that, between 1995 and 2014, the export share of state-owned companies dropped from 67 percent to 11 percent. However, many critical and strategic sectors such as banking, infrastructure, and some upstream sectors are still largely controlled by state-owned companies. Some people attribute China's economic success to the strong role of government in managing the economy, and name this path of economic development the "China model." Because the state-owned sectors are the major participants implementing the government's strategies, many economists and policymakers in China begin to emphasize the importance of state-owned sectors in national development and international expansion. The emphasis on state-owned enterprises in China is not a surprise given what was stated in the above-mentioned Decisions of 2013, but it raises a renewed concern of the retreat of private sectors, which have been the true engine of the economic growth in China over the last several decades.

Although Xi probably has no intention to reverse the course of China's market reforms, he doesn't seem to emphasize the importance of continued economic reforms and the development of private sectors, not to say political reforms. Due to the close relationship between government and state-owned sectors, a natural consequence is a system favoring state-controlled firms. In recent years, the "advancement of state-owned sectors and the retreat of private sectors" (guo jin min tui) are particularly worrisome.

The retreat of private sectors may not be the intention of the government, but rather a side effect of the over-emphasis on the importance of state-owned sectors. This problem can be driven by a few factors. One of them is the 2008 world financial crisis. Against this backdrop, countries including China implemented the against-wind macroeconomic policies through rescue plans, quantitative easing, stimulus programs, etc. In China, state-owned companies have played an important role in implementing the stimulus policies while private sectors were reluctant to invest.

In addition, to switch from the original development strategy built on low wages and labor-intensive industries, the Chinese government has been trying to redirect resources toward more high-tech sectors. Due to externalities, the lack of resources, and less favorable economic prospects since the 2008 financial crisis, private firms – except a small number of large ones – have little incentive to invest in high technologies. State-owned companies naturally become "better" candidates in fulfilling the goal of climbing the technology ladder and industrial upgrading. Accordingly, state-owned companies backed by the government also receive preferential treatment in the areas such as financing.

On the contrary, private sectors find it increasingly difficult to compete against state-owned companies to secure loans, especially those with good terms. As documented by Lardy (2019), 57 percent of loans went to private firms and 35 percent to state-controlled firms in 2013 when Xi just assumed office. By 2016, state-controlled firms received 83 percent of loans, compared with 11 percent for private firms. This is also shown by Harrison et al. (2019): currently state-owned firms receive more subsidies and lower interest rates than formerly state-owned firms, which in turn, are favored relative to always-private firms. This happened despite the fact that the profitability of private-sector firms is more than double that of state-controlled companies. Much of this lending came from state-owned banks. The induced inefficiency can be huge. This is why many entrepreneurs and economists in China called for "competitive neutrality" to make sure that private and state-owned sectors receive similar treatment and are on a level playing field.

Finally, some market-oriented reforms have unintended consequences. For example, the sudden crackdown of shadow banking seems to be a move in the right direction, but could block the only access of small private firms to credit, and indirectly provide state-owned sectors even more favorable conditions relative to private sectors in the credit market.

The government can intervene in the economy in many ways. Besides regulations, monetary and fiscal policies used in typical market economies, a government can lay a heavy hand on the economy through other means such as state-owned or sponsored enterprises, industrial policies, and government procurement. Industrial policy is the major channel through which the Chinese government implements its development strategies, which culminates with the recent Made in China 2025 Initiative.

MIC2025 first appears in the 2015 Report on the Work of the Government and again in the reports of 2016 through 2018. The Report (2015) states, "We will implement the 'Made in China 2025' strategy; seek innovation-driven development; apply smart technologies; strengthen foundations; pursue green development; and redouble our efforts to upgrade China from a manufacturer of quantity to one of quality." The Report (2016) states, "We launched the 'Made in China 2025' initiative to upgrade manufacturing, set up government funds to encourage investment in emerging industries, and to develop small and medium-sized enterprises, and establish more national innovation demonstration zones." The Report (2017) states, "We developed and launched a plan for completing major science and technology programs by 2030…. We will intensify efforts to implement the 'Made in China 2025' initiative… we will adopt a variety of supportive measures for technological upgrading and re-energize traditional industries." The Report (2018) states, "Implementation of the 'Made in China 2025' initiative has brought progress in major projects like the building of robust industrial foundations, smart manufacturing, and green manufacturing, and has accelerated the development of advanced manufacturing."

As an ambitious plan to upgrade the Chinese economy by climbing the technology ladder, the "Made in China 2025" initiative lays out the strong state-directed industrial policies.

Industrial policies have been used by most of the countries in the world at certain stages of development. We have seen more failures than successes. These policies often create tension among countries in the era of globalization, especially when a country is large, because firms in different countries and sectors may no longer be on a level playing field. Depending on how domestic firms acquire their technologies, the protection of intellectual property rights also becomes a concern of many western companies that are strongly against forced technology transfers and infringement of intellectual property rights. This is why MIC2025 has attracted so much attention and is one of the major reasons behind the 2018 U.S.-China trade war. This is probably why a similar statement on MIC2025 disappears from the 2019 Report on the Work of the Government to avoid further escalation of such disputes. The Chinese government seems flexible enough to accommodate the requests and concerns from other nations.

However, this by no means implies that China has abandoned its MIC2025 Initiative. It is unrealistic to stop the practice of industrial policies in China (or any other major economy), so the best we could do is probably to develop an approach for open discussions. To ensure effective negotiations, countries should at least have a mutual understanding of information sharing and fairness.

I end this section with a discussion of the so-called "China model" or "Socialism with Chinese Characteristics" with strong government involvement. This strategy has its advantage in certain countries at particular states of economic development. Besides addressing market failures such as public goods and externalities, the government can help gather limited resources and make concerted nationwide efforts to target specific development goals so that a developing country can catch up with advanced countries more quickly. The more centralized system and state-owned companies have played important roles in the economic development in China, especially in certain areas like infrastructure. Tighter regulations and the gradual opening of financial markets help to contain risks and avoid large-scale financial crises. China's economic success has offered valuable insight to both developing and developed countries around the world.

However, placing too much confidence in government- and state-owned sectors is dangerous. As stated in my original essay five years ago, this ignores the basic fact that China's economic miracle has been driven by market reforms rather than government control. It is important to realize that the so-called the market economy with Chinese characteristics is a transition period from a destined-to-fail socialist regime to a more efficient market regime. Its outstanding performance during the last several decades in China should not be over-emphasized. On the contrary, China's success demonstrates how severely the economic capacity of

China was depressed under the socialist policy before the reform. The Chinese economy took off and prospered when the government gradually released its control. The past success can be a poor guide for the future. To ensure continued economic prosperity, China needs deeper market reforms, not a reversal of this policy with a stronger hand of government on the economy.

**Trade War between the U.S. and China**

Global free trade is a natural extension of a free market economy within a country. The benefits from trade are now well understood. China's economic size (GDP) has grown 10 times larger from about $1.4 trillion since its 2001 entry into the World Trade Organization to about $14 trillion in 2019 (predicted). When China grows into a global power, its domestic policies have important international implications. The "China model" featured with state capitalism can clash with western market economies. In state capitalism, the government owns and provides preferential treatment to businesses in critical sectors in the name of industrial policies. Although many countries in the west also implement certain industrial policies – such as the support to high-tech or green technologies – their polices are relatively more transparent than in developing countries like China. The combination of state capitalism and the lack of transparency in China, as well as the influence of interest groups through lobbying in many western economies, pose tremendous challenges when the international community seeks to promote an open, competitive and fair system through multilateral talks under the WTO framework. Large countries like the U.S. may abandon multilateral trade talks and initiate a trade war. I believe that this is a fundamental reason behind the trade wars initiated unilaterally by the Trump administration.

To make things worse, in the international sphere, Xi has abandoned the policies under previous leadership since Deng Xiaoping by keeping a low profile and focusing on domestic economic reform and development. Instead, Xi seems to be more interested in advocating the "China model" for other developing countries to emulate as an alternative to western market capitalism. Xi has spelled out openly his ambitious plans to exert a greater influence on the rest of the world through strategies like "One Belt One Road" and MIC2025 initiatives. Although these initiatives are considered strategic plans for the future in China, the goals are more or less incompatible with other statements, e.g., the claimed developing country status that makes China qualified for preferential treatment under various international agreements, such as the WTO. As a result, China has paid the price: the 2018 trade and economic war between the U.S. and China, among other international disputes and conflicts. As Reuters reported (Miles, 2019), the U.S. is drafting WTO reform to halt handouts for big and rich states that claim to be developing nations, including China, India, etc. Special and Differential treatment (S&D) under the WTO entitles developing countries to longer time periods for implementing commitments, measures to increase trading opportunities, provisions requiring all WTO members to safeguard the trade interests of developing countries, support to help developing countries build the capacity to carry out WTO work, handle disputes, and implement technical standards, and provisions related to least-developed country (LDC) members. The WTO currently allows countries to self-designate as developing countries. The U.S. draft reform posted on the WTO website said current and future trade negotiations should withhold such special treatment from countries classified as "high income" by the World Bank, OECD members or acceding members, G20 nations and any state accounting for 0.5 percent or more of world trade.

The U.S.-China trade war has gone far beyond trade into many other areas including investment and technology. In 2018, the U.S. Congress passed the Foreign Investment Risk Review Modernization Act (FIRRMA), expanding the authority of the Committee on Foreign Investment in the United States (CFIUS) to include mandatory filings. FIRRMA is a legal hurdle to stop foreign firms from investing in the U.S. and acquiring American businesses in key sectors: filing fees, approval process, and expanded scope of coverage. In addition to the FIRRMA legislation, the Export Controls Act of 2018 was also passed to mitigate technology transfer activity from the U.S. to China. The U.S. had proposed sanctions against the Chinese state-owned company ZTE, but defused after agreement, and then placed sanctions against other Chinese firms including Huawei. Recent accusations of forced technology transfers, discriminatory licensing of American firms in exchange for market access in China, unfair ruling of IP disputes, government-facilitated acquisition overseas, cyber-attacks, stealing of technology and trade secrets (e.g., the investigations of the scholars in the 1000 Talents Program and even proposed restrictions on the exchanges of students and scholars), and violations of Iran sanctions by Chinese companies such as ZTE and Huawei. Under the pressure, China has agreed to revise IPR rules and step up IP protection and grant more market access.[1]

In the following part of this essay, I will focus on the 2018-2019 trade war between the U.S. and China. We know that China has been running a huge trade surplus with the U.S. The main concerns of the U.S. are China's exchange rate manipulation, industrial subsidies, and slow delivery of WTO commitments in the areas of market access, government procurement, and subsidy notifications. I don't think the Trump administration has any intention to change the U.S.'s open trade policy. Tariffs are just a means for the U.S. to demand a level playing field from other countries including China, India and allies such as the EU, Japan, and Canada, although different countries may have different interpretations of fairness in trade. The U.S., of course, could bring the case to the WTO as has been done numerous times in the form of anti-dumping or countervailing charges. But the process can be long, especially given the lack of transparency in China's economic policies. As the U.S. claimed, China hasn't made much progress on delivering subsidy notifications to the WTO. Without sufficient information and a formal channel to obtain the required information, it is hard to resolve the conflicts through appropriate channels recommended by the WTO. Together with the pressure to get reelected, this is probably why the Trump administration sets aside the WTO and approaches China directly through bilateral trade wars and talks.

Note that, in this essay, I focus on issues that require international cooperation, keeping in mind that the U.S. domestic policies are also responsible for its large trade deficit.[2]

Given the obvious costs of the trade war, the right solution is still multilateral (WTO) or bilateral negotiations. After many rounds of high-level talks, several threats and setbacks, the U.S.-China trade negotiations have been going through a scary roller coaster ride. Although the two parties agreed at the G20 meeting in late June 2019 to sit down again to negotiate, the prospect is still unclear. Just recently, Donald Trump announced a new round of tariffs on imports from China that would go into effect September 1, 2019. Although this leaves a short window for the two parties to try to work out their differences, it is a tough task. Progress could be made if China starts to buy more American products, strengthens IPR protection, speeds up financial market liberalization, grants more market access to American firms, and refrains from manipulating currency, and the U.S. removes tariffs on Chinese products over time. Resolving some other issues such as transparency on subsidies, information-censoring, and the modification of China's laws, however, may require drastic economic and even political reforms, which the Chinese government is reluctant to do, at least in the short run. Despite the differences in opinions, the intertwined economic interests make the trade war too costly for both countries to afford. But the process to achieve free trade can be a long one.

One insight we gain from the U.S.-Japan trade negotiation in 1980s is that it can take a long time for two economic powers to settle trade disputes. China has learned the lesson from Japan and will likely refuse to make drastic changes such as currency appreciation, so this can make the U.S.-China negotiation even more prolonged. Therefore, both the U.S. and China should be patient throughout this process. In recent years, we have seen an increasing divide between the U.S. and China on the timing for a resolution to address these issues.

At an international symposium to commemorate the 40thAnniversary of Normalization of U.S.-China Diplomatic Relations at The Carter Center in Atlanta in early 2019, I raised the concern about the possible escalation of the U.S.-China trade war and suggested a gradual approach for the bilateral negotiation. Mr. Craig Allen (President of the U.S.-China Business Council) pointed out that the time for U.S.-China trade talk is running out. He said that China prefers to follow a gradual approach and needs another 10 or 20 years to implement deeper reform and open policies, while the U.S. has lost patience saying that China has delayed fulfilling its commitments at the entry of the WTO for a long time and these should have been done yesterday. Facing this stalemate, the two countries were dragged into a trade war in 2018.

Initially, as stated in a draft framework for negotiation by the U.S. Delegation (2018), the U.S. demands "China immediately remove market-distorting subsidies and other types of government support that can contribute to the creation or maintenance of excess capacity in the industries targeted by the Made in China 2025 industrial plan." The U.S. demands that China eliminate specified policies and practices with respect to technology transfer within a few months and must concede to the U.S.'s enforcement mechanisms without retaliation. In addition, China must abandon its state-led economic development model, which would be politically difficult to swallow in China because a large part of the economic success of China is based on this type of policy. Indeed, accepting U.S. demands likely would require not just a policy paradigm shift, but also a regime change, which is impossible to accomplish in the short run. The U.S. cannot expect that China will scrap its economic model overnight. With the intertwined interests and complicated relations, we have to be patient with U.S.-China negotiations.

On the other hand, if the U.S. condones China's state capitalism, this would legitimize a system that puts U.S. firms at a permanent disadvantage. To be realistic, the U.S. needs to continue to press China to speed up its economic reforms through bilateral and multilateral talks, but at the same time have patience to work things out with China, probably following the approach of the U.S.-Japan negotiations in 1980s.

China should take U.S. demands seriously and make meaningful changes as quickly as possible. To address its large trade imbalance, China should adopt a more market-determined exchange rate policy, continue with structural reform by transforming an investment- and export-driven economy to a domestic consumption-driven economy, and contain the risk from excessive borrowing and underperforming state-owned sectors.

It is important to understand China before pressing the government for a deeper reform and drastic changes. The last part of this essay will address this issue in a broader context, not just the trade war. China has been following a gradual approach in its economic reform and opening. It has proved to be very successful during the past several decades, not only helping China to reap the benefits from having an increasingly market-oriented system, but also avoiding the sudden shocks from drastic reforms. Despite being authoritarian politically, China has managed to transfer powers peacefully and maintain a very stable economic and political environment. But whether China should continue with this approach is controversial. The potential dividend from this approach has largely been redeemed. To revive the economy, China now needs a new approach that encourages innovation in a competitive economic and political environment, without relying heavily on cheap excess labor and distortive government policies. This new development model requires deeper institutional reforms. Although most people believe China should eventually embrace a fuller market economy, the timing is hard to judge. A drastic reform will create a series of new problems and hence may face opposition in both business and political circles. For example, as mentioned earlier, a drastic change in regulation in the credit markets by prohibiting shadow banking seems to be a sign of progress in China, but it can do more harm to small private businesses if other accompanying policies are not in place.

Since the 1980s, the Chinese government has claimed to continue to pursue an open and reform policy. Even under the current administration, the 2017 Report of Work of Government states, "We will make big moves to improve the environment for foreign investors. We will revise the catalog of industries open to foreign investment, and make service industries, manufacturing, and mining more open to foreign investment. We will encourage foreign-invested firms to be listed and issue bonds in China and allow them to take part in national science and technology projects. Foreign firms will be treated the same as domestic firms when it comes to license applications, standards-setting, and government procurement, and will enjoy the same preferential policies under the Made in China 2025 initiative. Local governments can, within the scope of the powers granted them by law, adopt preferential policies to attract foreign investment. We will build 11 high-standard pilot free-trade zones, and widespread practices developed in these zones that are proven to work... China's door is going to keep on opening wider, and China will keep working to be the most attractive destination for foreign investment."

## Concluding Thoughts

Despite the claims or promises by the Chinese government, other countries have been concerned about the actual implementation and the political constraint, even though China's continued economic success has disappointed many people who predicted China's collapse. China has actually done pretty well in keeping promises and carrying out the open and reform policies, but it becomes increasingly difficult to implement deeper reforms. This problem has become more evident during the past decade. In the case of the trade war, even if the U.S. and China successfully sign an agreement later this year, the implementation will certainly be a central issue for discussion. The U.S. and some other countries have accused China of not implementing promised changes that were part of its commitments for entry into the WTO.

As another example, in the original essay (Liu, 2014), I mentioned particularly the Shanghai Pilot Free Trade Zone. Adopting a negative list approach, this is demonstration of the decentralization of power in areas including trade, investment, financial reforms, and regulations. It is useful to look at what has been achieved during the past five years, but it turns out not much has been done. On banking services liberalization, for example, due to many regulations and slow opening of Chinese market, the presence of foreign banks and their services are still very limited in China as compared to domestic state-owned banks. The essence of these free trade zones is minimal government intervention, which is hard to achieve in China. The implementation of the free zone polices requires deeper economic and even political reform and changes in related laws and regulations on foreign companies and joint ventures. This explains why it has not been as successful as the first round of special economic zone experiments under Deng Xiaoping in the 1980s.

As a final note, China should have already realized that it needs to make significant and meaningful changes in its policies, but it is unlikely that it will make drastic economic and political reform to satisfy all of the demands from the U.S. and other western countries. Given the size and importance of China's economy, however, western countries cannot afford an economic decoupling with China. Therefore, a practical approach in multilateral and bilateral negotiations is needed. This can be a long process and may become the new norm. A minimum requirement for successful negotiations is transparency in policies. For example, all nations including China and other developing countries should disclose their industrial policies and notify other WTO members regarding their subsidies as required by the WTO.

This is easier to say than to do. Transparency is actually a tough issue to address in China because it will eventually involve political reforms. Instead of relying on censorship and firewalls to block citizens' access to information, Chinese leaders should be more confident to embrace an open society. This will benefit China's long-run growth, and also help China to integrate better with other countries in today's globalized economy.

### Notes

1    *China's tariff level is not very high overall, but China still has many non-tariff barriers (NTBs), especially in services sectors. Better transparency on NTBs is needed.*

2    *People have paid much attention to China's large trade surplus with the U.S. Overall, however, China's trade surplus is not that large, actually approaching zero in early 2019, because China has run sizable trade deficits with other countries such as Korea. China's trade surplus with the U.S. is on par with other countries, so the U.S. trade deficit is not going to be resolved simply through negotiations with China. The U.S. should focus on its economic problems to improve its domestic economic environment and increase firms' export competitiveness.*

## References

Harrison, Ann, Marshall Meyer, Peichun Wang, Linda Zhao, and Minyuan Zhao, 2019. "Can a Tiger Change Its Stripes? Reform of Chinese State-Owned Enterprises in the Penumbra of the State." NBER Working Paper No. 25475

Lardy, Nicholas, 2014. Markets over Mao: The Rise of Private Business in China. Peterson Institute for International Economics, Washington D.C.

Lardy, Nicholas, 2019. The State Strikes Back: The End of Economic Reform in China? Peterson Institute for International Economics, Washington D.C.

Liu, Xuepeng, 2014. "Market vs. Government in Managing the Chinese Economy." China Currents 13(2). Source: https://www.chinacenter.net/2014/china_currents/13-2/market-vs-government-in-managing-the-chinese-economy/

Miles, Tom, 2019. "U.S. drafts WTO reform to halt handouts for big and rich states." Source: https://www.reuters.com/article/us-usa-trade-wto/u-s-drafts-wto-reform-to-halt-handouts-for-big-and-rich-states-idU.S.KCN1Q426T

The Report on the Work of the Government of People's Republic of China (2015). Source: http://english.gov.cn/archive/publications/2015/03/05/content_281475066179954.htm

The Report on the Work of the Government of People's Republic of China (2016.) Source: http://english.gov.cn/premier/news/2016/03/17/content_281475309417987.htm

The Report on the Work of the Government of People's Republic of China (2017.) Source: http://www.xinhuanet.com/english/china/2017-03/16/c_136134017.htm

The Report on the Work of the Government of People's Republic of China (2018.) Source: http://en.people.cn/n3/2018/0403/c90000-9445262.html

U.S. Delegation, 2018. "Balancing the Trade Relationship between the United States of American and People's Republic of China." Source: https://xqdoc.imedao.com/16329fa0c8b2da913fc9058b.pdf

---

*Dr. Xuepeng Liu is Professor of Economics at Kennesaw State University and an Associate of the China Research Center.*

# New Trends in China's Media Control at Home and Public Diplomacy Abroad

*Hongmei Li*
*Vol. 18, No. 1*
*2019*

This essay analyzes new trends in China's media control mechanism and public diplomacy efforts in the past five years since the country issued its media and cultural policies pertaining to the 18th Party Congress' 3rd Plenary Session's Decision in 2014. It is built on my previous essay published in China Currents five years ago (Li, 2014). In that essay, I examined the intersection between cultural and media policies and the push and pull between the party-state and market-oriented media producers. Specifically, I highlighted potential changes in six areas: (1) media control mechanisms, (2) the prescribed nature of a media organization, (3) media censorship, (4) media consolidation and economies of scale, (5) the entry of private capital into the Chinese media industries, and (6) China's soft power and public diplomacy.

This essay only focuses on media control at home and public diplomacy abroad because these two areas have seen the most change and can offer a sharp contrast between China's state-centric, nontransparent domestic policies and the participatory more democratic foreign policies (Li, 2006, 2016).

## Media Control

As I argued in my 2014 essay, media control has been gaining ground despite "potential seeds for at least a partial reordering of the dynamic tension between impulses demanding control." Indeed, since Xi Jinping came to power in 2013, media censorship in China has been tightened not only in traditional media but also more apparently in new media sectors.

In traditional media, the two-pronged control system (the state and the party) continues to censor content ranging from news to entertainment through the unified organization State Administration of Press, Publication, Radio, TV and Television of China (SAPPRFT) and the local and national branches of the Central Propaganda Department. Content considered vulgar and conducive to the promotion of blatant materialism is forbidden (Li, 2016), and new lists of forbidden programming are constantly added to a long list of already censored topics. For example, SAPPRFT issued an order in 2018 that forbids video dramas of power fights at royal courts (宫斗剧). Recently it issued a new order that further forbids a wide range of costume dramas, including those dealing with martial arts, fantasy, history, mythology, time travel, and other topics ("Zhongguo Zuijin," 2019, March 24). As a result, several dozen costume dramas may be unable to be aired over TV or the internet.

The most stringent control occurs in the new media arena, especially on Weibo and WeChat. While the Chinese authorities found it challenging to control the internet in the early 2000s, and internet users employed parodies and spoofs to criticize and poke fun at the Chinese government (Li, 2011), information control online and over mobile phones has gained momentum. Such control aims not only to censor information but also to shape public opinion (引导舆论) through flooding these spaces with officially sanctioned and "desirable" information. In this way, the Chinese state and party hope to set the agenda and guide the formation of public opinion.

Chinese authorities are especially worried about social instability and disruptions before and during large national events and anniversaries of sensitive events. For example, China hosts the National People's Congress and the Chinese People's Political Consultative Conference each year, and the Chinese authorities spare no effort in making sure that these meetings are held without any problems. The anniversary of the Tiananmen Square movement (also called the June 4thmovement) always attracts increasing police scrutiny and media censorship. Information about the movement is purged from history books, traditional media, and the internet. Terms associated with this event such as "64,""89," and "Tiananmen" are filtered by China's great firewall. This year – 2019 – is the 30thanniversary and Chinese authorities and media operators took more stringent measures to ban public discussion. Not only did traditional media mention nothing about this movement that mobilized millions of protesters who demanded free press and democracy, but social media platforms were also compliant in tightening information. Many WeChat groups—capped at 500 each—were banned because members posted information—such as videos, articles, and comments—about the movement.

For such banned groups (often called half-ban, 半封), users of accounts registered within China cannot view or post any new content, but users of overseas accounts can continue to view and post new information. This method creates two separate spaces within the same group, thus separating users overseas and those in China. However, if all users are registered in China, the group will be completely dissolved, resulting in a complete ban. Another way is to ban accounts registered overseas and users of such accounts can only view others' posts, but cannot post content. This method is called mouth-ban (封口). The third way is to ban an account completely (called account-ban, 全封) and the account cannot be revived in the future.

Online video programming is also tightly censored. In January 2019, China Netcasting Services Association issued an order that regulates online video, including title, commentary, dubbing, emoji, background, and other information. It includes 100 articles, specifying content that will be banned such as information attacking China's political and legal systems, opposing the "one-China" policy, damaging the national image, damaging the image of revolutionary leaders and heroes, leaking national secrets, disrupting social instability, damaging ethnic and regional unity, opposing national religious policies, and other information (China Netcasting Services Association, 2019, January 9).

Even online emojis and pictures are subject to censorship. For example, following Xi Jinping's and U.S. President Barack Obama's two-day summit in California in June 2013, a Chinese artist noticed the resemblance between a picture of Xi and Obama strolling together and the cartoon characters of Winnie the Pooh and Tigger the Tiger walking together. The artist put these images together to show the similarities. Chinese censors immediately deleted the cartoon image from the Chinese internet. Various versions of Winnie the Pooh have since been blacklisted, suggesting that even harmless fun can be viewed as a challenge to Xi Jinping's authority (Lee, 2017, July 16; Luedi, 2016, March 29). Gradually, the fictional bear has become a meme and a symbol of resistance against Xi Jinping. Because of this, Shanghai Disneyland reportedly removed Winnie the Pooh at the request of Chinese authorities (Stolworthy, 2018, November 30).

The ban is part of a broader campaign that supports the government and Xi Jinping's consolidation of power (Luedi, 2016, March 29). In February 2018, China announced it would drop the term limit on the presidency, suggesting that Xi has absolute power to rule the country indefinitely. While this shocking move motivated many Chinese to search for opportunities to immigrate to other countries, state-owned Chinese media gave supportive coverage. What's more, various measures were taken to make sure that resistance was suppressed. For example, many journalists were imprisoned, and overseas dissidents were silenced by targeting their families at home.

In addition to China's continuing block of foreign sites such as The New York

Times, Facebook, YouTube, Twitter, and many others, China's control over virtual private network (VPN) services has also become more stringent. While visitors and dissidents could use VPN to bypass China's great firewall in the past to access foreign sites, the Chinese government has cracked down on VPN, culminating in Apple's deletion of all VPN apps from its App Store in 2017. Chinese internet service providers such as China Mobile, China Unicom, and China Telecom were all ordered to block access to VPNs.

Furthermore, new laws are implemented to punish the "wrong" use of social media. For example, the Amendment (IX) to the Criminal Law of the People's Republic of China was adopted at the 16th Session of the Standing Committee of the 12th National People's Congress of the People's Republic of China on August 29, 2015 and became effective on November 1, 2015. A paragraph added in Article 219A states:

Whoever makes up any false information on the situation of any risk, epidemic disease, disaster or emergency and spreads such information on the information network or any other media, or knowingly spreads the aforesaid false information on the information network or any other media, which seriously disrupts the public order, shall be sentenced to imprisonment of not more than three years, criminal detention or surveillance; and if serious consequences have resulted, shall be sentenced to imprisonment of not less than three years but not more than seven years.

Criminalizing online information dissemination can further force people to censor themselves. Any WeChat group founders are legally responsible for information disseminated in the group. Anyone who spreads rumors to 500 people (the upper limit of a WeChat group) or more could face legal consequences. Several people were reportedly detained for spreading false information. As a result, WeChat group founders reportedly transferred the group administration right to members in other countries to avoid the risks. An overseas Chinese person reportedly became the administrator of more than 70 WeChat groups overnight in 2017 after the new rule was publicized (Qiao, 2017, September 13).

Freedom House's report in 2018 gave China 14 out of 100 in Freedom in the World Scores (0 = least free, 100 = most free). Among them, China's political rights score is the least free, 7 out of 7 (1 = most free, 7 = least free); civil liberties score is 6 out of 7; and overall freedom rating is 6.5 out of 7. The reports states (Freedom House, 2018):

China's authoritarian regime has become increasingly repressive in recent years. The ruling Chinese Communist Party (CCP) is tightening its control over the media, online speech, religious groups, and civil society associations while undermining already modest rule-of-law reforms. The CCP leader and state president, Xi Jinping, is consolidating personal power to a degree not seen in China for decades. The country's budding civil society and human rights movements have struggled amid a multiyear crackdown, but continue to seek avenues for protecting basic rights and sharing uncensored information, at times scoring minor victories.

In addition to the tightening of media control, the Chinese leadership has also developed new technology-driven instruments of control called the Social Credit System. While this system is not completely new, its recent development aims to utilize big data and collect any information of individuals and organizations, ranging from financial information to activities that cover economic, social, and political conduct of individuals and organizations. Specifically, the National Development and Reform Commission has already built a national credit system through sharing data and blacklisting businesses and individuals who break laws and social expectations. Other private credit entities have also been established, such as Alibaba's Sesame Credit, Tencent Credit, and Kaola Credit, suggesting that both state and commercial agencies collaborate with each other to increase surveillance in Chinese society.

The control system involves a wide range of government agencies, commercial entities, and partnerships with private organizations. It aims to establish a comprehensive surveillance system that facilitates the development of a moral society supported by a legal and administrative monitoring system. While the primary purpose of the social credit system is to modernize China's legal and administrative governance, it can be used to further suppress the voices of dissidents and freedom of expression. In this way, organizations' and individuals' political, social, and economic activities are under constant monitoring by the state through data aggregation and automation. While the credit system in the United States only collects financial data, the social credit system in China collects all kinds of data, thus making it a more powerful and dangerous surveillance instrument. Such a system has caused a lot of concern among scholars over China's capacity to finally realize its total control over society (Creemers, 2018; Liang, Das, Kostyuk & Hussain, 2018).

### China's Soft Power, Public Diplomacy, and Challenges

China has been paying increasing attention to its soft power since 2000 (Li, 2012). As I stated in my previous essay, China has attempted to increase its soft power through foreign aid, cultural programs, and various other global programs in order to gain more attraction among foreign publics. China has also allocated huge resources to increase the international influence of Chinese media such as Xinghua News Agency, China Central TV, and Shanghai Media Group. However, China's global outreach and projection of soft power have encountered many challenges. Specifically, I will discuss the Confucius Institute, China's corporate globalization, and the One Belt and One Road Initiative.

Recently, China's Confucius Institute has been under great scrutiny, especially in the United States. Launched in 2004 by the Office of Chinese Language Council International (called Hanban), the Confucius Institute has been increasingly criticized for its relationship to the Chinese Communist Party, ranging from concerns over academic freedom, institutional autonomy, control over curriculum, China's use of it as a propaganda instrument, and the quality of the teaching faculty. As U.S.-China tensions intensify, Washington has called for American higher education institutions to close the institutes down. At least 10 have closed or announced plans to close the Confucius Institutes since 2018 (Redden, 2019, January 9). While some American educators still believe the Confucius Institute offers valuable resources for cultural exchange and that the politically motivated criticisms are unsubstantiated, such scrutiny means that China's soft power strategy has experienced a huge backlash.

The global expansion of Chinese companies has also proved to be challenging. Since around the 2000s, the Chinese government has supported Chinese companies in going global (Li, 2016). Many companies such as Lenovo, Huawei, and Haier have established their global presences. However, the way business is conducted in China has proved to be an inherent obstacle for these companies' global expansion, especially in the West. One example is Huawei. While Huawei is a leading global provider of information and communication technology and smartphones, its entry into the U.S. market has been constantly blocked mainly based on the alleged security risk because of Huawei's perceived close relation with the Chinese state and party. Huawei's 5G network has also been banned in Australia.

However, the difficulty facing Huawei is not unique. Any Chinese telecommunication and technology companies planning to enter the American and Western markets may encounter similar challenges. After all, the boundary between a government agency and a commercial entity in China is not as clearly marked as in the United States and European countries. With the Chinese government's tight control, no company can become completely independent. Even foreign companies doing business in China are required to obey Chinese laws regarding media control and censorship. In this sense, the government practices at home actually become a hindrance when a Chinese company goes global.

Another high-profile project that China has launched recently is the Silk Road Economic Belt and the 21stCentury Maritime Silk Road, called the One Belt and One Road Initiative (OBORI). The OBORI is the most ambitious global project launched by China since the country started to open itself to capitalism in 1978. The area covers 65 percent of the world population and one-third of global GDP. Since 2013, various measures have been implemented to support this initiative, including the founding of Asian Infrastructure Investment Bank and the New Development Bank.

However, views toward this initiative are mixed. For example, while some countries in Europe are receptive to China's investment, other European countries are more cautious and insist that China must "follow international standards and not exclusively pursue its geostrategic interests" (Le Corre, 2017). This initiative also marks China's divergence from its old foreign policy cultivated by Deng Xiaoping asking China to bide time for development and to keep a low profile. The initiative is generally viewed as having not only economic importance, but also geopolitical significance in shaping global trade policies. While it is hard to tell whether OBORI will be successful, China will definitely face tremendous political, cultural, and economic challenges to implementing the plan both at home and abroad.

Interestingly, there is a sharp contrast between China's domestic policies and foreign policies. While China's foreign policies often advocate for a multipolar global order that enables smaller countries to have voices so that China can increase its influence and benefit from broader global political participation, China's domestic policies are characterized by tight control and non-transparency. The inconsistency often causes the international community to be concerned about China's promotional rhetoric of global political participation. In order to gain credibility internationally, China has to seriously transform its own domestic policies and make them more transparent and democratic.

## Conclusion

I argue that China's control over traditional and new media has tightened tremendously since I first examined this in 2014, making China one of the least free countries in the world. China's data-driven social credit system has the capacity to even further intensify the monitor and surveillance mechanism, thus allowing the Chinese government to have a total control over citizens and corporations. While China has actively encouraged the companies to go global, the very nature of the domestic business environment makes Chinese companies the target of suspicion because of the lack of separation between the government and the corporate world. As a consequence, China's efforts to increase its global soft power through economic means and corporate diplomacy will encounter tremendous challenges.

*References*

China Netcasting Services Association (2019, January 9). *Review Guidelines and Criteria of On-line Short Video (*网络短视频内容审核标准细则*). Accessed June 21, 2019. http://www. cnsa.cn/index.php/infomation/dynamic_details/id/69/type/2.html*

Creemers, R. ( 2018, May 9 ). *China's Social Credit System: An Evolving Practice of Control. Available at SSRN: https://ssrn.com/abstract=3175792or http://dx.doi.org/10.2139/*

*ssrn.3175792*

Freedom House (2018). *Freedom in the World 2018: China Profile. https://freedomhouse.org/report/freedom-world/2018/china*

Le Corre, P. (2017, May 23). *Europe's mixed views on China's One Road, One Belt Initiative. https://www.brookings.edu/blog/order-from-chaos/2017/05/23/europes-mixed-views-on-chinas-one-belt-one-road-initiative/*

Li, H. (2006). *Advertising and Consumption in Post-Mao China: Between the Local and the Global. Dissertation, University of Southern California.*

Li, H. (2011). *Parody and resistance on the Chinese internet. In D. Herold & P. W. Marolt (Eds.), Online society in China (pp. 71-88). Routledge.*

Li, H. (2012). *The Chinese diaspora and China's public diplomacy: Contentious politics for the Beijing Olympic float in the Pasadena Rose Parade. International Journal of Communication, 6, 2245–2279.*

Li, H. (2014). *Chinese media and culture: Dancing with chains. China Currents, 13(2). Available: http://www.chinacenter.net/2014/china_currents/13-2/chinese-media-and-culture-dancing-with-chains/*

Li, H. (2016). *Advertising and consumer culture in China. Cambridge, UK: Polity.*

Liang, F. Das, V. Kostyuk, N. & Hussain, M. M. (2018) *Constructing a Data-Driven Society: China's Social Credit System as a State Surveillance Infrastructure. Policy & Internet, 10 (4): 415-453*

Luedi, J. (2016, March 29). *Why China banned Winnie the Pooh and why it matters. https://globalriskinsights.com/2016/03/china-blacklists-winnie-pooh/*

McDonell, S. (2017, Oct. 16). *"中国政府如何审查你的思想？" (https://www.bbc.com/zhongwen/simp/chinese-news-41634026)*

Qiao, L. (2017, September 13). *微信群主"移民"海外避险. https://www.rfa.org/mandarin/yataibaodao/meiti/ql1-09132017112957.html*

Redden, E. (2019, January 9). *Closing Confucius Institute. https://www.insidehighered.com/news/2019/01/09/colleges-move-close-chinese-government-funded-confucius-institutes-amid-increasing*

Stolworthy, J. (2018, November 30). *Winnie the Pooh 'banned from Disneyland in China' due to Xi Jinping meme. https://www.independent.co.uk/arts-entertainment/books/news/winnie-the-pooh-disneyland-china-ban-xi-jinping-meme-shanghai-president-a8660461.html*

Zhonguo Zuijin Gongbu "Xian Gu Ling": Guzhuang Ju Quanmian Jin Bo (2019, March 24). *Reprinted from Ziyou Shibao. https://www.wenxuecity.com/news/2019/03/24/8183297.html*

---

*Dr. Hongmei Li is Associate Professor and the coordinator of Strategic Communication at Miami University of Ohio.*

*Appendix*

*Image 1: Xi Jinping and Barack Obama at the Sunnyvale Summit in 2013 and the image of Winnie the Pooh and Tigger strolling together*

*Special Issue: Vol. 18, No.1, 2019: The CCP 19th Party Congress*

# China's Continued War on Air Pollution

*Eri Saikawa*

*Vol. 18, No.1*
*2019*

## Introduction

Since Prime Minister Li Keqiang declared war against air pollution in March 2014, five years have passed. Last year, reports were coming out spreading good news. For example, concentrations of fine particulate matter with an aerodynamic diameter of 2.5 microns or less, known as PM2.5, were down, on average, by 32 percent from 2014 to 2018(Greenstone, 2018). Awareness about air pollution has also skyrocketed, so much so that no Chinese would likely tell me that the air pollution we see in the sky is just fog, as they used to in 2006 when I first visited Beijing. Some were going so far as to state that China was winning in the war on air pollution based on the significant progress it has made on improving air quality at the beginning of 2018.

As clearly seen in Figure 1 (BeijingAirNow), the number of days with heavy or extremely heavy pollution in Beijing have reduced substantially since 2013, and days with excellent air quality have increased over the five years. In Beijing, the annual average PM2.5concentrations dropped to 58 micrograms per cubic meter (µg/m3) in 2017, meeting the 2013 action plan to improve air quality in the region around the capital(Xu and Stanway, 2018). Of course, the data need to be taken with a grain of salt as the standard used here for PM2.5in Beijing is an annual average concentration of 75 µg/m3 or less, which is substantially higher than the official national standard of 35 µg/m3, as well as the standard of the World Health Organization (10 µg/m3), the U.S. (12 µg/m3), or EU (10 µg/m3), as I discussed in 2014 (Saikawa, 2014). Still, Beijing's PM2.5 was 35 percent lower in early 2018 compared to 2013, and such a decrease is significant; some argue that it is equivalent to the change that took 12 years in the U.S. (Greenstone, 2018).

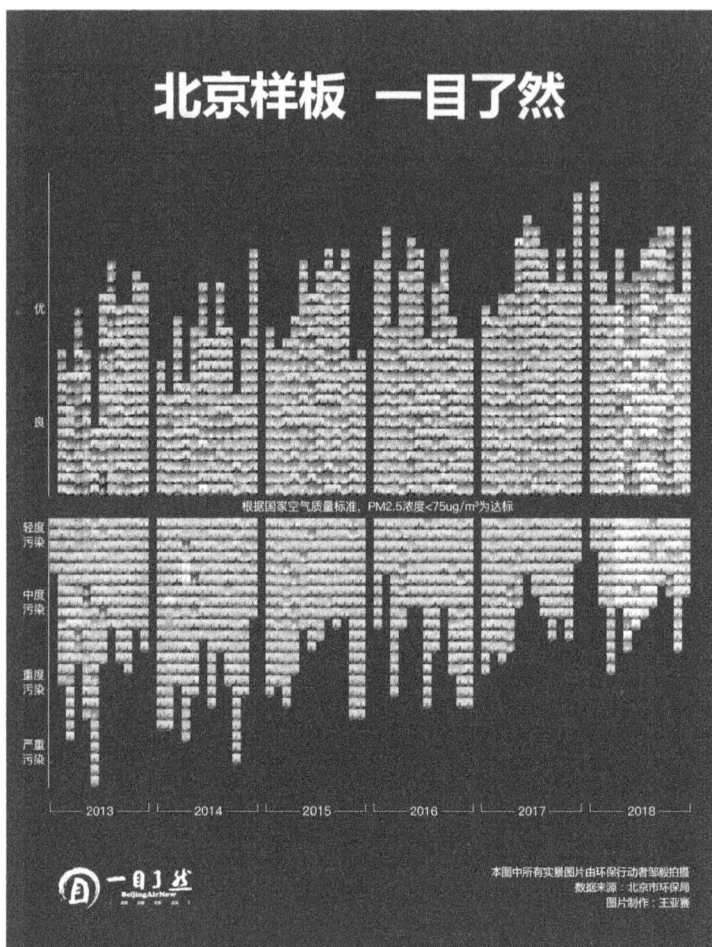

*Figure 1. Difference in air quality in five years in Beijing*

**Air Pollution Policies**

What has been done to combat air pollution in China? One of the major changes was probably the replacement of the main household energy source from coal to natural gas. Since 2017, the Chinese government says around four million homes in the North have seen the change (Yu, 2018). This energy transition is important because it impacts not only ambient air pollution but also household air pollution (HAP). After all, we are interested in reducing air pollution mainly because of the large health problems it creates. Exposure to air pollution leads to substantial adverse health impacts, such as cardiovascular and respiratory diseases. The latest Global Burden of Disease (GBD) study estimated that in 2017, more than 1.6 million deaths were attributable to HAP exposure from solid fuels, and 3.4 million deaths were attributable to ambient air pollution (Stanaway et al., 2018).

For the past five years, my research group has worked on measuring HAP in three different parts of Tibet. We have been interested in assessing residents' exposure to HAP, their awareness of HAP, and the link between the two. Until the late 1990s, most Tibetan nomads lived in black woven yak hair tents. Today, these yak hair tents are scarce in all nomadic villages we visited, as most nomads have transitioned to store-bought plastic tarp tents, which are lighter, better waterproofed, and easier to set up, or to temporary houses that are more spacious and comfortable. This transition is important because of the type of stove used in each household. In yak hair tents, residents have an open fire using an iron ring or a homemade adobe mud stove with an opening in the ceiling of the tent for ventilation (Sclar and Saikawa, 2019). Tarp tents or temporary houses, on the other hand, utilize improved cast iron cookstoves with stovepipes that vent the smoke through the ceiling. In Nam Co in the Tibetan Autonomous Region, we found that four households out of 23 used natural gas instead of yak dung (Xiao et al., 2015). Those households had the lowest six-hour mean PM2.5 concentrations (43 µg/m3) compared to others varying from 178 – 1530 µg/m3, and those were also the only houses meeting the national 24-hour standard of 75 µg/m3. In some households in Tibet, the instantaneous PM2.5concentrations went as high as 157,000 µg/m3 (Sclar and Saikawa, 2019). It clearly showed that the fuel type was an important factor for HAP, and the transition to natural gas was reducing both HAP and ambient air pollution at the same time.

While the residential sector clearly plays an important role for PM2.5, industry is also equally or more important, especially for those areas close to it. Steel, aluminum and cement producers were told to cut output by as much as 50 percent in the winter of 2016-2017 (October-March) in the region surrounding Beijing to avoid smog (Lelyveld, 2018). This was a part of the "Airborne Prevention and Control Action Plan (2013-17)," which targeted Beijing, Tianjin, and Hebei to reduce emissions by implementing strict policies (Greenstone, 2018). A similar action plan was issued for the Fenwei Plain and also in the Yangtze River Delta region as well.

In 2013, $277 billion was pledged by China's Academy for Environmental Planning to mitigate urban air pollution (Yu, 2018). In addition to closing down industry, China prohibited new coal-fired power plants, restricted the number of cars on the road, banned high-emission vehicles, and shut down coal mines (Greenstone, 2018, Xu and Stanway, 2018). These strategies make sense, as two other important sectors for air pollution are power and transport (Saikawa et al., 2017).

**Air Quality Trends in Cities**

Unfortunately, the air quality trend has not continued to improve from 2018 onward. Although the clear sky was visible at the start of 2018, by the end of November, smog was thick again in the sky, with pollution levels 10 percent higher than in 2017(Stanway, 2018). In the 2018-2019 winter period, for example, air pollution levels increased by 10 percent from the previous year(Hu, 2019).

It is not fair, however, to blame a lack of policies or enforcement because air quality does not solely depend on emissions. Terrain and meteorological conditions are also important. Researchers have found that atmospheric transport of pollution to downwind areas and stagnant meteorological conditions are equally important factors linked to the severe air pollution episodes in northern China (Zhang and Cao, 2015, Sun et al., 2016, Wang et al., 2017). It is also important to note that this past winter was one of the coldest years on record in China, with snow in Shanghai, which most likely also increased the heating demand across the country (Leister and Richards, 2018). Henan province government officials had a point when they explained their 27 percent increase in PM2.5concentrations, which was the highest across China, as a result of "unfavorable weather conditions (Stanway, 2019)."

Despite the closures of coal-fired power plants across China in 2017, there was a report of satellite imagery showing pre-construction and/or construction phases of new coal-fired power plants again. It appeared that the quick and stringent regulations backfired and led to the national government loosening restrictions on these plants in five provinces in early 2018 (Hao, 2018). The 13th Five-Year Plan limits the total coal power capacity to 1,100 gigawatts. The current capacity is 993 gigawatts. Adding 46 gigawatts found in pre-construction and construction mode and 57 gigawatts of shelved projects would bring the total to 1,096 gigawatts, allowing China to stay just below the plan ceiling by 2020 (Hao, 2018).

Despite last year's early celebration that China was winning in the war on air pollution, the war does not seem to be ending just yet. In the summer of 2018, China published a new three-year action plan on air pollution that added no new targets to the existing policies (Ma, 2018). The question now is whether China can maintain its commitment to improving air quality. With the signs of renewed construction of coal-fired power plants, what we should be prepared for may be higher PM2.5 concentrations again this coming winter.

**Complicated Problems**

China's war on air pollution is also not just about PM2.5. Some researchers are finding that even when PM2.5 concentrations were going down, another important air pollutant, tropospheric ozone (O3), was going up. Stratospheric ozone, higher up in the atmosphere, is a good ozone, protecting us from the harmful ultraviolet radiation. Tropospheric ozone, on the other hand, is a bad ozone and is an air pollutant, having harmful health impacts. O3is not directly emitted but is produced in the atmosphere through a chemical reaction under sunlight. Li et al. (2018), for example, have shown that O3increased since 2013 after the decrease in PM2.5 concentrations, especially in megacities such as Beijing and Shanghai. The researchers explain that this increase may be due to the decrease in PM2.5 concentrations reducing the sink of hydroperoxyl radicals and enhancing O3 production.

In our work, we also found a similar trend of increased O3 concentrations in future simulations (Zhong et al., 2019). We assessed the sensitivity of health estimates due to PM2.5 and O3 exposure in China in 2050 to various uncertainties, including emissions, concentration-response function linking the relationship between air pollution exposure and health impacts, and population projections. We found that concentration-response function is the largest source of uncertainty for PM2.5-related health estimates, while future emissions are the greatest source of uncertainty for estimated O3-related health outcomes in China. Other parameters are much less influential compared with emissions. Our results highlight the importance of constraining emissions to better assess PM2.5– and O3-related human health impacts. It is important to mention that the projected changes in future O3 are much more variable. Eight out of 12 cases show that at least 50 percent of future population will be exposed to higher O3, while in all cases, more than 80 percent of the future population would be subjected to reduced PM2.5 exposure.

The Chinese government also recognizes the increase in O3 concentrations and made a statement that in 74 cities, they (Ministry of Ecology and Environment, 2017). Among 338 areas, 59 cities observed O3 levels above the second national standard. In 2017, based on the increasing trend, the Chinese government emphasized the importance of volatile organic compounds (VOCs) emission reduction. Nitrogen oxides (NOx) and VOCs are the major sources of O3 production. The chemical reaction to produce O3 is non-linear and thus the effective control depends on the existing mix of chemicals. China's case illustrates an example of where the efficient O3 reduction results from a reduction in VOCs, and not in NOx (Saikawa et al., 2017).

It is important to realize that both PM2.5 and O3 also affect climate and so we are not just dealing with air pollution. Reducing O3 concentrations can improve air quality and climate at the same time. However, to make the matter more complicated, PM2.5 can both cool and warm the atmosphere, depending on its chemical composition. So, reducing PM2.5 concentrations does not necessarily translate to a win-win situation of improving air quality and mitigating climate change at the same time. Considering the health impacts associated with PM2.5

exposure, reducing their concentrations is important for human welfare, but more efforts are also essential to reduce greenhouse gas emissions and to mitigate climate change.

Air pollution is complicated and is also linked to other problems, such as food production. Crop yields can be significantly reduced by being exposed to air pollution, especially O3 (Van Dingenen et al., 2009, Avnery et al., 2011). In China, because of the change to natural gas in residential homes, domestic fertilizer production was also directly affected in 2017. China is the largest nitrogen fertilizer consumer in the world (International Fertilizer Association, 2019) and it has relied on its domestic fertilizer production. However, because of the shortage of natural gas this winter, fertilizer production was cut in half. This decline led to a spike in agricultural production costs and a sharp increase in prices for urea, synthetic ammonia, and compound fertilizers(Gu and Mason, 2018).

## Looking Ahead in the War on Air Pollution

Many of the studies give us more reason to look at the inter-related issues of pollution holistically rather than to focus on one specific problem. It is probably time to start linking multiple problems. These can include air pollution, climate change, and water pollution, but we might also start linking ecosystem conservation and sustainable production, and other social issues. Multiple improvements in diverse fields would be possible; it is important to look at our environment as a complex system, with multiple components. One such mechanism might be to find food production methods that do not emit so much greenhouse gas and air pollutants. China's large fertilizer consumption is leading to large nitrous oxide emissions from farms (Saikawa et al., 2014). It is a great beginning to switch household fuel from coal to natural gas, but it is also time to emphasize the need for reduced fertilizer use in China's agricultural fields. We forget how agriculture is linked to air pollution and soil pollution sometimes and yet, it is significant. Individuals can also do things to make our planet more sustainable. Instead of relying on the governments, maybe it is also time to consider what different ways are available for us to be closer to more blue-sky days in the coming years.

### References

Central People's Government of PRC. "History of Christianity in China." Accessed July 18, 2015. http://www.gov.cn/test/2005-07/26/content_17214./htm.

---

*Dr. Eri Saikawa is an associate professor in the Department of Environmental Sciences and the Rollins School of Public Health at Emory University, and an Associate of the China Research Center.*

## There Is and Must Be Common Ground
## between the United States and China

*Yawei Liu*
*Vol. 18, No.1*
*2019*

**An Interview with Yawei Liu conducted by Sun Lu**

*Liu Yawei is the director of the China Program at The Carter Center in the United States and member of the China Research Center's Board of Directors. Sun Lu is an associate professor at the Institute of International Relations at the Communication University of China. The interview was conducted in Chinese in 2019 and translated by Baker Lu, Cindy Cheng and Caroline Wang.*

*Q: President Carter not only built the diplomatic relationship between the U.S. and China, but he also kept promoting U.S.-China relations even after he left the White House. In particular, President Carter wrote a letter to President Trump about the importance of U.S.-China relations and offered suggestions about how to repair this relationship under the current circumstances. What are the implications for the bilateral relations between U.S. and China after reviewing the history of President Carter and Vice Premier Deng Xiaoping's decision to establish diplomatic relations and President Carter's continuous efforts to promote U.S.-China relations after he left the office?*

A: I think there are three things we can learn from history — from the Nixon 1972 ice-breaking trip to the 1978 establishment of diplomatic relations.

First of all, the normalization of diplomatic relations with China was actually easier for Nixon. He became involved in politics by embracing the anti-communist doctrine. Nixon would not have begun his political career, served as the vice president under the Eisenhower administration, or been elected as the president in 1968 if he had not shown his anti-communism sentiment. Therefore, when Nixon said that he was in contact with China, nobody suspected that he was colluding with the Chinese Communists. People believed that he did this to protect the national security.

For Carter, it was much more difficult to negotiate with China. Soon after the Chinese Communist Party (CCP) won the civil war in 1949, the Republicans immediately initiated a big discussion about "Who lost China," accusing the Democrats of being pro-communist. This atmosphere led directly to the proliferation of McCarthyism. All U.S. State Department diplomats who had contact with the CCP during World War II and the Chinese Civil War were were cast aside or even fired. As a result, the Democratic Party was blamed for allowing the CCP to take power because of its softness toward the CCP. This is also the reason neither President Kennedy nor Johnson improved diplomatic relations with Beijing.

Therefore, when President Carter began secret negotiations with Deng Xiaoping, some of Carter's assistants informed him that building diplomatic relations with China would definitely cause him to lose the 1980 election. However, Carter still established relations with China for the sake of the national interest. As for Deng Xiaoping, the pressure he faced was no less than Carter.

Based on this historical background, President Carter and Vice Premier Deng showed us that politicians must have vision and courage. Also, politicians and leaders need to grasp the necessity of compromise. Sometimes a temporary compromise can lead to a broader consensus, and this consensus can promote a win-win situation. For instance, on how to solve Taiwan issue, both Carter and Deng showed great vision and courage.

Second, mutual interests are the engine of U.S.-China relations. When the leaders of China and the United States established diplomatic relations, they faced a common enemy: the Soviet Union. Back then, Moscow's threats to the well-being of the U.S. and China brought these two countries, which had completely different histories, cultures and political systems, together. Today, although the Soviet Union no longer exists, we face far more dangerous and uncontrollable common enemies. For instance, climate change, terrorism, Iran and other chaos in the Middle East will put the whole world in turmoil and bring disaster to the global economy.

Decades ago, China and the United States had common interests. Today, there are even more common interests between China and the United States. These common interests do not allow Washington and Beijing to part ways, and if China and the United States do not work together to face these challenges, the world might become less secure than it was during the Cold War. Back then we had certainty and predictability under a superpower duopoly, but now the world has become unpredictable and less stable because of nationalism and various other factors. Therefore, under the current circumstances, China and the United States cannot let domestic factors, especially on the U.S. side, break the ties between them.

Third, President Carter has said in his books and on the recent phone call with President Trump that many of the problems faced by the United States come from its own belligerent and failed foreign policies. On the other hand, the rise of China is precisely due to the fact that China has taken a peaceful approach to development. The shortage of money for U.S. domestic development, therefore, is caused by the vast fiscal investments in war and conflicts. The U.S. should mind its own business if it wants to become stronger and to make its politics rational again.

On the Chinese side, although it has made tremendous achievements in the past four decades and the total size of its economy is approaching the United States, its economy still faces the problem of sustainable development, which is mainly caused by challenges in deepening and expanding its economic reform and opening up. As a result, despite the fact that some of the current difficulties in Sino-U.S. relations have an international dimension, the main reasons for these difficulties are the political and economic challenges within these two countries.

Donald Trump vows to make the United States great again, to revitalize U.S. manufacturing, to boost the U.S. economy, and to make blue-collar workers proud. Xi Jinping keeps talking, from last year's Boao Forum to this year's One Belt One Road Summit, about how to deepen reform and expand openness, how to enhance the role of the market in the Chinese economy, and how to meet the interests and ensure fair competition with foreign companies in China. Therefore, Americans should understand that if China achieves all reform goals proposed by President Xi, the trade war will end. The truce and renegotiations achieved in the Osaka meeting between President Trump and Xi Jinping further demonstrate that in order to develop, these two leaders need to stop confronting each other and solve the problem through dialogue.

In other words, the current low point in Sino-U.S. relations actually isn't a diplomatic problem; it stems from the externalization of domestic issues.

In the United States politicians shift domestic problems and find scapegoats by accusing China. In China domestic special interest groups caused China to miss the window for a second opportunity of reform. Therefore, as President Trump said at the press conference in Osaka, as long as China improves the environment for investment, China and the United States will be strategic partners, not opponents or enemies.

**Q: *During the Osaka Summit, although there was no agreement between the U.S. and China on trade, the two countries decided to resume negotiations. How do you analyze the results of this summit?***

A: I think the result of this summit is like an old saying from a Chinese poem: "Find the silver lining at the end of our tethers." After the breakdown of Sino-U.S. trade negotiations in early May, both sides actually thought about the worst outcome. The rhetoric that China and the United States will completely break their ties is rampant in both countries. However, after looking at media reports of the summit, it is possible that both China and the U.S. have gotten what they want, so both sides can find ways out. The following specific questions to be negotiated should then be dealt with by experts in the relevant fields.

Based on the comments from the American Chamber of Commerce, the two sides had reached consensus on more than 90% of the issues before the sudden breakdown of negotiations in May. The last 5%-6% are only about the details of how to implement, advance and verify the agreement. However, China and the United States have different views on these final parts. For example, there are reports that the United States has asked China to change its law to ensure its commitments to the agreements. Unsurprisingly, since this is about China's sovereignty and dignity, China did not accept the U.S. request on this matter. Some Chinese even argue that if the government had signed this agreement, it would have been the second version of the Treaty of Shimonoseki.

After the pause of negotiations, anti-American propaganda films "Shang Ganling" and "Heroes and Children" were broadcasted on Chinese TV channels. In addition, the People's Daily also issued scores of comments criticizing and attacking the United States. However, prior to the Osaka Summit, CCTV started to show films depicting U.S.-China friendship, like "Yellow River Love." During the summit, we observed that Xi Jinping talked about ping-pong diplomacy and Trump praised Xi Jinping as one of most outstanding leaders in China and claimed that a trade deal could be "historic." From all of these changing signals, we can say that the two leaders once again stopped the Sino-U.S. relationship from deteriorating and diverted it from possible confrontations to serious and equal dialogue.

When Xi Jinping met with Trump, he mentioned ping-pong diplomacy from 48 years ago and the establishment of diplomatic relations between China and the United States 40 years ago. His words implicitly suggest that the reason why Mao Zedong, Zhou Enlai, Deng Xiaoping, Nixon, Kissinger and Carter could build the new era of the U.S.-China relations was that they had mutual respect, found common ground while putting aside differences, compromised and had fine negotiations. Today, like the mentioned great leaders, President Trump and Xi must have similar courage, vision and skills to bring Sino-U.S. relations to another new era. As an observer, I greatly admire them for their untraditional, responsible and unconventional actions.

As for those who say Trump is a "player" who just does loose talk, claim Xi Jinping's domestic structural reforms will face great obstacles, argue that it is easy for these two leaders to say things in Osaka but it will be difficult for their assistants to do anything in Beijing and Washington D.C., my answer is that it took eight years from the ice-breaking to the establishment of diplomatic relations between the U.S. and China. In the following forty years after the establishment of diplomatic relations, the U.S. and China have written the most brilliant page of shared peace and prosperity in human history. The relationship between the two countries is intertwined and critical for the stable development of the world. Therefore, unlike some people's rhetoric, the bilateral relationship's importance prevents it from being broken too easily. This requires the most capable and courageous leaders to do their best to keep continuous development of this bilateral relationship, and both Trump and Xi have done this.

**Q:** *Both the face-to-face talk between Trump and Kim Jong-Un in the Korean Demilitarized Zone and the Kim-Xi meeting in North Korea have been given lots of attention recently. What role do you think that China could* *still play in solving the North Korea nuclear crisis?*

A: Even though I am not an expert on the Korean Peninsula, I do believe that China is willing to play a role, and its influence will be decisive.

As we look to the past, the reason why North Korea could navigate its path under the intense pressure of international sanctions was the Chinese irresolute attitude towards the situation on the Korean peninsula. Some decision makers argue that the enemy's enemy is a friend. In other words, North Korea's nuclear weapons threat is recognized as China's trump card that could be used to exercise restraint over the United States at any time. If the U.S. really needs to involve China in the process of denuclearization of the Korean peninsula, it should be prepared to make some concessions, such as the abolishment of Taiwan Relation Act. If China is determined enough, it has the power to wreck the economic system of North Korea, even though there are the concerns about the refugee influx crossing the Yalu River into the northeast of China.

Until 2017, the Chinese government still categorized the Korean peninsula crisis as a "none of my business" issue. As a Chinese adage suggests, "untying a bell needs the one who ties the knot in the beginning." The North Korea nuclear crisis should remain a problem between North Korea and the United States. It is the potential threat that the U.S. has imposed upon North Korea that causes the problem. As a result, as long as the two countries build mutual trust, this issue will be solved naturally without too much help that China could offer. However, the situation has started to change since the surprise visit of Kim to China last year. Kim-Xi meetings have happened four times. Two took place before Donald Trump met Kim. From my perspective, even though the "shake hands and say hello" between Trump and Kim after the G20 Summit seemed largely unplanned, this decision must have been related to the recent Xi-Kim meeting. For China, the only way to maximize its gains is to actively participate in the Korean peninsula issue. A separate peace between the U.S. and North Korea is the worst thing for the country's political interest. Akin to what China did 66 years ago — signing the Korean Armistice Agreement — there is no denying that the country plays a critical role in carrying out a new peace treaty in North Korea. Even though China cannot guarantee the same protection that the U.S. promises for Seoul, the situation could still be greatly altered if China could convince Kim to give up military plans and start to rejuvenate the domestic economy.

After all, we should never forget the blood-cemented historical relationship between China and North Korea. Today, China serves as the essential provider and passage of goods for North Korea. Passing Beijing is a must for North Korean officials who travel abroad for foreign affairs. Moreover, China is also the test field that proves the huge success of economic reforms. For me, it's unwise to simply hold these advantages. In fact, under the gathering cloud of Sino-America tension, China should be more actively involved in Washington's effort to denuclearize the Korean Peninsula through a combination of sanctions and diplomatic activities. Only by doing so can China reduce the perception held by the American elite that it is not a responsible great power. China needs to convince Washington that it is doing its best to share the burden of denuclearization and peaceful development on the Korean Peninsula.

**Q: One female officer in the United States State Department pointed out that the conflict between China and the United States is a clash of civilizations. This is an unprecedented viewpoint for the discussion of Sino-America relationship. How do you interpret this perspective?**

A: "Clash of civilizations" first appeared in the famous argument of Samuel P. Huntington. Before the publication of his book in 1996, the mainstream argument was rooted in Francis Fukuyama's book, The End of History and the Last Man, in which he argues that the end of the Cold War and the end of the history is symbolized by the triumph of western democracy represented by the United States over the socialism represented by the Soviet Union. However, Huntington holds different opinions, advocating that the world faces more deeply-rooted conflicts than the battle between different ideologies: the clash of civilizations. After the 9/11 attack, the Fukuyama's argument was gradually replaced by Huntington's. In the 21st century, the global village is more turbulent. There is not only the western culture dominated by America but also Chinese civilization, Islamic civilization, and others. It's reasonable to predict that the clash of civilizations will be more uncertain, the contradictions will be more irreconcilable, and the corresponding fissures will be more intensive.

Kiron Skinner, the Director of Policy Planning at the U.S. Department of State, once grandiloquently described the great power competition during the Cold War as a "fight within the western family." Today, the competition with China is completely different, since China is the first competitor for the U.S. that is "not Caucasian" and not predominately white. This is the real clash of races, ideologies, and civilizations. With a Ph.D. earned from Harvard University and as a political science professor at Carnegie Mellon University, Skinner makes herself a mockery by advocating such a hilarious argument. It's even more ironic that, as an African American, she criticizes the cultural collision between white and black people. Prejudice is farther away from truth than ignorance. Skinner boasts herself as the follower of Condoleezza Rice, the former U.S. secretary of state, who has claimed numerous times that she is the direct beneficiary of the Civil Rights Movement. According to her, if there had been no magnificent movement led by Martin Luther King, there would not have been possible for her to achieve the outstanding academic outcomes and brilliant political career (the first black secretary of state in the U.S.). I have no idea how she will comment on her student and whether she will call the severe contradiction between the American white and black people that still exists after the abolishment of slavery 165 years ago, as the "clash of civilizations" as well.

By no means should we deny that China and the United States have great differences in history, civilization and political systems and incompatibilities caused by the characteristics of distinctive civilizations. This cannot be avoided. However, this does not mean that the two countries will end up with a civilization clash. I am convinced that leaders, scholars and ordinary citizens of China and the U.S. could through exploration find ways to combine the advantages of the two civilizations and overcome the respective deficiencies.

As China has always suggested, the two countries should seek agreement and peaceful coexistence while shelving differences. Once standing at the same position of Skinner, George Kennan was in charge of planning U.S. long-term foreign policy. If Skinner regards current Sino-American friction as the clash of civilizations, this preconceived prejudice will definitely thwart the possible reconciliation of the two countries.

Different civilizations have coexisted in the world for centuries. Even though there have been contradictions and wars, the general progress of human civilization continues to develop in an inclusive and eclectic era. After not formally recognizing China for 30 years, the United States eventually discovered the possible foundation of collaboration with China. In the following 40 years, the two countries together have built the East Asia and Pacific area into the brightest spot of peace and prosperity. I believe that these two civilizations will create more brilliant moments in the future, exploring unprecedented paths for the establishment of the community of shared future for mankind.

*Q: I would like to ask about a new trend in the field of American colleges and universities. Emory University, which is cooperating with The Carter*

**Center, recently dismissed several Chinese professors. Yesterday, the U.S. National Public Radio reported that the FBI recommended that American universities should supervise Chinese scholars and students on campus. What do you think about this trend?**

A: First of all, let's look back at what has happened: the U.S. FBI director said in testimony before Congress last February that China's threat to the United States is a threat to the entire society and that a U.S. counterattack should also target the entire society. On October 4, Vice President Pence delivered a speech saying that China's threat to the United States is government-wide, so the U.S. counterattack against China's threat should also be government-wide. On November 28, the Hoover Institution and Asia Society, both famous think tanks, co-sponsored and co-authored "The American Interests, China's Influence," which argued that China is engaging in large-scale, fruitful penetration and erosion of the United States, including universities. Subsequently, the National Institutes of Health (NIH) issued a document requesting that research institutions receiving funding from China should review whether they were violating regulations. Following the dismissal of several Chinese-American and Chinese scholars at the Anderson Center, a famous cancer research institution in Houston, Emory University also ordered a Chinese-American couple to leave.

All these subsequent statements and actions remind people of the 1882 Chinese Exclusion Act and the McCarthyism of the 1950s. The discrimination against the Chinese in the past seems to have reemerged. In the United States, Chinese communities, other minority organizations, and many prestigious universities have expressed concern that they will not allow such a policy discriminating against a race to continue to expand.

Second, since the establishment of diplomatic relations between China and the United States 40 years ago, the greatest cooperation has actually been in education and scientific research, as well as cooperation in economy, trade, culture, politics, security and other fields. Chinese students have been the largest group of international students on American campuses for many years. Chinese scholars, especially those who have blended into American society after receiving a degree in the United States, are located at almost all the American universities and research centers. Chinese students have made great contributions to the prosperity of American universities. The research carried out by Chinese-American and Chinese scholars certainly helps put the United States at the forefront of innovation and invention.

Have Chinese scholars in the United States violated relevant laws and regulations and transferred their research results without disclosing them to their institutions or without the approval of their institutions? This surely has happened, but only involving a very small number of people. The United States should not just look at the trees and disregard the forest. I believe that American universities and scientific research institutions will not pursue the dead end of "Science with Borders" and will not give up the key that allows them to dominate the world's scientific research, which is valuable because all talented people can realize their dreams in the United States.

Finally, Americans should not just calculate their own trade deficits. Instead, they should also calculate their own education and research dividends. Tuition paid by Chinese students to American universities each year are a huge bonus in the United States. The research dividends created by Chinese scholars for the United States should be astronomical.

At present, anti-China and anti-Chinese voices are constantly rising, but I believe that the United States will neither make the same mistake made in 1882 again nor allow McCarthyism to reemerge. All Chinese who have been educated and have done research in the United States, whether they will be in the United States or China in the future, are bridges between China and the United States, bind two different civilizations together, and are the engines of the Chinese and American efforts to create a new civilization for mankind.

**Q: Beijing held the second Belt and Road summit in April. You have recently visited Africa several times. How do local people respond to the Belt and Road, and what do you think of this initiative?**

A: The first thing to say is that the role of the Belt and Road has been infinitely magnified in China. The Belt and Road has become a basket, and everything can be put into it. Fundamentally, the Belt and Road is actually using China's own production capacity and capital advantages to add to the development of China and improve China's infrastructure. Beyond that, it can increase trade, lower tariffs, reduce non-tariff barriers, deepen mutual understanding between China and the countries along the Belt and Road, and finally form a situation in which the tide lifts all boats, and all countries embrace sufficiency. If we follow this way of thinking to implement the Belt and Road initiative, it will not only benefit China but also benefit all developing countries and increase trade and other associations between developing and developed countries. President Xi Jinping has repeatedly pointed out that China is the biggest beneficiary of economic globalization, and the Belt and Road allows countries that have not yet fully integrated to the economic globalization to check in and board the train.

If the story of the Belt and Road is like this, many countries that maliciously attack the initiative, especially the leaders of the United States, may become speechless. Countries along the route must also be consistent with China in the ultimate goal of the Belt and Road initiative and tell the story of the initiative together with Beijing. If they do not recognize the view that the Belt and Road initiative is a so-called debt trap and conspiracy to plunder resources and invade the sovereignty of small countries, China will win more friends and partners.

Last week, the World Bank released an evaluation report on the Belt and Road. The report concludes that "One Belt, One Road" is a project that benefits the world but not without risks and challenges. The four major risks mentioned by the World Bank are debt, environment, management, and social unrest. If the sponsor nations of the Belt and Road initiative design the top-level well, increase the transparency of project loans and fair bidding on projects, understand, digest and implement projects and provide relevant information for the domestic people, the final success of the project will be more guaranteed. The Chinese Ministry of Foreign Affairs is very positive about this report, indicating that the Chinese government has become more mature and pragmatic regarding the Belt and Road initiative.

In fact, the second Belt and Road summit hosted by Beijing shows that Chinese leaders have realized the challenges that the initiative has encountered and will face in the process of promotion. They have become more objective and practical in its promotion. At the same time, China has also begun to expand the circle of friends and partner groups of the Belt and Road.

The United States is not a country involved in the Belt and Road, and the United States has gradually transitioned from ignorance to misunderstanding and hostility. We cannot underestimate the ability of the United States to use its own strength and power to interfere with and undermine the Belt and Road initiative. In the past two years, the chief leaders of the U.S. State Department have warned the leaders of participant countries during their visits to those developing and developed countries that they should not board Beijing's train because the train only leads to one station – the debt station. To break through the U.S. blockade of the Belt and Road initiative, China must, as mentioned earlier, break the U.S. decision-making and media portraits that demonize the initiative. Second, China should actively provide the U.S. government, think tanks, and NGOs with information about and conditions of development. Third, China should actively invite American companies to participate in bidding for projects and discuss with the U.S. government and non-governmental organizations about engaging in trilateral cooperation in the countries that join the Belt and Road. The United States asserts that China is doling out stories in the African countries and Latin America to set debt traps there. For example, East Africa is an important node on the maritime silk road. China should cooperate with the United States in Kenya, Ethiopia, and Djibouti to increase mutual trust and cultivate the habit of cooperation in various forms. In this way, China and the U.S. can make good contributions to building Africa as a new continent with sustainable development in the world economy.

# China's Recent Engagement in Latin America and the Caribbean: Current Conditions and Challenges

*Enrique Dussel Peters*
*Vol. 19, No.1*
*2020*

## Introduction

Since the beginning of the 21st century, China's presence in Latin America and the Caribbean (LAC) has been substantial in practically all socio-economic fields: cultural, bilateral, and multilateral political issues, as well as trade, foreign direct investments, academic exchanges, and other areas. The main objective of this essay is to analyze the effects of China's presence in the region in terms of sustainable and long-term development. I will include a diagnostic to understand some of the specificities of the LAC-China socioeconomic relationship, followed by the conclusion with a series of proposals.

The first section of the paper will examine four issues that are relevant to understanding general and specific topics about the China-LAC relationship:

1. China's increasing geopolitical competition with the U.S. in LAC.
2. China's proposal of a globalization process;
3. Particular developments and structures in trade, foreign direct investment, financing and infrastructure; and
4. The institutional framework between LAC and China.

The second part of the paper focuses on the concept of "new triangular relationships" and LAC's challenges given increasing tensions between the United States and China.

**Four topics to understand the current China-LA relationship**

Since the beginning of the 21st century, there has been a qualitative change in China's global presence, including in LAC. While it is true that China is still a developing country in terms of GDP per capita and other socioeconomic indicators, the size of its population and of its economy, along with its medium- and long-term initiatives, have all allowed China to become a serious global competitor to U.S. hegemony. From a LAC perspective, it is true that the U.S. is still by far the most important "qualitative" actor in the region, with long historical ties with the regional elites, militaries, and academics, and plays an important role in cultural terms. It is also true that China is increasing its presence in LAC, with or without diplomatic ties. Less than a decade ago Chinese scholars argued that China would respect the U.S.'s "backyard" (Wu 2010). Since then, however, China's presence has not only increased in socioeconomic terms (as we shall see below), but it has also emerged as an additional actor breaking the duopoly of the European Union and U.S. presence in the region. China has become an additional point of reference in terms of economy, culture, education, and even in military terms, such as in the case of Venezuela (Koleski and Blivas 2018).

**China's proposal of a globalization process with Chinese characteristics**

China's increasing global presence in the context of profound domestic social, economic, and political reforms since the 1970s has also been reflected in the increase of Chinese activities and responsibilities in the United Nations Security Council, in the acknowledgement of China's relevance in the international financial system through its membership in 2016 and inclusion of the renminbi as part of the Special Drawing Rights (SDR), and by its increasing leadership at the G20. From this international perspective, the launch of the Belt and Road Initiative (BRI) at the end of 2013 is crucial to understanding China's proposal and ambition of a globalization process with Chinese characteristics. The BRI is China's key international cooperation strategy with countries in Asia, Africa, Europe, and Latin America since January of 2018, when China formally recognized Latin America at the CELAC-China Forum, specifically through five areas of cooperation: policies, roads and highways, trade, currency, and people-to-people (Long 2015). The BRICS countries (Brazil, Russian Federation, India, China and South Africa) New Development Bank (NDB), as well as the Asian Investment and Infrastructure Bank (AIIB) are some of the new powerful instruments of this global strategy.

The conclusions of the XIX National Congress of the Communist Party of China (CPC) at the end of 2017 and the two CPC sessions in 2018 are relevant to these initiatives (Anguiano Roch 2018, 2019). They not only emphasize a long-term socialist development of China for 2035 and 2050 and elevate Xi Jinping's thought as part of the CPC, but they also underline the importance of BRI as part of the domestic and global strategy of China. After the Second BRI Forum in April of 2019, 130 countries had joined the BRI (Belt and Road Portal 2019), 17 from LAC. The Asian Infrastructure Investment Bank (AIIB), on the other hand, accounts for 70 members, including 44 regional members and 26 non-regional members, plus 27 prospective members (six regional and 21 non-regional).

As part of these strategies, China has signed an increasing number of trade agreements and today has 10 free trade agreements, including those signed with Chile, Costa Rica, and Peru, in addition to the agreements with the Special Administrative Region of Hong Kong and Macao, as well as negotiations with Pakistan and Israel. From an Asian regional perspective, China has been also leading efforts within the Asia-Pacific Economic Cooperation (APEC) and the Association of Southeast Asian Nations (ASEAN). However, in recent years China has prioritized the Regional Comprehensive Economic Partnership (RCEP) with 16 member countries, including the Philippines, Japan, Korea, Australia, India, and Vietnam. So far, no LAC country participates in that initiative.

China has proposed a group of specific initiatives toward LAC. On the one hand, the Chinese public sector published two "White Books" for LAC in 2008 and in 2016 (GPRC 2011, 2017). They integrate a group of issues relevant for this analysis, including 13 priorities on economic and trade topics (GPRC 2017:7-11), among them: the promotion of trade in high-value-added products and with high technological content, cooperation in industrial investment and productive capacity, cooperation in infrastructure and in manufacturing, and cooperation between chambers and institutions to promote trade and investment (GPRC 2017:9). Interestingly, the 2016 White Book states that Chinese firms should "promote linking the productive capacity with quality and advantaged equipment from China to the necessities of the countries of LAC to help them in improving their development capacity with sovereignty" (GPRC 2017:7) and to enhance infrastructure projects and public-private partnerships "in transport, trade logistics, storage installations, information and communication technologies, energy and electricity, hydraulic works, urbanism and housing, etc." (GPRC 2017:8) China also focuses on cooperation in the manufacturing sector to "establish lines of production and sites for the maintenance of construction material, of nonferrous metals, machinery, vehicles, communications and electricity equipment, etc." (GPRC 2017:9)

More relevant in the specific context of Chinese proposals of cooperation with LAC is Xi Jinping's cooperation scheme "1+3+6," which stands for: 1 plan (CELAC's Cooperation Plan for 2015-2019), 3 driving forces (trade, investment, and financial cooperation), and 6 key fields of cooperation (energy, resources, infrastructure projects, manufacturing, scientific innovation, and technical innovation). The CELAC-China Forum Cooperation Plan for 2015-2019 includes a wide range of tools for cooperation in politics, culture, education and economic issues, among others. It also includes enhancing micro, small and medium firms, financial institutions, infrastructure and transportation, industry, science and technology, as well as specific sectors such as the aeronautics, information and communication industries. The plan also makes explicit reference to the "joint construction of industrial parks, science and technology, special economic zones and high-tech parks between China and CELAC member states, with the goal to improve industrial investments and the generation of industrial value chains" (CELAC 2015:4). Those initiatives will be accompanied by several forums and funding options, including the Forum on Development and Industrial Cooperation China-LAC, the Fund for China-LAC Cooperation, the Special Credit for China-LAC Cooperation, and other options according to the cooperation priorities. Most of these instruments, as well as new ones, were renewed in the Working Program of the China-CELAC Forum (CELAC 2018).

In this context, China's presence in the region has been highlighted and criticized from a number of different perspectives, notably using the argument of a "debt trap" and environmental challenges.

### China's Socioeconomic presence in LAC

The LAC-China socioeconomic relationship since the beginning of the 21st century can be understood as a series of four phases (Salazar-Xiranachs, Dussel Peters, and Armony 2018):

1. The stage that starts in the 1990s with a rapid intensification of the trade relationship and China becoming LAC's second trading partner;
2. The stage of 2007-2008, parallel to the global financial crisis, during which China became a major regional financial source for LAC;
3. In the same period (2007-2008) China also became a very important source for overseas foreign direct investment (or Chinese OFDI); and
4. The stage starting in 2013, in which China is developing massive infrastructure projects in the region, also as part of a series of Chinese global initiatives.

### Increased trade between China and LA

At least four topics are relevant in this area:

1. China's share in LAC's trade increased from less than one percent in the 1990s to 14.08 percent in 2017, and China has been LAC's second trading partner since 2013, displacing the European Union. In addition — and a topic that has received little attention so far — LAC has increased its share in China's trade becoming China's second trading partner, mov-

ing from less than four percent in the 1990s to 9.52 percent in 2017, second only to the U.S.

2. LAC's trade with China is characterized by an increasing trade deficit — above $80 billion since 2012. These trends are a result of the disaggregated composition of trade. LAC's main three import goods (according to the Harmonized Tariff System) from China — automobiles, electronics, and auto parts — have increased significantly their share over total imports, from 26.67 percent in 1990 to 38.63 percent in 2000 and 56.85 percent in 2017. LAC's exports to China are significantly more concentrated. LAC's main three export goods — soya, minerals and copper — account for at least 65 percent of total exports since 2007.

3. The specific content of LAC-China trade is critical. The content of LAC imports and exports from/to China differs dramatically by its technological share. While LAC's share of medium and high technological exports to China account for less than five percent of total exports in the last decade, imports from China accounted for more than 60 percent. Trade figures with the United States show that LAC's trade has not only closed its gap in terms of medium- and high-technology goods, but has achieved substantial results, exporting more medium- and high-tech goods than it imported.

4 The U.S. has been the main loser as a result of increasing competition between China and the U.S. in LAC's imports. During 2000-2017, the U.S. share of LAC's trade fell from 53.57 percent to 40.76 percent, while China's increased from 1.72 percent to 14.08 percent (Dussel Peters 2016). The decline of U.S. exports to LAC has generated an annual loss estimated at around 840,000 jobs, particularly in manufacturing and the auto parts-automobile global commodity chain (Dussel Peters 2015).

**China's OFDI in LAC**

A series of recent studies on Chinese outward foreign direct investment (OFDI) in LAC highlights regional and national characteristics. Some case studies include analysis of particular areas of the global value chains and firms (Dussel Peters 2014; Jiang 2017), with methodological and statistical differences between international, Chinese, and Latin American sources (Ortiz Velásquez 2016). With these relatively detailed discussions on LAC and China in mind, the Monitor of China's OFDI in LAC (Dussel Peters 2019) provides the following trends for 2001-2018:

1. The People's Republic of China has issued methodological regulations to record the final destination of OFDI (MOFCOM, NBS and SAFE 2015). Such regulations, however, have not yet resulted in the official

statistics to record Chinese OFDI.

2. Total Chinese OFDI fell in 2018 for the second year in the last decade, as well as to LAC (from 31 percent to eight percent in 2018) and represented 51.66 percent of 2016.

3. Chinese firms invested $121.7 billion from 2000 to 2018 in 402 transactions that generated 324,096 jobs, particularly during the most recent period 2010-2018.

4. Recent results on China's OFDI include an increased share of mergers and acquisitions (M&A) (72.2 percent in 2017 and 74.8 percent in 2018), and they show an increased diversity of China's OFDI, particularly in services and manufacturing (in 2010-2018). For example, raw materials' share of total OFDI in LAC accounted for only 36.2 percent of total OFDI, and the increased share of private OFDI within the total OFDI, from 29.8 percent during 2000-2018 to 93.7 percent in 2018.

Disaggregating by country, China's OFDI also reflects interesting recent changes, including increased diversification in target countries, with an increased presence in Chile and Peru, while the share and absolute value of Chinese OFDI to Argentina, Brazil, and Mexico fell substantially in 2018.

**China as a major source of financing for LAC since 2007-2008**

A group of authors and institutions, particularly Kevin Gallagher at the Global Economic Governance Initiative (GEGI), have contributed substantially through transaction and country-level analysis, with comparisons on the conditionality of financing, as well as national and sectorial distribution of financing (Gallagher, Irwin and Koleski 2013; Gallagher 2016; Myers and Gallagher 2019; Stanley 2013). In general, China's financing to LAC during 2005-2018 has been highly concentrated. China Development Bank and Exim Bank have provided more than $140 billion. Most resources in 2018 were channeled to Venezuela, focusing significantly on infrastructure projects. As with OFDI trends, however, Chinese finance to LAC has fallen substantially in 2017 and 2018.

The RED ALC-China (Dussel Peters, Armony and Cui 2018) has provided a detailed analysis and discussion of Chinese infrastructure projects in LAC. The presentation of firm-level statistics and analysis of case studies in several countries results in a wide range of experiences and policy suggestions at the firm and sector level. Until 2017, China had pursued 69 infrastructure projects in LAC, accounting for more than $56 billion and generating more than 214,000 jobs in the region. Argentina, Venezuela, Ecuador, and Brazil have had the most Chinese infrastructure projects in the region, while other countries in Central America and Mexico have, so far, received fewer.

The more qualitative and case study work of Dussel Peters, Armony, and Cui (2018) reflects the pragmatism of Chinese firms through infrastructure projects in the region and the ability to operate in very different labor conditions, subcontracting networks and relations with clients depending on each country's context. In several cases the same Chinese firms — all of them public firms — generate very different conditions in different countries of the region. In some cases, Chinese firms are able to subcontract all major civil engineering segments of the projects to local and national firms, and subcontract with local suppliers for major segments of the respective infrastructure projects. Workers and working conditions are thus generated by local firms. In several cases, the employees do not know they are working for a Chinese infrastructure project. In other cases, the totality of the project is run by Chinese firms, including the design of the project, financing, subcontracting, workers, engineering activities, construction, and post-construction services. While Chinese firms have the ability to offer these "turnkey projects," in most cases it depends on the specific conditions of the host country. The involvement of local and domestic firms, workers, and specialized activities, and particularly the contracts defined and accepted by host countries, may in some cases even allow for learning processes and technology transfer. Development, from this perspective, is highly dependent on the host country and government that proposes and signs these contracts. A rather small group of Chinese public firms are the core of these infrastructure projects in the region.

### Weak and insufficient institutions in LAC, China, and the U.S. on the LAC-China relationship

Rather surprisingly, while socioeconomic and political relations between China and LAC have increased dramatically, public, private, and academic institutions working on China in LAC and LAC in China, as well as bilateral institutions between China and specific LAC countries and in the U.S., have not reflected the same dynamism. In general, there is a wide gap between public, private, and academic institutions analyzing the China-LAC relationship both in LAC and in China and socioeconomic growth (Arnson et. al 2014; Dussel Peters and Armony 2015). Beyond the fashion of studying the China-LAC relationship, in general, there are many authors and institutions in LAC, China, and the U.S., including think tanks, that do not review the massive, albeit insufficient, literature in China and Latin America and the Caribbean of the last four decades. WÅith few exceptions, such as the Consejo Empresarial Brasil-China (CEBC), the Institute for Latin American Studies of the Chinese Academy for Social Sciences (ILAS/CASS), the China Institutes of Contemporary International Relations (CICIR), the Center for Chinese-Mexican Studies (CECHIMEX) at UNAM, and the Academic Network of Latin America and the Caribbean (RED ALC-China), the institutional analysis in the public, private, and academic sector is weak, with few attempts to develop a qualitative learning process beyond the institutional competition, and those based on the existing analysis in LAC and China. The best example of the existence of these limited institutions is the CELAC-China Forum (Cui and Pérez 2016). Its presidency rotates annually, it lacks a technical secretariat, and it depends annually on a different ministry of foreign affairs from a LAC country. As a result, the learning process in terms of analysis and proposals is weak, the technical and qualitative learning process is limited, and so are the implementation, evaluation, and proposals on very specific items discussed and proposed by the CELAC-China Forum since 2015.

## Looking to the future: a new triangular relationship

Acknowledging these trends along with the concept of "New Triangular Relationships" (Dussel Peters, Hearn and Shaiken 2013) is critical for LAC today. The region and each of its countries, with no exception, has to understand, deal with and negotiate within this "new triangle." In some cases, the presence of the U.S. is still very strong, such as in the Caribbean, Mexico, and Central America. In others, the presence of China is considerable, such as in Cuba and Venezuela. Nevertheless, in all cases LAC countries must consider increasingly difficult strategies in their foreign relations given the increasing tensions between China and the U.S. None of the LAC countries can exclude the U.S. or China as important strategic partners. New governments (such as in Argentina and Brazil) have attempted to distance themselves from China recently, with little success. Venezuela, on the other hand, until the recent crisis still had substantial economic linkages with the U.S.

From this perspective, many countries in LAC are at a crossroads and in the middle of the U.S.-China competition. Vice President Mike Pence (2018) highlights: The U.S. will be "heightening our scrutiny of Chinese investment in America to protect our national security from Beijing's predatory actions." … "A new consensus is rising across America …" and putting enormous pressure on countries worldwide, including LAC. In 2017 and 2018, three LAC countries — Dominican Republic, El Salvador, and Panama — established diplomatic relationships with China. In response, the U.S. in September 2018 recalled its top diplomats from all three countries and threatened 17 additional countries that still have diplomatic ties with Taiwan, mainly in Central America, the Caribbean, and the Pacific, proposing new legislation in the Senate to "downgrade U.S. relations with any government that shifts away from Taiwan, and to suspend or alter U.S. assistance" (Reuters 2018).

The situation is particularly stressful for countries in LAC that are geographically close to the U.S., such as Mexico and those in Central America, with long historical, political, and economic ties with the U.S. and that are experiencing an increasing presence of China. In the case of Mexico, the renegotiation of the North American Free Trade Agreement in 2018 has led to the signing of the United States-Mexico-Canada Agreement, or USMCA, which still has to be ratified by the legislatures of the respective countries and includes an "Anti-China chapter" (chapter 32.10) that practically prohibits free trade agreements with China (as a "non-market economy") (Dussel Peters 2018).

Acknowledging the potential risks of their relationships with either China or the U.S., LAC countries might find themselves in the future under strong pressure to choose sides. However, that would make little sense from an LAC perspective given the presence of both powers in all countries of the region.

## Note

*This essay along with the essays by Haibin Niu and Margaret Myers and Rebecca Ray focus on China's expanding relationships in Latin America and the Caribbean. All three were first published in longer versions by The Carter Center as part of the China Research Center and The Carter Center's joint organization of the Sixth Annual Meeting of the International Consortium for China Studies held in Atlanta May 31- June 1, 2019.*

## References

Anguiano Roch, Eugenio. 2018. "El 19 Congreso Nacional del Partido Comunista de China". *Cuadernos de Trabajo del Cechimex 1, pp. 1-24.*

Anguiano Roch, Eugenio. 2019. "La Iniciativa Una Franja-Una Ruta: evolución visible". *Ciclo de Conferencias del Cechimex, April 4th.*

Arnson, Cynthia, Jorge Heine and Christine Zaino (edits.). 2014. *Reaching Across the Pacific: Latin America and Asia in the New Century. Washington, D.C.: Woodrow Wilson Center.*

CELAC (Community of Latin American and Caribbean States). 2015. *Cooperation Plan (2015-2019). CELAC, Beijing.*

CELAC. 2018. *Plan de Acción Conjunto de Cooperación en Áreas Prioritarias CELAC-China (2019-2021). Santiago de Chile: CELAC.*

Cui, Shoujun and Manuel Pérez García. 2016. *China and Latin America in Transition. Policy Dynamics, Economic Commitments, and Social Impacts. Beijing: Springer.*

Dussel Peters, Enrique (coord.). 2014. *La inversión extranjera directa de China en América Latina: 10 estudios de caso. México: Red ALC-China, UDUAL y UNAM/Cechimex.*

Dussel Peters, Enrique. 2015. *Testimony before the Joint Subcommittee Hearing of the Committee on Foreign Affairs, Subcommittee on the Western Hemisphere and Subcommittee on Asia and the Pacific, US States House of Representatives, September 10th.*

Dussel Peters, Enrique (coord.). 2016. *La nueva relación comercial de América Latina y el Caribe con China, ¿integración o desintegración comercial? México: Red ALC-China and UNAM/Cechimex.*

Dussel Peters, Enrique. 2018/a. *Comercio e inversiones: la relación de Centroamérica y China ¿Hacia una relación estratégica en el largo plazo?. Ciudad de México: CEPAL, Sede Subregional en México.*

Dussel Peters, Enrique. 2018/b. "The New Triangular Relationship Between Mexico, the United States, and China: Challenges for NAFTA". In, Dussel Peters, Enrique (coord.). *The Renegotiation of NAFTA. And China? Mexico: Red ALC-China, UDUAL, and UNAM/Cechimex,* pp. 87-99.

Dussel Peters, Enrique. 2019. *Monitor of Chinese OFDI in Latin America and the Caribbean 2018. Red ALC-China: Mexico.*

Dussel Peters, Enrique, Ariel C. Armony and Shoujun Cui (coord.). 2018. *Building Development for a New Era. China's Infrastructure Projects in Latin America. Mexico: Red ALC-China and University of Pittsburgh.*

Dussel Peters, Enrique, Adrian H. Hearn, and Harley Shaiken. 2013. *China and the New Triangular Relationship in the Americas. China and the Future of US-Mexico Relations. Mexico: University of Miami/CLAS, University of California Berkeley/CLAS and UNAM/CECHIMEX.*

Gallagher, Kevin. 2016. *The China Triangle: Latin America's China boom and the fate of the Washington Consensus. Oxford University Press: Boston.*

GPRC. 2017. *"Documento sobre la Política de China hacia América latina y el Caribe". Cuadernos de Trabajo del Cechimex 1, pp. 1-12.*

Jiang, Shixue. 2017. *"La inversión china en América Latina y el Caribe: características, mitos y prospectos". In, Pastrana Buelvas, Eduardo y Hubert Gehring (coord.). La proyección de China en América Latina y el Caribe. Editorial Pontificia Universidad Javeriana: Colombia, pp. 267-292.*

Koleski, Katherine, and Alec Blivas. 2018. *China's Engagement with Latin America and the Caribbean. Washington D.C.: U.S.-China Economic and Security Review Commission.*

Long, Guoqiang. 2015. *"One Belt, One Road: A New Vision for Open, Inclusive Regional Cooperation". Cuadernos de Trabajo del Cechimex 4, pp. 1-8.*

MOFCOM (Ministry of Commerce), NBS (National Bureau of Statistics) and SAFE (State Administration of Foreign Exchange). 2015. *Statistical Registry Procedure OFDI. Beijing: MOFCOM, NBS and SAFE.*

Myers, Margaret, and Kevin Gallagher. 2019. *Cautious Capital: Chinese Development Finance in LAC, 2018. Washington, D.C.: Inter-American Dialogue and Global Development Policy Center.*

Ortiz Velásquez, Samuel. 2016. *Methodological Differences in Chinese OFDI. Monitor de la OFDI China in LAC. Red ALC-China: Mexico.*

Reuters. 2018. *"U.S. recalls diplomats in El Salvador, Panama, Dominican Republic over Taiwan". Reuters, September 7.*

Salazar-Xirinachs, José Manuel, Enrique Dussel Peters, and Ariel C. Armony (edits). *Efectos de China en la cantidad y calidad del empleo en América Latina (2000-2018). Lima: OIT.*

Stanley, Leonardo. 2013. *"El proceso de internacionalización del RMB y el nuevo protagonismo del sistema financiero chino". In, Enrique Dussel Peters (edit.). América Latina y el Caribe – China. Economía, comercio e inversiones. México:*
Red ALC-China, UDUAL and UNAM/CECHIMEX, pp. 147-169.

Wu, Hongying. 2010. *"Has Latin America Become China's Backyard?". Contemporary International Relations 19(3), pp. 16-26.*

---

*Dr. Enrique Dussel Peters is a Professor at the Graduate School of Economics, Universidad Nacional Autónoma de México.*

## Building Development Partnership: Engagement between China and Latin America

*Haibin Niu*
*Vol. 19, No.1*
*2020*

The full-fledged economic ties between China, Latin America, and the Caribbean are important indicators of China's role as a global player. In the ongoing and heightened debate about China's rise, China's impact on Latin America is being discussed by scholars and policy-makers worldwide. Though there are doubts about China's intentions and impact on Latin America, China has developed a more substantial and meaningful policy framework to build development partnership with the region.

### An Emerging Development Partnership

Latin America's ties to China are characterized by their economic dimensions instead of the fully-fledged ties between the region and the United States. The economic agenda has taken a high profile in the Sino-Latin American relationship since the establishment of the China-Brazil strategic partnership in 1993. The most visible achievements of the strategic partnership are economic in nature. For example, China surpassed the United States as Brazil's largest trade partner in 2009. Additionally, China and Brazil are founding members of the newly established multilateral investment banks such as the New Development Bank (NDB) and the Asian Infrastructure Investment Bank. China's Free Trade Agreements (FTAs) with Chile, Peru, and Costa Rica clearly show the primacy of the economic agenda in the relationship. China's economic growth strategy is to integrate itself into the world economy, and Latin America is an increasingly important partner for China, and vice versa.

This is not to say that political, cultural, and military exchanges between China and Latin America are not important, but other dimensions are overshadowed by this prominent economic linkage. In the context of this deepening economic relationship, both sides are engaging with each other on other dimensions such as culture, politics, and security. While the relationship is supported by economic ties, it needs to become more comprehensive and sustainable in order to continue to develop. To achieve this goal of a stronger relationship, China has strengthened its political will and increased the amount of economic resources in order to support its overall relationship with the region.

There are some new features of this prominent economic linkage. Firstly, the economic ties are going beyond the initial trade dimension. China is the largest trade partner for Brazil, Peru, and Chile. China is also an increasingly important creditor and investor for the region's various economic sectors. Research by Inter-American Dialogue and Boston University found that Chinese state-to-state finance has exceeded the sovereign lending from the World Bank and the Inter-American Development Bank (IDB) since 2005.[1] Secondly, China is pursuing economic ties in a sustainable manner by paying more attention to infrastructure, innovation, and renewable energy, which is mainly achieved via China's diversified investment in the region. Thirdly, the economic ties are used by both sides to build a kind of solid development partnership. Both China and regional countries are treating their economic ties from a perspective of not only commercial interests, but also development opportunities. An important indicator in this regard is the increasing number of countries from the region that are joining the Belt and Road Initiative, designed by the Chinese leadership as a platform for international cooperation.

All these new features are happening in the context of China's gradual rise. In the past, China and Latin America were highly dependent on the advanced economies. In the long period after China initiated its reform and opening up process in the late 1970s, China's main economic partners were developed economies who could offer China much-needed capital, technology, management, and export markets. Latin America also depended on advanced economies and was a low priority region for China in the last century because it didn't have the capital, technology, or management skills China needed. Without China's rise within the international economic system, it would have been impossible to build such a dynamic development partnership with a region that is geographically remote from China.

From a perspective of domestic and external nexus, China's projection in Latin America is always influenced by the strategic environment of the international system. Historically, China's interaction with Latin America was quite loose since China lacked the capacity and intention to project its presence into Latin America. The famous maritime silk road (1565-1865) between China and Mexico was mainly conducted by European traders, and trade relations between China and Mexico were connected via the European-controlled Philippines. In the 19th century, thousands of Chinese migrants were traded to Latin American countries by European colonists. These Chinese laborers contributed greatly to railway and canal construction. They also became the targets of racist attacks, prompting the Qing dynasty to deploy a warship to the region in 1911.[2]

After the establishment of the PRC in 1949, China's major external relationship was concentrated on the Soviet Union group for a long period because of the blockade imposed by the Western countries. China's interaction with Latin America during that period mainly happened in the cultural and economic sectors. China's intentions in Latin America during that period were also questioned by some regional countries because of their domestic communist activities. The establishment of the China-Cuba diplomatic relationship in 1960 also fit the Soviet Union-U.S. bipolar power structure. The China-Cuba relationship suffered from the Moscow-Beijing rivalry through 1970s and 1980s until the normalization of the Soviet Union-China relationship in the late 1980s. China's booming diplomatic relationship with Latin America came about in the 1970s in the context of the improved Sino-U.S .relationship and China's return to the United Nations as a permanent member of the Security Council. From this geo-strategic perspective, some scholars argue that China's foreign policy toward Latin America has been primarily driven by a one-dimensional concern: global geopolitics from a historical perspective.[3] In general, the bipolar world power structure constrained the potential of the China-Latin America relationship.

It is fair to say that a substantial relationship with Latin America became possible only when both China and Latin America could act as independent players on the global stage. Even when China implemented its famous opening up policy in 1978, it took at least two decades for China to have the capacity to engage substantially with remote developing regions such as Africa, the Middle East, and Latin America. China's growing economic capacity and strategy to integrate itself into the world economy are what allowed China to build a substantial relationship with Latin America. Therefore, it was at the start of the 21st century that a substantial economic trade relationship began to emerge between China and Latin America as China integrated itself into the global value chains. During this time, Latin America mainly provided raw materials to China as China developed into a world-class manufacturing center. Later, China's sizable emerging middle class's growing domestic demands, accumulated capital, management and technology, and increasingly capable "going global" enterprises began to be new major drivers of China's economic ties with Latin America. China's social dynamism includes a significant population of 700 million that left poverty in recent years; its increasing demands for meat, dairy, cereal, and soy products were very attractive for the region's agricultural sector.

In 2016, China became the second-largest source of outward Foreign Direct Investment (FDI) for the first time, and its FDI outflows were 36% more than the amount of its inflows. China remained the largest investor in the least developed countries (World Investment Report 2017). The importance of China for the developing world including Latin America and the Caribbean (LAC) was well recognized by international organizations.[4] In its 13th Five-Year Plan (2016-2020), China set some important goals regarding the developing world. They include the goal of reaching a volume of trade in services that accounts for at least 16% of total foreign trade, establishing overseas production centers and cooperation zones for major commodities, and encouraging international cooperation on production capacity and equipment manufacturing. China will promote opening up of capital markets and encourage Chinese financial institutions to increase their overseas presence. China's transition from world factory to innovation center will also affect its economic relationship with the rest of the world. In the future, Chinese investments will focus on more advanced and value-added industries.

The rise of China is a new reality for Latin American countries when they think of the future. Since the beginning of this century, most Latin American countries turned their eyes to East Asia and especially to China for commerce and trade opportunities. They were trying to engage with China bilaterally and multilaterally. The agenda with China goes beyond economic areas to global issues such as climate change, fighting poverty, etc. China also treated Latin America as an important region in the global system. With this vision in mind, China built many types of strategic partnerships with individual countries from the region and coordinated with regional countries in international forums such as APEC, BRICS, and the United Nations. To facilitate cooperation with the whole region, China initiated the China-CELAC Forum. Latin American countries were also invited to join the Belt and Road Initiative, which is a flagship initiative of the Chinese government led by President Xi Jinping.

## Challenges for the Future

In deepening cooperation with LAC countries, China needs to pay attention to several factors. First, in order to avoid investment risks, both sides need to do a better job of policy consultation and cooperate in a transparent and sustainable manner that is committed to long-term engagement. Second, considering the diversity of the LAC countries and different approaches to regional integration, China needs to continue to mix its bilateral and multilateral approaches to address this diversity. Third, in order to reach real development cooperation, China should encourage and support the potential partner's domestic debate on issues and policies regarding cooperation with China. Finally, China's engagements with Latin America should continue to build a comprehensive and sustainable development partnership. Both sides should work together to safeguard an open world economy in an era full of doubts about the benefits of globalization.

Aside from economic considerations, political interests are also playing an important role in China's engagement with Latin America. China highly values Latin America's overall importance in the international system. In 1988, Deng Xiaoping had the foresight to state that the 21st century should be the century of both the Pacific and Latin America. As a rising global power, China needs support from more countries to make China's rise acceptable and legitimate to the rest of the world. As both China and Latin America are developing, China thinks there are more common interests between the two than with established powers. China doesn't look for allies with Latin American countries to challenge the current international order. What China expects from Latin America is political understanding of its domestic development approach and its international profile. Exchanging ideas on domestic governance has been an important aspect of cooperation, and it helps Latin American people better understand China's political system rather than exporting it to Latin America. China also needs Latin American countries to understand its domestic and international agenda.

China's historical relationship with Latin America has been deeply affected by the international environment. Clearly, whether China has a geopolitical strategy towards Latin America or not, global geopolitical situations—especially major power relations—have a structural impact on the China-Latin American relationship. To understand China's current dynamic presence in Latin America, we need to understand how China perceives the current international system and how the system's factors affect China's projection in Latin America. In the first 15 years of this century, economic globalization, the rise of the global south including the emerging economies, and a pro-globalization G20 constituted a benign international environment for the China-Latin America relationship to blossom.

Under the George W. Bush and Obama administrations, the United States held an officially objective and inclusive attitude towards the deepening relationship between China and Latin America, which was quite helpful for the relationship. Though the region has been largely overlooked since the U.S. has been primarily focusing on the anti-terrorism agenda in Central Asia, the U.S. generally thought of China's presence in the region as a natural result of its economic expansion rather than a security threat. China participated in the OAS and Inter-American Development Bank with the support of the U.S. The U.S. also held regular dialogues with senior Chinese officials on Latin American affairs to exchange their concerns and interests. When the United States formally abandoned its 190-year-old Monroe Doctrine in 2013 and made adjustments to its policy to Cuba, both

China and Latin America welcomed this new posture of the U.S. towards the region. China also expressed its open and supportive attitude of cooperation with third parties in Latin America.

In this favorable international context, China's approach to Latin America was supportive of economic globalization and international cooperation. Therefore, China's presence in Latin America was not perceived as a threat to the region's peace and prosperity. China's growing ties with Latin America were built in this relatively peaceful environment and were based on a mutually beneficial economic logic from the beginning of the 21st century. Different from East Asia's competitive strategic environment, China's economic engagement with Latin America was less affected by the geostrategic competition from the United States and its allies. Most Latin American countries were embracing globalization and building a diversified external relationship by looking for more international partners, including China. China also identified itself as a beneficiary of the current international system and followed a peaceful rise approach. Major international economic institutions also recognized that the robust growth in Latin America in the past decade was partially due to its connections to China.[5]

However, this optimistic atmosphere totally changed when the Trump administration adopted a new strategy towards both China and the LAC region. The "America First" doctrine distanced the U.S. from both China and Latin America by emphasizing trade protection and economic protective measures. Furthermore, the U.S. is holding an increasingly suspicious and unfriendly attitude towards China's presence in Latin America by publicly criticizing China's intention, practices and impacts in the region and persuading regional partners away from cooperation with China, especially on digital technologies. The U.S. rolled back many important and positive measures initiated by the Obama administration. It reversed the engagement with Cuba and reasserted the Monroe Doctrine, which caused a fundamental change to the geostrategic environment of the Western Hemisphere. This kind of strategic and policy-level change might affect the trilateral relationship among China, the U.S., and Latin America negatively in several aspects.

While there are many challenges with a shifted American approach, it is noteworthy that both China and Latin America share a goal of achieving autonomy in international affairs. It is in the interest of both Latin America and China to pursue autonomy by building diversified international partnerships. China has increasingly presented itself as a full-fledged global player, which is naturally reflected in the comprehensive agenda of the Sino-Latin American relationship. China's presence in Latin America will definitely create some geopolitical implications for the region even if it might not be China's original intention. A strong and sustainable China and Latin America relationship serves to create the strategic international space that enhances their domestic development.

A good, stable, and rule-based China-U.S. economic relationship will be important for Latin American economies. Though countries such as Brazil and Argentina might benefit from the trade disputes between the United States and China in the short term, the uncertainties and the possible trade deal's impact are worrisome for the region's policymakers and private sector. A trade deal between China and the U.S. might reduce China's import of energy and agriculture products from Latin America. The deal's impact on the role and rules of the WTO is still unclear. As the weaker and vulnerable part of the world economy, developing economies including China and Latin America are more dependent on WTO regulations and rulings.

To ensure a sustainable China-Latin America relationship, it is also important to avoid strategic rivalries between China and the United States in Latin America. From a geostrategic point of view, an accommodative United States will offer more space for China and Latin America countries to engage with each other. In a highly integrated world, most countries in Latin America prefer to have good relations with both major world economies rather than take sides between China and the United States. In a larger context, it is a game of managing balance-of-power shifts in the region considering the rising autonomy of the region and more capable external and internal players emerging in the region. Considering the issues in the U.S.-Latin American relationship, China's economic engagement with the region could provide more favorable conditions to solve the issues of illegal immigration, drug trafficking and energy security. It takes time for all relevant stakeholders to build a mutually beneficial trilateral relationship among China, the U.S., and LAC.

China's approach to Latin America will continue in its pragmatic way with its preference for national interests rather than ideology. Latin America is a region full of market economies and democracies that was highly influenced by Western culture and values. China respects these institutional and cultural choices of Latin America when it seeks to deepen its relationship with the region. China still holds a neutral approach to engage with Latin American countries regardless of their ideological differences. China's strategic partnerships in Latin America are based on partners' development potential, regional influence, and global capacity rather than their political types or anti-U.S. attitude. By respecting national interests, China's relationship with those countries represents a huge shift in leadership. What China looks for in Latin America is international cooperation, mutual respect and common development. Thus, it is highly possible for China to keep a politically neutral attitude to regional affairs in Latin America.

## Notes

1   *Margaret Myers and Kevin P. Gallagher, "Cautious Capital: Chinese Development Finance in LAC, 2018," China-Latin America Report, February 2019. https://www.thedialogue.org/wp-content/uploads/2019/02/Chinese-Finance-in-LAC-2018-2.pdf.*

2   百度百科词条：“托雷翁惨案”, *https://baike.baidu.com/item/%E6%89%98%E9%9B%B7%E7%BF%81%E6%83%A8%E6%A1%88/9112881?fr=aladdin&ivk_sa=1022817p.*

3   *XIANG, Lanxin, "An Alternative Chinese View", in Riordan Roett and Guadalupe Paz, eds., China's Expansion into the Western Hemisphere, Brookings Institution Press, 2008.*

4   *OECD, UN, CAF, Latin American Economic Outlook 2016: Towards a New Partnership with China, 2015. http://www.oecd.org/dev/Overview_%20LEO2016_Chinese.pdf.*

5   *The World Bank (2011), Latin America and the Caribbean's Long-Term Growth: Made in China? Washington, D.C.: The World Bank/LAC.*

## References

*De la Torre, etc., "Latin America and the Rising South: Changing World, Changing Priorities," Overview booklet, World Bank, 2015.*

*Enrique Dussel Peters, "China's Evolving Role in Latin America: Can It Be a Win-Win?" Atlantic Council Report, September 2015.*

*Evan Ellis, US National Security Implications of Chinese Involvement in Latin America, Army War college Strategic Studies Institute, 2005.*

*Global Issues, November 2016.*

*Jiang Shixue, "New Development of China-Latin America Relations," China Quarterly of International Strategic Studies, Vol. 1, No. 1, 2015, pp. 149-153.*

*Jiemian Yang ed., China's Diplomacy: Theory and Practice, NJ: World Century Publishing Corporation, 2014, pp. 415-476.*

*Jorge Guajardo, Manuel Molano, and Dante Sica, Industrial Development in Latin America: What is China's Role? Washington DC: Atlantic Council, 2016.*

*Margaret Myers and Kevin P. Gallagher, "Cautious Capital: Chinese Development Finance in LAC, 2018," China-Latin America Report, February 2019.*

*Mario Esteban ( coord.), "China in Latin America: Repercussions for Spain", in Real Instituto Elcano Working Paper, No.3, October 2015.*

*Mercedes Garcia-Escribano, Carlos Goes, and Izabela Karpowicz, "Filling the Gap: Infrastructure Investment in Brazil," IMF Working Paper, WP/15/180, July 2015.*

*National Security Strategy of the United States of America, December 2017.*

*OECD, UN, CAF, Latin American Economic Outlook 2016: Towards a New Partnership with China, 2015.*

*Peter Hakim, "Is Washington Losing Latin America?" Foreign Affairs, Vol. 85, No. 1, 2006.*

*Riordan Roett and Guadalupe Paz, eds., China's Expansion into the Western Hemisphere, Brookings Institution Press, 2008.*

*Ted Piccone, "The Geopolitics of China's Rise in Latin America," Geoeconomics and The World Bank, Latin America and the Caribbean's Long-Term Growth: Made in China? Washington, D.C.: The World Bank/LAC, 2011.*

*WU, Baiyi, Opportunities Along with Transformation: A Multi-Perspective Analysis of the China-Latin American Relations, Economy and Management Publishing House, 2013*

---

*Dr. Haibin Niu is senior fellow and deputy director of the Institute for Foreign Policy Studies, Shanghai Institutes for International Studies.*

# China in Latin America: Major Impacts and Avenues for Constructive Engagement: A U.S. Perspective

*Margaret Meyers and Rebecca Ray*
*Vol. 19, No.1*
*2020*

## Introduction

Over the past two years, U.S. officials have frequently pointed out China's negative effects on the Latin American and Caribbean (LAC) region's development and stability. U.S. Secretary of State Mike Pompeo typified this approach when he said during a trip to Mexico City in October 2018, "China has invested in ways that have left countries worse off" (Jourdan, 2019).

China's effects on regional development are decidedly mixed. China's contributions to the region's economic growth are well-documented: China is LAC's second-most important trading partner, second-most important source of M&A FDI, and top source of development finance. Nonetheless, Chinese demand for raw materials has accentuated regional dependence on commodities, in a process of "re-primarization" in South American economies, with troubling implications for the region's long-term development prospects. Chinese investments have transformed the energy sectors in some countries, but the environmental effects of hydroelectric and other projects will be long-lasting in certain cases.

To achieve a wide range of development objectives — economic, environmental, and social — LAC must depend on increasingly well-planned and coordinated engagement from all of its major economic partners, including China. This is especially true in times of growing uncertainty, as the region grapples with humanitarian and migration crises, relentless corruption, and climate change, among other factors.

## China's Effect on Latin American Development

This report aims to qualify China's effect on key development indicators in LAC, using the United Nations' 17 Sustainable Development Goals (SDGs) as a basis for analysis. The sections below consider relationships around aid, finance, investment, and trade, in turn.

### Chinese Aid to LAC

Chinese development assistance to LAC, including concessional finance, grants, technical assistance and aid, has undoubtedly affected development outcomes in the region, especially in targeted communities. Chinese disaster assistance was critical after the 2016 Ecuador earthquake, for example, and China-funded housing projects in Venezuela have enhanced the lives of their beneficiaries. Chinese technical assistance, including in agricultural technology and telecommunications, is rising in step with Chinese capacity in these sectors. A growing number of Chinese companies, including China National Petroleum Corporation (CNPC) in Peru and the Industrial and Commercial Bank of China (ICBC) in Argentina, provide occasional donations to local communities, such as CNPC's "Sinfonías del Mar" music program for unprivileged students in Piura. Barbara Stallings (2017) estimates that from 2010 to 2012, LAC was somewhat over-represented among recipients of Chinese official development assistance (ODA) (Stallings, 2017). LAC accounted for 8.4 percent of Chinese ODA compared to seven percent of its trade and just 2.8 percent of its FDI. Considering the focused nature of Chinese aid on targeted communities, these efforts have supported decent work, quality education, and health and well-being SDGs (Goals 3, 4, and 8).

### Chinese Finance in LAC

China has provided more than $141 billion in development finance commitments to LAC governments and state-owned firms since 2005, more than the World Bank, Inter-American Development Bank (IDB), or CAF — the Development Bank of Latin America (Gallagher and Myers, 2019). It has done so primarily through the China Development Bank (CDB) and the Export-Import Bank of China (China Exim Bank), two national development finance institutions (DFIs).

These two DFIs have financed highway, transportation, and renewable energy projects, as well as mega-dams in Ecuador (Coca-Codo Sinclair), Colombia (Ituango), and Argentina's (Condor Cliff) mega-dam, as well as high-tension power lines associated with Brazil's Belo Monte mega-dam (Gallagher and Myers, 2019). This trend will likely continue, as LAC nations join the Belt and Road Initiative, signaling their interest to work with China on finance and investment projects. To date, 14 Latin American and Caribbean countries have signed onto the initiative, including some of the region's more prominent economies of Chile, Peru, Costa Rica, and Panama.

Despite some clear benefits of China-backed projects to the region, the U.S. has criticized China's overseas finance, noting a Chinese tendency for "predatory economic practices" (Jourdan, 2018). Washington is especially focused on China's role in Venezuela, where CDB and China Exim are thought to have enabled government-level mismanagement. In January, U.S. Secretary of State Pompeo accused China of "propping up a failed regime" there through "ill-considered investments" in the oil-rich nation (Gehrke, 2019).

U.S. concerns are sometimes warranted. The lack of transparency in Chinese state financing may facilitate corruption in certain countries. CDB and China Exim Bank have often extended finance though credit lines without publicly specified purposes, creating a transparency challenge for domestic constituencies. For example, these arrangements have stoked allegations in Venezuela that the funds have disappeared, without benefitting the Venezuelan population.[1]

Concerns regarding debt sustainability of CDB and China Exim finance appear to be less well-founded. Despite its significant finance presence in the region, China has not had a serious impact on the region's overall debt sustainability. If anything, China stands to lose money from Venezuela, the main LAC recipient of Chinese finance. Analysts have predicted a default on Chinese oil-based payments as early as this year (Grisanti, and Lalaguna, 2018). More broadly, Ray and Wang (2019) show that even as Bolivia, Guyana, and Ecuador increased their Chinese debt between 2004 and 2016, their total external public and publicly guaranteed debt fell. In other words, Chinese credit substituted for traditional sources of credit, but each of these three countries ended the time period with less external debt than they had in 2004. Moreover, while aggressive creditor action gains more news coverage than debt forgiveness, China has shown itself willing to engage in debt restructuring many times recently. Hurley, Morris, and Portelance (2018) document 84 cases of Chinese debt renegotiation, restructuring, or forgiveness since 2000. Kratz, Feng, and Wright (2019) calculate that this activity sums to approximately $50 billion in debt relief.

Finally, Chinese DFIs have exposed themselves to significant environmental and social risk in infrastructure finance in LAC. Like many national DFIs, CDB and China Exim Bank do not apply their own binding environmental and social standards when operating abroad. For example, the China-financed Rositas dam in southern Bolivia was recently suspended amid allegations of insufficient prior consultation with indigenous communities that would have been displaced for the dam (Hinojosa, 2018). Colombia's Ituango dam collapsed during construction, requiring the evacuation of downstream communities, though effective early-warning systems prevented casualties (Ray 2018). The Coca-Codo Sinclair dam project in Ecuador has been the subject of environmental, labor-related, and technical scrutiny. Furthermore, China's deferential approach to environmental and social risk management has enabled Latin American governments to seek Chinese financing for higher-risk projects which, like the Rositas dam, did not attract financing from western DFIs (Ray, Gallagher, and Sanborn, 2018).

Overall, Chinese finance in LAC has facilitated regional transport and energy expansion, improving livelihoods and energy access (SDGs 7 and 8). But the extent to which these projects support local job creation (SDGs 1 and 8) and environmental sustainability (Goal 11) depends greatly on the contract negotiation and performance oversight by LAC governments, and it varies widely across the region.

### China's Investment Impact

Chinese foreign direct investment (FDI) has bolstered the LAC region, bringing much-needed capital and creating an estimated two million jobs (Salazar-Xirinachs, Dussel Peters, and Armony, 2018). However, as with any transition of this size, it has not always been a smooth process. Chinese investors are relative newcomers and have faced steep learning curves in adapting to local labor and cultural expectations, as in the cases of Shougang mining in Peru and Golden Dragon copper in Mexico (Sanborn and Chonn, 2017; Schatan and Piloyon, 2017). Despite considerable reference to environmental and ecological cooperation in China's LAC policy, and China's own progress in recent years on the environmental SDGs, Chinese engagement in LAC appears to continue to struggle with sustainability.

LAC's environmental and social standards are among the most ambitious in the world, and Chinese investors have at times struggled to meet them, especially when enforcement has been lacking from LAC national governments, as in the case of Sinopec in Colombia (Rudas Lleras and Cabrera Leal, 2017). In other cases, Chinese investors have been willing to take on environmentally risky projects proposed by LAC governments, even as signs of potential environmental conflict brew around them. For example, Sinohydro's hidrovía amazónica commercial water investment project in Peru will reportedly alter the dynamics of the affected rivers and their capacity to sustain lakes in natural parks such as the Pacaya Samiria (DAR 2019).

For more than 20 years, the U.S. has expressed concern regarding the strategic impact of Chinese investment, including the prospect for Chinese dual (civilian-military) use of port and other investment projects in Latin America. Concerns surfaced in 1998 about Hong Kong firm Hutchinson Whampoa running ports on either end of the Panama Canal, for example (United States Senate, 1998). Chinese billionaire Wang Jing's canal adventures in Nicaragua were also closely monitored in Washington starting in 2013. Attention has focused more recently on Chinese investment in a deep space monitoring facility in Neuquén, Argentina, and its implications for U.S. security (Londoño, 2018).

U.S. concerns have tangible implications for LAC countries, as regional governments are encouraged to avoid engagement with China in favor of partnership with traditional allies. There are indeed drawbacks associated with the Chinese model, including the negative impacts of insufficient due diligence in certain infrastructure investment projects. The Nicaragua Canal project, for example, has been all but abandoned facing widespread public protests and unforeseen financing difficulties. However, U.S. pressure to limit economic options and partnerships could have unfortunate consequences for the region's overall economic growth.

*The Trade Story*

Latin America's trade relationship with China has also grown precipitously in the last decade. Chinese demand now accounts for more than 10 percent of LAC exports, including over 15 percent of LAC agricultural exports and more than 25 percent of LAC extractive exports such as minerals and oil (Ray and Wang, 2019). In fact, China's soaring demand for these commodities was strong enough to drive a global rise in minerals prices (Roach, 2012; Streifel, n.d.), further boosting export revenue in minerals-exporting countries globally, including in LAC (Arezki and Matsumoto, 2015). Moreover, the rise of China as an export market represented significant geographic diversification of Latin America's exports, cushioning the blow from the U.S. recession of 2008-2009 (Jenkins, 2010; Wise Armijo, and Katada, 2015; Pastor and Wise, 2015).

Nonetheless, China's imbalanced demand for raw materials from Latin America, coupled with its own development into a powerhouse of manufactured exports, has contributed to a process of re-primarization of LAC economies: a retreat from industrialization and toward primary commodity production. The rise of China as a global trading giant has created "winners" and "losers" in LAC countries' trade balances, based on whether each country's export profile is complementary or competitive with China (Jenkins, Dussel Peters, and Mesquitia Moreira, 2008). Those countries with histories of exporting mineral and agricultural goods — particularly in South America — have seen those sectors bolstered. Meanwhile, Mexico and Central America, whose exports include an important share of manufactured goods destined for the U.S. market, have struggled to maintain that market in the context of strong competition from Chinese manufactured goods (Gallagher and Porsecanski, 2011). However, imports of Chinese energy technology, especially in renewable energy, has allowed for the dramatic expansion of the solar power industry in Chile, as well as electric transportation throughout LAC (Borregard et al 2017; Bermúdez Liévano 2019).

Of course, the China-led expansion in LAC agro-industrial and extractive activity is not solely an economic phenomenon, but also an environmental and social one. The expansion of agro-industrial and extraction activities into areas previously occupied by peasant and forest communities has come at a cost to those same communities, which have often been displaced and dispossessed of the natural resources necessary for their livelihoods, as reflected in environmentally-based conflicts surrounding that expansion throughout LAC (Bebbington and Bury, 2013; Roberts, Thanos, and Helvarg, 2003; Edwards, Roberts, and Lagos, 2015). More broadly, the expansion of these economic frontiers into tropical forests has brought an end to years of progress in reducing Amazonian deforestation, with important climate implications for the planet as a whole (Fuchs et al, 2019). Thus, the region's boom in agricultural and extractive exports, fueled by demand from China, has come with significant economic, social, and environmental costs for rural communities in the region, as well as environmental costs for the planet.

The overall impact of the China-LAC trade boom has been decidedly mixed from the perspective of SDGs. Progress toward economic SDGs, including poverty and hunger reduction, employment and growth (Goals 1, 2, and 8), has been boosted significantly in "winning" countries in South America, but faced challenges in "losing" countries such as Mexico, as well as in pockets of negatively impacted rural communities in South America. Progress on climate and local environmental justice goals (Goals 11, 13, and 15) has also been lopsided, advanced by Chinese renewable energy technology imports but weighted down by the expansion of carbon-intensive agricultural and extractive industries, which compete for access to natural resources with traditional communities.

## Conclusion

Until at least the spring of 2019, U.S. government officials had articulated concerns about Chinese engagement with Latin America. Most recently, then-Assistant Secretary of State for Western Hemisphere, Kimberly Breier, made reference to the China-Latin America relationship in a April 26, 2019 speech at the Council of the Americas in Washington, D.C., noting China's distorted market practices; the generational impact of 5G-related decision-making on national security, economy, and society; Chinese support for authoritarian regimes and surveillance states; and China's responsibility for the worsening the crisis in Venezuela, among other issues (Breier, 2019). Breier added that while some Chinese projects are not "malign," "a mere promise of 'high-quality development'" was outweighed by a poor track record.

China's messaging vis-à-vis Latin America, as articulated most recently in the Chinese Ministry of Foreign Affairs "2018 Policy Paper on Latin America and the Caribbean" and a handful of other commonly referenced proposals, such as the "1+3+6 Cooperation Framework" portrays a decidedly different perspective. It describes a partnership supportive of common development objectives and shared global interest, including climate change mitigation and upgrading global economic governance.

In practice, Chinese activity in LAC has had varied effects on the region's development prospects. Chinese engagement appears to at least partially support several SDGs, including those related to employment, poverty, and economic growth. However, trade patterns between China and LAC have reinforced LAC's traditional focus on commodities exports, and China's investments in infrastructure and extractives raise environmental and social risks.

China nonetheless appeals to the region on the basis of equal partnership, south-south goodwill, and support for alternative development paths suited to countries' "own conditions." Some in LAC share U.S. skepticism of China's intentions in the region, but the prospect for collaborative partnership with a fellow developing nation remains attractive to many others. Sustained interest in partnership with China, along with regional demand for Chinese investment and trade, will ensure stronger relations in the years to come. China would also appear fully committed to continued engagement, having recently extended the BRI to Latin America.

With China very much in the region to stay, LAC's development outcomes are best supported by engagement from a range of partners, and growing commitment from both regional governments and external actors to sustainable, long-term development initiatives. Collaboration on areas of shared interest, whether by the U.S., China, and LAC, or by LAC governments and other partners nations, will help to promote positive development outcomes while reducing negative ones.

For example, East-West collaboration on aid efforts can take advantage of existing complementarities. Chinese and U.S. disaster responses and readiness exercises already resemble each other and could benefit from greater coordination. The November 2010 China-Peru bilateral medical exercise Angel de Paz resembled U.S. Southern Command-led joint exercises, and the Chinese "Peace Ark" hospital ship and the USNS Comfort pursue parallel operations (Ellis, 2017). In the long term, it would be beneficial to avoid unproductive duplication and build long-term ties among agencies operating in the same aid arenas.

LAC's environment ministries already support each other through the Red Latinoamericana de Fiscalización y Cumplimiento Ambiental (REDLAFICA), and the United States' Environmental Protection Agency's cooperates with REDLAFICA, organizing workshops on combatting environmental crimes like the illegal logging that has driven conflict throughout the Amazon basin. For its part, China has a history of collaborating with peers through the China Council for International Cooperation on Environment and Development (CCICED) but has not worked closely with REDLAFICA. Bridging this gap can help ensure that collaborating toward shared goals of sustainable development through LAC's "China boom."

Finally, DFIs also have an important role in cultivating greater joint progress toward shared goals. Collaboration between Chinese and western DFIs can pair Chinese DFIs' size and flexibility with the local experience, access, and technical abilities of western institutions. As Ma, Studart, and Vasa (forthcoming 2020) explain in detail, each of these types of actors has complementary institutional strengths, all of which are needed for the development of climate-savvy, socially-inclusive infrastructure. Chinese DFIs offer competitive capital costs and sizable financial resources, along with a wealth of technical expertise in the design and implementation of infrastructure projects. Western MDBs also have abundant access to capital, as both the World Bank and IDB have AAA bond ratings. What CAF is lacking in this regard it partially offsets through its perfect history of borrower repayment, emphasizing its excellent relationships with regional governments (Ray and Kamal, 2019). Finally, LAC NDBs have unique vantage points for identifying and cultivating feasible and sustainable projects. By working together to identify, finance, and oversee the next generation of LAC infrastructure, these various types of DFIs can help ensure that these projects facilitate LAC's progress toward the Sustainable Development Goals.

## Notes

1    Author (Myers) interviews with Venezuelan journalist and former PdVSA personnel, May 2016.

## References

Arezki, Rabah and Akito Matsumoto. 2015. "Metals and oil: A tale of two commodities." Washington, DC: Brookings Institution. https://www.brookings.edu/blog/africa-in-focus/2015/09/16/metals-and-oil-a-tale-of-two-commodities/.

Bebbington, Anthony and Jeffrey Bury. 2013. Subterranean Struggles: New Dynamics of Mining, Oil, and Gas in Latin America. University of Texas Press.

Bermúdez Liévano. 2019. "El año en que los buses eléctricos llegaron (finalmente) a América Latina." Diálago Chino, 4 February. Accessed 17 October 2019 from https://dialogochino.net/21995-latin-american-cities-finally-embrace-chinese-electric-buses/.

Borregaard, Nicola, Annie Dufey, María Teresa Ruiz-Tagle, and Santiago Sinclair. 2017. "Chinese Incidence in the Chilean Solar Power Sector" in China and Sustainable Development in Latin America: The Social and Environmental Dimension, Rebecca Ray, Kevin P. Gallagher, Andrés López, and Cynthia Sanborn, Eds. London: Anthem Press.

Brieir, Kimberly. "Remarks: Assistant Secretary of State for Western Hemisphere Affairs Kimberly Breier," Accessed 1 May 2019 from https://www.as-coa.org/articles/remarks-assistant-secretary-state-western-hemisphere-affairs-kimberly-breier.

Ellis, Evan, "Cooperation and Mistrust between China and the U.S. in Latin America," in Margaret Myers and Carol Wise, eds., The Political Economy of China-Latin America Relations in the New Millennium, Routledge: New York, (2017).

Dammert, Juan Luis. 2018. "Financing Infrastructure Projects in the Southern Amazon of Peru: its relation with environmental and social safeguards." Boston: Boston University Global Development Policy Center Working Paper. http://www.bu.edu/gdp/files/2018/10/GEGI_GDP-Peru-WP.pdf.

Derecho, Ambiente, y Recursos Naturales, "Sinohydro's social and environmental policies on the ground," DAR web site, accessed 13 March 2019 from https://www.dar.org.pe/en/news/sinohydros-social-and-environmental-policies-on-the-ground/.

Edwards, Guy; J. Timmons Roberts and Ricardo Lagos. 2015. *A Fragmented Continent: Latin America and the Global Politics of Climate Change.* MIT Press.

Fuchs, Richard, Peter Alexander, Calum Brown, Frances Cossar, Roslyn C. Henry, and Mark Rounsevell. 2019, "Why the US–China trade war spells disaster for the Amazon." *Nature*, 27 March. Accessed 17 October from https://www.nature.com/articles/d41586-019-00896-2.

Gallagher, Kevin P. and Margaret Myers. 2019. "China-Latin America Finance Database," Washington, DC: Inter-American Dialogue. https://www.thedialogue.org/map_list/.

Gallagher, Kevin P. and Roberto Porzecanski. 2011. *The Dragon in the Room: China and the Future of Latin American Industrialization.* Stanford University Press.

Gehrke, Joel. 2019. "Pompeo denounces Russia, China over support for Venezuela's Maduro." *Washington Examiner.* Accessed 1 May 2019 from https://www.washingtonexaminer.com/policy/defense-national-security/pompeo-denounces-russia-china-over-support-for-venezuelas-maduro.

Grisanti, Alejandro and Gorka Lalaguna, 2018. "El arte de la deuda: China, más cerca del default que de nuevo financiamiento." *Prodavinci.* Accessed 1 May 2019 from https://prodavinci.com/el-arte-de-la-deuda-china-mas-cerca-del-default-que-de-nuevo-financiamiento/.

Hinojosa, Josué. 2018. "ENDE suspende proyecto Rositas por el rechazo de las comunidades." *Los Tiempos*, 4 October. http://www.lostiempos.com/actualidad/economia/20181004/ende-suspende-proyecto-rositas-rechazo-comunidades.

Hurley, John, Scott Morris, and Gailyn Portelance, "Examining the Debt Implications of the Belt and Road Initiative from a Policy Perspective," Center for Global Development: Washington, DC (2018). https://www.cgdev.org/sites/default/files/examining-debt-implications-belt-and-road-initiative-policy-perspective.pdf.

Jenkins, Rhys, "China's Global Expansion and Latin America," *Journal of Latin American Studies* 42 (2010): 809-837. https://doi.org/10.1017/S0022216X10001379.

Jenkins, Rhys, Enrique Dussel Peters, and Mauricio Mesquita Moreira. 2008. "The Impact of China on Latin America and the Caribbean." *World Development* 36:2 (February), 235-253. https://doi.org/10.1016/j.worlddev.2007.06.012.

Jourdan, Adam. 2018 "China denounces Pompeo's 'malicious' Latam comments amid influence battle." *Reuters.* Retrieved 1 May 2019 from https://www.reuters.com/article/us-usa-trade-china-latam/china-slams-pompeos-malicious-latam-comments-amid-influence-battle-idUSKC-N1MW03Q.

Londoño, Ernesto. 2018. "From a Space Station in Argentina, China Expands Its Reach in Latin America." *New York Times*, 28 July. Retrieved October 14, 2019 from https://www.nytimes.com/2018/07/28/world/americas/china-latin-america.html

Ma, Xinyue, Rogerio Studart, and Alexander Vasa. Forthcoming 2019. "Cooperation between Development Finance Institutions in China and Latin America and the Caribbean: Triangular Green Finance Cooperation – Evolving Lessons from Cooperation Models." Boston: Boston University Global Development Policy Center.

Myers, Margaret and Kevin Gallagher, "Cautious Capital: Chinese Development Finance in LAC, 2018," Inter-American Dialogue: Washington, DC (2018).

Pastor, Manuel and Carol Wise. "Good-bye Financial Crash, Hello Financial Eclecticism: Latin American Responses to the 2008–09 Global Financial Crisis," *Journal of International Money and Finance*, vol. 52 (April 2015), pp. 200–217.

Ray, Rebecca and Rohini Kamal. 2019. "Can South–South Cooperation Compete? The Development Bank of Latin America and the Islamic Development Bank." *Development and Change* 50:1 (January), 191-220. https://doi.org/10.1111/dech.12468.

Ray, Rebecca, Kevin P. Gallagher, and Cynthia Sanborn. 2018. "Standardizing Sustainable Development? Development Banks in the Andean Amazon." Boston: Boston University Global Development Policy Center. https://www.bu.edu/gdp/files/2018/04/Development-Banks-in-the-Andean-Amazon.pdf.

Ray, Rebecca, Kevin Gallagher, Andrés López, and Cynthia Sanborn. 2017. *China and Sustainable Development in Latin America: The Social and Environmental Dimension.* Anthem

*Press.*

Ray, Rebecca. 2017. "The Panda's Pawprint: The Environmental Impact of the China-led Re-primarization in Latin America and the Caribbean." *Ecological Economics 134 (April),* 150-59. *https://doi.org/10.1016/j.ecolecon.2016.12.005.*

Ray, Rebecca. 2018. "Colombia Megadam Collapse Highlights Need for Comprehensive Standards." *Diálago Chino, 12 July. https://dialogochino.net/11354-colombia-megadam-collapse-highlights-need-for-comprehensive-standards/.*

Ray, Rebecca and Kehan Wang. 2019. "China-Latin America Economic Bulletin, 2019 Edition," *Boston University, accessed 1 May 2019 from https://www.bu.edu/gdp/2019/02/21/2019-china-latin-america-economic-bulletin/.*

Roach, Shaun. 2012. "China's Impact on World Commodity Markets." *Washington, DC: IMF Working Paper.*

Roberts, J. Timmons, Nikki Demetria Thanos, and David Helvarg. 2003. *Trouble in Paradise: Globalization and Environmental Crises in Latin America. Routledge.*

Rudas Lleras, Guillermo and Mauricio Cabrera Leal. 2017. "Colombia and China: Social and Environmental Impact of Trade and Foreign Direct Investment" in *China and Sustainable Development in Latin America: The Social and Environmental Dimension, Rebecca Ray, Kevin P. Gallagher, Andrés López, and Cynthia Sanborn, Eds. London: Anthem Press.*

Salazar-Xirinachs, José Manuel, Enrique Dussel Peters, and Ariel C. Armony, Eds. 2018. *Efectos de China en la Cantidad y Calidad del Empleo en América Latina. Lima: ILO Regional Office for Latin America and the Caribbean. http://www.dusselpeters.com/133.pdf.*

Sanborn, Cynthia, and Victoria Chonn. 2015. "Chinese Investment in Peru's Mining Industry: Blessing or Curse?" in *China and Sustainable Development in Latin America: The Social and Environmental Dimension, Rebecca Ray, Kevin P. Gallagher, Andrés López, and Cynthia Sanborn, Eds. London: Anthem Press.*

Schatan, Claudia and Diana Piloyan. 2015. "China in Mexico: Some Environmental and Employment Decisions" in *China and Sustainable Development in Latin America: The Social and Environmental Dimension, Rebecca Ray, Kevin P. Gallagher, Andrés López, and Cynthia Sanborn, Eds. London: Anthem Press.*

Stallings, Barbara, "Chinese Foreign Aid to Latin America: Trying to Win Friends and Influence People," in *Margaret Myers and Carol Wise, eds., The Political Economy of China-Latin America Relations in the New Millennium, Routledge: New York, (2017).*

Streifel, Shane. (no date). "Impact of China and India on Global Commodity Markets Focus on Metals & Minerals and Petroleum." *Washington, DC: World Bank. http://www.tos.camcom. it/Portals/_UTC/Studi/ScenariEconomici/39746563551035393/ChinaIndiaCommodityImpact.pdf.*

Stuart, Elizabeth. 2015. "China has almost ended urban poverty – a promising start for the SDGs." *ODI, 19 August. https://www.odi.org/blogs/9803-china-has-almost-ended-urban-poverty-promising-start-sdgs.*

United States Department of Defense. 2018. "Military and Security Developments Involving the People's Republic of China 2018." *Annual Report to Congress. Retrieved 14 October 2019 from https://media.defense.gov/2018/Aug/16/2001955282/-1/-1/1/2018-CHINA-MILITARY-POWER-REPORT.PDF.*

United States Senate. 1998. "The Panama Canal and United States Interests." *Hearing before the Committee of Foreign Relations of the United States Senate on June 16, 1998. Accessed 1 May 2019 from https://www.govinfo.gov/content/pkg/CHRG-105shrg49528/html/CHRG-105shrg49528.htm*

Wise, Carol, Leslie Armijo, and Saori Katada, eds.. *Unexpected Outcomes: How Emerging Economies Survived the 2008–09 Global Financial Crisis (Washington, DC: Brookings Institution Press, 2015).*

---

*Dr. Margaret Myers is director of the Asia and Latin America program at the Inter-American Dialogue in Washington, DC. Dr. Rebecca Ray is a researcher at the Boston University Global Development Policy Center.*

# The Wolf Warriors Films:
# A Single Spark. A Prairie Fire?

*Jie Zhang*

*Vol. 17, No.2*
*2018*

Wu Jing, 44, the director and action star of Wolf Warriors (2015) and Wolf Warriors II (2017), did not set out to make China's highest-grossing film in history. He reportedly had to take out a second mortgage on his apartment to produce the first Wolf Warriors film. His foremost concern was "Why couldn't China have one?" One being a "tough guy" on the big screen. As tough as Bruce Willis, Stallone, Schwarzenegger, or Tom Cruise.[1] A tough guy with a Chinese face.

Leng Feng, the Chinese special ops soldier played by Wu, has since become China's new favorite action hero. Leng follows his own honor code, gulps maotai liquor, flirts with his boss, and leaves behind piles of enemy bodies. The enemies are merciless drug dealers plaguing China's southern border, pirates at sea, foreign mercenaries, and African insurgents. But Leng is always smarter. He is also cooler, dodging kicks, arrows, bullets, grenades, and tanks. And he magically recovers from an Ebola-like virus overnight, becoming fit to fight again.

Chinese audiences have fervently embraced these two thrilling action flicks. If Leng's heroism appears too clichéd and implausible, the director and star suggested, one should blame Hollywood. "In Hollywood, the hero can take on a whole army. Why can't my character take on a dozen mercenaries?" Wu said in an interview with NPR.[2] On his controversial use of the Chinese national flag in Wolf Warriors II, he argued, "American movies can raise the flag, but if my character does it, I'm Red China. Why?"[3] Wolf Warriors II was China's official submission to the Academy Awards in 2017. It is deeply ironic that a Chinese variation of the white savior trope was sent to Hollywood for approval. In Wu's version, the hero single-handedly saves Chinese and African civilians as well as a Chinese-speaking American woman in a fictional African country plagued by an epidemic and a civil war.

Wu's movies are neither subtle nor apologetic in expressing patriotism. The ancient Chinese phrase "Whoever offends China will be wiped out no matter how far away" is articulated several times, conveying an increased level of confidence in China's military prowess. One of the last utterances of Leng's nemesis (played by Scott Adkins) in Wolf Warriors is: "The Chinese army is not as lame as I have thought." In Wolf Warriors II, Big Daddy (played by Frank Grillo) dies only after Leng reclaims agency in history. "People like you will always be beaten by people like me. Get used to it. Get fucking used to it!" Big Daddy hollers, pressing a sharp dagger on Leng's throat. A furious Leng lunges back, grabs the dagger, and kills Big Daddy in a frenzy of stabs, before he has the final words, "That's fucking history!"

For decades the patriotic feelings expressed in Chinese cinema have taken on the forms of victimhood and anxiety. The humiliation of the Opium Wars in the 1840s has been imprinted in the Chinese public mentality. Many films portray Japan's brutal occupation of China during WWII. The legitimacy of the Chinese government partly depends upon fomenting this type of resentment. The Wolf Warriors films, refreshingly, capture "a new, muscular iteration of China's self-narrative."[4] The films construct China as not only militarily capable but also diplomatically prevailing. "Stand down! We are Chinese! China and Africa are friends!" China's ambassador to the African country where Wolf Warriors II takes place calmly declares to a crowd of red-scarfed rebels pointing guns at them. The crowd then reluctantly retreats. "China is a permanent member of the U.N. Security Council and I need them on my side if I'm to take political power," the rebel leader cries later on in the film, scolding his mercenaries for having killed a Chinese doctor in a China-bonded hospital in his country. Plenty of dialogue in the films evokes the feeling of being given a lecture about China's greatness.

"China has never seen such a moment, when its pursuit of a larger role in the world coincides with America's pursuit of a smaller one," New Yorker writer Evan Osnos points out in explaining why some Chinese audiences gave Wolf Warriors II standing ovations and sang the national anthem after the screenings.[5] Rachel, the Chinese-speaking doctor whom Leng rescues in Wolf Warriors II, tries to call the U.S. consulate for help after bloodthirsty rebels have occupied the hospital. "We are sorry. We are currently closed!" is the voice message she receives. To Osnos, it is not coincidental that the films became a hit in China during an age of "America First," when Trump withdrew from the TPP and reduced U.S. contributions to the U.N. while China's Belt and Road initiative has expanded the country's global impact to an unprecedented extent. With a fatter budget, Wolf

Warriors II drives home its thinly disguised political message even more effectively in a new-colonial context. The film prominently sentimentalizes China's economic and humanitarian presence in Africa while, as some have critiqued, portraying African lives as disposable through numerous sensational scenes of massacre and epidemic outbreak against the exotic African landscape. An African boy called Tundu, Leng's godson, begs Leng to rescue his mother, who is stuck in a China-sponsored factory taken over by rebels. Leng promises to get her back safely in 18 hours. Leng has to complete the mission alone because the Chinese Navy has to get U.N. approval before they can take action. The message is clear. China is a powerful player that strictly abides by international law and executes only perfectly moral actions. A Chinese viewer's words best summarize the intended response: "It feels good to be on the side of justice."[6]

The hybrid of Rambo-style heroism, John Woo-style sentimental violence, and Chinese mainstream-style nationalism reaches its peak at the end of Wolf Warriors II. Leng wraps a Chinese flag around his arms and leads wounded Chinese and African citizens through an active war zone. The film closes with the shot of a Chinese passport, poignantly captioned with the announcement, "To the citizens of the People's Republic of China: When you find yourself in danger in a foreign country, never give up hope. China's strength will always support you."

"The patriotic kindling in people's hearts has been dried as far as it can be, and I, Wu Jing, have taken a small match or spark and dropped it on, lighting up all of you," the director said in an interview with a Chinese website.[7] The metaphor of a single spark igniting a prairie fire dates back to a Confucian classic but has been most widely known through Mao's letter in 1930 intending to boost the morale of the Red Army.

The Wolf Warriors films have provided a model to combine patriotic spectacle and box office miracle. The first movie cost $12 million and took in $90 million in China. The second, with a worldwide gross of more than $870 million, is not only China's highest-earning film but also the "only non-Hollywood movie to crack the world's 100 highest-grossing movies of all time."[8] For decades many Chinese audiences, the movie market on track to be the world's largest, have preferred Hollywood over domestic productions. Thanks to Wolf Warriors II, domestic films "for the first time prevailed over foreign imports in terms of combined box-office receipts," reaching almost 55 percent of the total gross in 2017.[9] Having risen to be a superstar, Wu has gained the political capital to build his Wolf Warriors franchise. Chinese government-sponsored cultural offices, film associations, and film research institutions have hosted symposiums to study Wu's success, in the hope of replicating the box office miracle, using films to promote the "Chinese Dream," and boosting China's global soft power. More than 500 reports, interviews, essays, and articles on the films have been published in China.

Collaboration between film producers and military bases—the first Wolf Warriors film was sponsored by the Nanjing Military Base, where Wu shadowed for 18 months—has been identified as a new model of producing breathtaking blockbusters with military themes.[10] It is reported that the script of Wolf Warriors III has been submitted for approval.

Can the Wolf Warriors films be considered "a turning point for China's movies to go global?"[11] While Wolf Warriors II ticket sales were overwhelmingly from China and overseas Chinese communities, Wu does not reject the idea of making films for global audiences. Wolf Warriors II employed prominent Hollywood talent, including Joe and Anthony Russo as consultants, Sam Hargrave ("Captain America: Civil War") as stunt director, and Joseph Trapanese ("Tron: Legacy") as composer.[12] "As Americans working in the China market, you have to be really respectful of their storytelling," Joe Russo said.[13] Evidently Wu knows how to make his Chinese audiences "feel good." And he believes action movies can transcend linguistic and cultural barriers and become universally appealing. In October 2017, Wu met Vin Diesel ("Fast and Furious") who later uploaded a Facebook video with himself beside Wu. "So the world, I want you to say hello to my friend," Diesel wrote.[14] To really be a friend, Wu will have to work hard to make his Western audiences "feel good" too. The practical question is whether he can actually do so without losing his Chinese base in the era of tariffs and threatened trade wars. The existential question is whether he is still himself if he makes Western audiences feel good.

## Notes

1    Rebecca Sun, "Meet China's New King of the Global Box Office." *Hollywood Reporter, vol. 423, no. 38, 06 Dec. 2017, 78-79.*

2    Anthony Kuhn, "Chinese Blockbuster 'Wolf Warrior II' Mixes Jingoism with Hollywood Heroism." *All Things Considered. Aug. 10, 2017. Url: https://www.npr.org/2017/08/10/542663769/chinese-blockbuster-wolf-warrior-ii-mixes-jingoism-with-hollywood-heroism. Accessed May 12, 2018.*

3    Rebecca Sun, ibid.

4    Evan Osnos, ""Making China Great Again." *New Yorker, vol. 93, no. 43, 08 Jan. 2018, 36-45.*

5    Evan Osnos, ibid.

6    Chris Buckley, "A Chinese Hero Beats Records (and Westerners)." *The New York Times, Aug. 17, 2017.*

7    Chris Buckley, ibid.

8    Rebecca Sun, ibid.

9    Thomas Schmid, "ASIA." *Film Journal International, vol. 121, no. 2, Feb. 2018, 56.*

10   Meng Lijing 蒙麗靜. "Chinese Film of Military Theme in the Blockbuster Era: Symposium Overview on Wolf Warriors" (走向大片時代的軍事題材影片: 電影<<戰狼>>討論會綜述). *Contemporary Cinema (當代電影), Jun. 1, 2015. 191-193.*

11   Li Nan, "Going Global: How Long Does It Take to Project Chinese Films onto the International Screen?" *Beijing Review, Sept. 21, 2017, 42-43.*

12  Patrick Frater, "China Mega hit Sparks Rethink Among Studios." *Variety*, Aug. 29, 2017, 16.

13  Rebecca Sun, ibid.

14  Rebecca Sun, ibid.

*Dr. Jie Zhang is associate professor of modern languages and literature at Trinity University.*

# Interview with China Scholar
# Dr. Deborah Davis, Yale University

*Penelope Prime*
*Vol. 17, No.2*
*2018*

Dr. Deborah Davis is the China Research Center's 2018 annual lecturer. Dr. Davis is Professor Emerita of Sociology at Yale University and a Distinguished Visiting Professor at Fudan University in Shanghai as well as on the faculty at the Schwarzman College at Tsinghua University. At Yale she served as Director of Academic Programs at the Yale Center for the Study of Globalization, Chair of the Department of Sociology, Chair of the Council of East Asian Studies, and co-chair of the Women Faculty Forum. Her past publications have analyzed the politics of the Cultural Revolution, Chinese family life, social welfare policy, consumer culture, property rights, social stratification, occupational mobility, and impact of rapid urbanization and migration on health and happiness.

This interview is based on a discussion in person and by email between Dr. Penelope Prime, the managing editor of China Currents, and Dr. Davis. The text has been edited for length and clarity.

***Penelope Prime: Dr. Davis, welcome to Atlanta. We are delighted to have you here and to learn from your expertise. We want to know how a sociologist sees what is going on in China today. The topic of urbanization runs throughout your work. What drew you to this topic and what have been the big takeaways?***

**Deborah Davis:** I like cities, and I like living in cities. Perhaps if I had grown up on a farm, I would have the same emotional attachment to rural as to urban living; but in my case, cities draw me in. My first job after I graduated from Wellesley was at the Chinese University of Hong Kong and after two years, I became even more attached to high-density living and the cultural variety of urban, public life. Subsequently at Harvard's East Asian master's program, I organized a reading group led by Alex Woodside to explore varieties of city life in East and Southeast Asia. In the mid-1970s when Americans couldn't live in China, I interviewed PRC migrants in Hong Kong for my doctoral thesis. As a family of three we lived in a tiny 100 square meter apartment overlooking a busy street, and we thrived on the energy and diversity of the city. When I finally could do fieldwork in China in 1979, the Chinese government so severely restricted our geographic movements that we couldn't even exit the final stop on the Beijing subway. One result was to turn my attention to analyzing the spaces and everyday life in the urban core.

Then after these early restrictions were lifted and Chinese and American scholars developed ongoing partnerships, professional and personal networks reinforced my initial focus on densely settled cities, and in particular on Shanghai. I first went to Shanghai in 1981 and then returned almost every summer between 1984 and 1995, following 125 households whom I first interviewed in 1986 and 1988. Over these 10 years, China took the first steps toward a rapid expansion of the urban population that by 2010 had created 160 cities with more than one million residents.

**PP: *You have also studied marriage. Is that urban marriage or just marriage generally?***

DD: In my first book "Long Lives," the core question was how the Communist revolution had impacted the elderly and their relations to their families in both rural and urban China. Previously many had assumed that collectivization of the economy and political campaigns against ancestor veneration had destroyed family solidarity. Drawing on documents and household interviews, I argued that the economic, legal, and health initiatives of the CCP between 1950 and 1976 had actually strengthened family connections because they promoted higher levels of marriage among all social classes, and more sustained interdependence between elders and their surviving sons and daughters than had been the norm during the three decades of war and dislocation before 1949.

**PP: *What are the big takeaways that you have found over these decades of studying marriage and cities and family relations?***

DD: First, I would stress that as a fieldworker focused as often on dynamics of daily life as on broad demographic and structural trends, I rarely can muster big takeaways. That is not to say I never generalize, but the level of generalization tends to be modest and contingent. For example, over the past decade I have focused on how the one-child policy, commodification of property relations, and enforcement of a new marriage law that reduced barriers to divorce have "privatized" the institution of marriage. But simultaneously, I have used focus groups and extended family interviews to probe the refined moral logics by which siblings and divorcing spouses divide domestic property as the party-state has granted individuals more privacy in how they conduct their intimate relationships. By listening to individual voices and placing these conversations within larger institutional spaces, sociologists work to understand both social process and personal agency.

**PP: *Do you have any observation of youth in China these days?***

As you know, currently I'm a visiting professor at Fudan University, and this year I will return for my third faculty appointment at Schwarzman College at Tsinghua University in Beijing. In these two university settings, as well as in interactions with newly arrived PRC students in the U.S., I get a glimpse into the ambitions and fears of those in their late teens and early 20s. Fifteen years ago, acceptance to university guaranteed a good job upon graduation. Now after rapid expansion of the tertiary sector, 30 percent of 18- year-old men and women continue their education beyond senior high school. Consequently, the value of a bachelor's degree has fallen and competition to enter specific majors in elite colleges has greatly intensified. China not only has the largest number of college and university students in the world, but it also has one of the highest percentages of secondary school graduates continuing to tertiary education. Higher education has become highly stratified, and the pressure on teens and their families is far more intense than for those only 15 years their senior. Therefore, the first thing I would say about "youth" in China today is that most teens in urban centers live in a pressure cooker, and the sorting process begins in the last years of primary school. Those who succeed in these academic competitions and whom I have taught at Fudan, Tsinghua, and Yale are extremely accomplished and ambitious; but even they worry intensely about their future. However, I would also stress that talent stretches across the whole country, and it is not concentrated in one or two megacities. China has no single metropole.

**PP: But that is a good thing.**

DD: Yes, overall such drive and ambition are good for this cohort and good for China and there is not a single province where one cannot find talent and drive.

**PP: You have done a lot of research on the ground over these years.  How have those opportunities and methodologies changed, or not?**

DD: Indeed.  When I first went to China in 1979 Chinese officials had no experience with foreign social scientists. Working with the U.N., the government had committed to making the 1982 census meet global standards, but virtually no officials who supervised foreign visitors championed random samples. As a result, until well into the 1980s, sociologists did a kind of "piecework" or what we more formally term "triangulation." We gathered every shard of evidence from as many sources and angles as possible, operationalized variables in multiple ways, and when the results aligned into a coherent pattern, confirmed or rejected our hypotheses. Today, we still need to "triangulate," but the methodologies in the study of Chinese society closely resemble those in the study of American society.

I drew my first random sample in 1986, when the Shanghai City Union sponsored me to write about the family life of newly retired textile workers. This project was negotiated at the local level. They had never heard of a random sample, but they wanted scientific methods. Over the next 18 years I went back eight times to that research site. Many of the original respondents had died or moved away. Yet in 2004 I was able to contact family members in 70% of the original 125 households.

The years between 1996 and 2016 represented a golden age. Excellent census data was publicly available, digitized statistical materials were accessible via the internet, and most importantly, many PRC born sociologists were leading research teams. The Chinese census is one of the best in the world and almost every Chinese academic journal can be searched online.  In one day, scholars working from the United States can gather trend data and run regressions that 20 years ago would have taken months to complete.  For example, in 2005 when I wanted to discuss how the government had understood and used the role of consumers after 1949, I spent a few hours with keyword searches of People's Daily to create the numerical trend and then a week to read all the articles in which the word "consumer" had been linked to discussion of "waste" between 1949 and 2003. To complete such an analysis 10 years earlier, I would have needed to travel to the rare library with a complete run of People's Daily, lifted every bound set, and spent hours to identify every article which discussed both consumption and waste. It would have taken months and would not have produced results that were as accurate.

**PP: *What advice would you give to young scholars these days who are interested in studying China?***

DD: I am not one to easily give advice, but I would note that the support and recognition for scholarship of contemporary China varies by discipline. Not so very long ago, donors to Yale had raised money to hire an economist who worked on the Chinese economy. Nevertheless, the economics department did not launch a search because most faculty believed that there was no suitable data on China to support frontier research in economics. Clearly, we no longer face the same data restrictions today, but some disciplines still provide more opportunities than others.

**PP: *What is your next project?***

DD: Currently my primary research focus is a multi-year study of how rapid growth of megacities and the inclusion of 400 million rural residents into urban settlements have impacted family life. I also will extend a 2015-2016 project that studied wedding ritual to understand changing urban kinship ties.

**PP: *Congratulations! From your vantage point, just to wrap up our discussion of this wonderful career that you've had, what is your sense of U.S.-China relations today?***

DD: We are challenged. Short statement. We are challenged. But we've been challenged before, and I think that the talent and the diverse players on both sides of the Pacific who are committed to the long term give me confidence that the future will be brighter.

**PP: *So, you are overall optimistic?***

DD: You have to be. What's the alternative? There are many reasons to be pessimistic but there is too much at stake, too many shared interests, to see only the dark side.

---

# Movie Review: Crazy Rich Asians

*Paul Foster*

*Vol. 17, No.2*
*2018*

Honestly, I'm a kung fu and action film fan, but I really enjoyed Jon M. Chu's Crazy Rich Asians, a film that proved to be a compellingly funny action-filled romantic comedy that economically sifted through a cornucopia of old Chinese culture set against the trappings of modern cosmopolitan wealth at its gaudiest extremes.

At the outset I admit that I have studiously avoided other reviews of this movie because I wanted to approach the experience with freedom to create my own interpretation. That said, it has been impossible to escape hearing in the news media about some casting issues that dovetail with current Hollywood film discourse about "white-washing." The minimum that can be said (with relief) is that the male lead, Henry Golding, is unmistakably not Anglo in appearance, despite his unmistakably Anglo name. His terrific acting also makes moot other angles in this discourse.

I'd love my language students to see this movie just for the soundtrack as all of the songs are in non-subtitled Mandarin Chinese. Included are at least two hits by the queen of classic Chinese ballads, Theresa Teng (Deng Lijun), as well as other Chinese language renditions of some famous rock and roll party classics. The more challenging task is for students to dissect the complexity of Chinese culture presented here, particularly in light of the intersections of non-Chinese ideology, religion, politics, geography, and history. There is a lot of historical baggage to examine outside the movie theater that is thankfully only hinted at within. This will make great fodder for classroom debate. For example, after an initial scene set in the childhood of the male lead, our introduction to the Young family matriarch, played by Michelle Yeoh (star of Crouching Tiger, Hidden Dragon [2000]), is set during a Bible study session at her mansion in Singapore, which she of course leads in reading. What is the role of Christianity in Asia, after all? This example merely hints at the idiosyncrasy of a film whose wealthy characters are international and cosmopolitan. However, we "commoners" with Western cultural backgrounds are set to readily identify with "commoners" throughout East Asia in mutual recognition of the eye-popping luxury and privilege presented among these crazy rich people.

So, is this an Asian movie? A Chinese movie? A Chinese American movie? A Chinese diaspora movie? To whom is this movie directed? The British-accented English beautifully spoken by all the main characters (except the Chinese American female lead played by Constance Wu) neatly parallels the Western obsession with royalty expressed by interest in royal marriages, the television series Downton Abbey, and the spurious assumptions regarding the assumedly higher intelligence of speakers of the Queen's English. It is all about perspective, right? Rich people must be really intelligent, so they speak that way, right? Intelligence aside, what commoner or aristocrat of any nationality wouldn't identify with the comeuppance of the London luxury hotel staff who discriminate against the Youngs, only to find the hotel bought by the matriarch (Michelle Yeoh) minutes later as revenge?

Why is this movie set in Singapore? The wealthy family (and extended family) are generally the product of British boarding schools, "old money" emigrated from pre-revolutionary China. This timing nicely sidesteps the issue of a hundred years of politics of the twentieth century, and also sidesteps the wealthy Taiwan as Chinese issue, as well as the fact of new money in the PRC today, which hosts the second-highest number of billionaires by nationality, a fact that would argue for titling the film "Crazy Rich Chinese." But could this be a "Chinese movie," given that the major tension of the movie runs along a class conflict motif presented by the already yearlong relationship between Rachel Chu, the New York-raised, working class, brilliant NYU game theory professor, and Nick Young, the scion of Singapore's leading family (unbeknown to her)? The title "Crazy Rich People" might be more appropriate as viewers watch Rachel and Nick return together for Nick's best friend's wedding, and Rachel is thrown into the lion pit of class conflict. The story then becomes how she either sinks or swims regardless of nationality.

The film portrays a cast of hot Chinese women with Baywatch bodies and men who are strong, ripped and stripped down in Bruce Lee style. They play in the idealized manner of really rich people anywhere, as depicted in the parallel bachelor and bachelorette parties. But the primary "love triangle" so to speak between Nick and Rachel, and matriarch Mrs. Young demonstrates the tension of traditional Chinese cultural norms of pre-May Fourth Movement (1919) gentry, whose parents must approve of suitably class-appropriate marriage partners. Who schools whom in this multigenerational game of romance presents the case for how to achieve "free [choice of] love," a revolutionary goal sought after with zeal for a hundred years since May Fourth era. Some things never change.

There is texture even among the rich. In addition to the stand-up performances by the leads, three excellent supporting actors demonstrate this variation. The first of these performances is found in the endearing new money comic role of Rachel's Singapore-native college friend, the semblance of a punk rocker type who name is Peik Lin. Equally endearing is the Young family coordinator, Oliver, who – with his insider knowledge of the various family dramas – is sympathetic to Rachel. Both these roles add a touch of realism as they widen the circle of relationships portrayed in this great game. The third stellar supporting performance is given by Astrid, Nick's closest female cousin who, in her tragic subplot, connects across class boundaries with Rachel as she herself valiantly struggles with the disintegration of her own "free love" marriage. These comic and tragic characters provide depth in their plot lines to demonstrate that despite the super wealth of these rich people, nothing is free.

The Singapore setting is spectacular, with fabulous architecture shot with production values that alone make the movie worth seeing, even if it comes off as a fantastic tourist infomercial. The food at the night market is appealing and multinational, with mouthwatering curry and other dishes portrayed lightly in a style reminiscent of Ang Lee's Eat Drink Man Woman (1994). And although the film is in English, the audience is treated to a menagerie of languages, from mostly Mandarin to Cantonese and perhaps some Hakka, generally with subtitles in English except for the songs.

All in all, the film has many nicely choreographed dichotomies, such as tradition versus modernity, new versus old money, as well a variety of supporting character types. The "healthy" love across class divide portrayed by Rachel and Nick stands as a critique of people whose self-image is virtually defined by their obsession with money and image. Crazy Rich Asians shows how a romantic comedy can address superficial culturally "universal" issues and stay out of thorny political and historical divides. That's the feel-good dimension, and what is left unaddressed are the political-economic foundations that make the crazy richness possible. Students of China on the rise should be crazy curious about these deeper-level dynamics, although this fun rom-com rightfully sidesteps these issues. Crazy Rich Asians demonstrates that regardless of our nationality or social class, we know that we "all" share similar dreams of such idealized riches, for better or worse. Perhaps this is the metaphorical lesson of Rachel's game theory lesson – the American Dream, the Chinese Dream, the Chinese American Dream, the

Asian Dream – we all share the color green.

---

*Dr. Paul Foster is Associate Professor of Chinese at Georgia Institute of Technology and an Associate of the China Research Center. He is author of Ah Q Archaeology: Lu Xun, Ah Q, Ah Q Progeny and the National Character Discourse in Twentieth Century China (Lexington Press, 2006).*

# On Grades

*Li Qi*
*Vol. 19, No.1*
*2020*

My six-year-old daughter learned about grading during my year-long sabbatical in Beijing. Grades and testing had been a foreign concept in her short educational experience in the U.S. The only tests she and her classmates took were designed to track progress, not evaluate performance, and they were reported only to parents.

School in Beijing was shock therapy.

My formerly clueless child quickly grasped the meaning of grades and all that implies. First, students are graded all the time. There is hardly any ungraded work (and there are tons of daily homework assignments and frequent exams). In fact, there is an obsession with quantifiable assessment on performance that reaches every position and worker throughout Chinese society (more on that later). My kid knows that every day a "showdown" time will come when she finds out how well she did in her homework or exam.

Second, these are not "soft" grades that give everyone credit for effort. Chinese schools don't do a lot of sugarcoating. I find that refreshing most of the time, but horrifying on some occasions. If your answer deserves only a 59, you should not expect an automatic round up to 60. As a college professor in the U.S., I often feel the pressure of arguing a case in front of the Supreme Court for giving a bad grade to a student.

Third, students' grades are essentially public knowledge among their classmates. I vividly remember one of my own Chinese teachers when I was a child used to give back the exams in descending order of the grades, so the entire class recognized the "best" and the "worst" instantly. I feel bad that my child was subject to the same practice decades later. She came back one day quite upset because one of her classmates (who was put in charge of returning exams!) taunted her for scoring the lowest grade in her class (77 out of 100). Holding back my anger and sadness, I asked her how she handled this. It turned out that my feisty girl said to the boy: "Well, I know you got only 73 a couple of weeks ago on a different exam!" Then she reported his "bullying" to the teacher.

As unhealthy and appalling as this sounds, I noticed that these sorts of incidents became a source of motivation for my daughter. The open knowledge of grades brews fierce competition. Somehow the seeds of wishing to score the absolute best (100!) were planted and she did succeed in obtaining that elusive 100 on her last exam before leaving China. I am glad and proud about how she reacted to this "negative" event, and on some level attributes the competitive environment with lighting a desire for self-improvement, although the public knowledge of grades must also discourage and "damage" many children.

When I was a child, a popular idiom among my classmates was "KaoKaoKao, Laoshi de Fabao; FenFenFen, Xuesheng de Minggen," which translates to "Test, Test, Test, a teacher's magical weapon. Grade, Grade, Grade, a student's lifeline." I find it still holds universal truth in China today.

Competition is always high among Chinese students due to the scarcity of good schools compared to the large number of students. Getting into a GOOD middle school, then a GOOD high school, a GOOD college, and ultimately securing a GOOD job gets progressively more difficult as one climbs the social pyramid. The competitive environment in Chinese schools mirrors that in the society, where most of the competition boils down to the quantifiable evaluation I referred above.

On most campuses in the U.S., the "tough love" approach is not a popular or well-regarded way of teaching and interacting with students. Sometimes I wonder whether we are sheltering them for too long from the real world, where effort is important, but performance is the key to success. Compared to our American students, their Chinese peers are confronted at a much younger age with real competition that translates to real consequences. Small children recognize that the grades correlate with respect, social standing, teachers' favor, and parents' approval. For older kids, this converts to chances of advancing to the next level of school and college, which ultimately links to income and social status as adults.

My daughter returned to her American elementary school with newfound enthusiasm and appreciation. Part of me was relieved, but part of me missed that striving energy I saw in her back at the Chinese elementary school. I still don't know how much competition and objective testing is healthy for young children. However, many Chinese children (and grown-ups) I encountered had that spirit of striving for self-improvement and held the belief that one could make a better life for themselves through hard work. That dream can be realized only if the playing field is level, the competition fair, and the rules transparent. And both China and the U.S. still have a lot work to do on that.

---

*Dr. Li Qi is Professor of Economics at Agnes Scott College and an Associate of the China Research Center.*

# U.S.-China Trade Pact President Trump Just Signed Fails to Resolve Three Fundamental Issues

*Penelope Prime*

*Vol. 19, No.1*
*2020*

U.S. President Donald Trump signed a trade deal with China on January 15, 2020, intended as a first phase toward a more comprehensive agreement between the two countries.

In exchange for some tariff relief, China promised to buy an additional US$200 billion in American goods and services over the next two years and make structural reforms that would provide more protection for U.S. intellectual property. It still leaves about $360 billion in punitive tariffs on Chinese imports in place – and more sanctions would be triggered if China fails to meet the terms of the deal.

Good news, right? The end of the trade war is nigh? Don't get your hopes up.

While business leaders in both countries will be temporarily relieved, the underlying tensions between them will not end easily.

As an economist who closely studies the U.S. relationship with China, I believe there are fundamental issues that won't be resolved anytime soon.

### Doing it in phases

Tariffs and other trade issues have received most of the attention during the trade war, but the more fundamental – and difficult – challenges are with lax intellectual property protection and China's industrial policy.

The U.S. is unhappy with China's use of these tools to develop its economy and to help its companies compete – unfairly, from the U.S. perspective. And many of the Trump administration's demands challenge China's normal business and policy practices.

China's leaders can't be seen by Chinese citizens as giving into the U.S., while Trump wants to show that he is tough on China as part his campaign for reelection. This makes the negotiations very sensitive on both sides.

That's why American and Chinese negotiators, who have been engaged in talks for almost two years, decided to try to get to an agreement in phases.

Phase one has focused on the trade balance and tariffs, with some provisions relating to technology transfer, intellectual property and opening China's economy to foreign business. Phase two is expected to then deal more deeply with intellectual property enforcement and economic reform in China.

Given the negotiations went on for so long, it's fair to ask, why are these issues so difficult to resolve? I believe there are basically three factors that have made finding much common ground difficult – and phase one won't change that.

## Government subsidies

First, China's successful growth has combined market competition with government-led industrial policy. For example, when China's leaders decided the economy needed more innovation, it created incentives and targets for companies and research institutes to create patents. The number of patents filed has soared as a result.

A wide range of government subsidies is used to direct and assist private as well as state investment in similar ways.

The U.S. does this as well but not on the same scale, and therefore views it as unfair.

From China's perspective, however, it is not reasonable for the U.S. to require China to change its development model in exchange for removing tariffs.

## Protecting intellectual property

Getting China to do more to protect the intellectual property of advanced technologies is another especially thorny issue.

Both countries are facing economic challenges that can be aided by improved technology. But since in many areas Chinese capabilities have caught up with those of the U.S., or are being rapidly developed, there is much more pressure from the U.S. for China to accept global norms on intellectual property rights.

Even while China's own IP protections have improved at home, there is ample evidence that Chinese companies have copied foreign technology without permission or payment, despite China's acceptance of IP protection as part of World Trade Organization membership.

Foreign companies also report being compelled to share advanced technology in order to do business in China. While, technically, the companies can decide to pull out of China's market, the U.S. argues that this hurts the competitiveness of U.S. businesses. It either means they must lose their technological advantage or not have access to the business opportunities that China's large market offers. There is no reciprocal requirement of Chinese companies doing business in the U.S.

The phase one agreement begins to deal with the IP issues and includes a complaint process, which is a step in the right direction. It remains to be seen, however, how extensive it will be and how quickly it'll be implemented given that Chinese companies will still face intense pressure from the government to advance China's domestic capabilities.

## Military concerns

Finally, technology capabilities are related to growing military concerns.

Many of the advanced technologies that China is racing to obtain have military as well as civilian uses. U.S. policy under the current administration has indicated a wariness about China's military intentions and is considering options.

This wariness has been bolstered by China's military buildup, especially naval capabilities in Asia. Some advisers to the Trump administration argue that China's ultimate long-term goal is to replace the U.S. as the dominant global power.

## China's rise

Conflicting differences in the U.S. and China's economic systems were less of a problem so long as Chinese companies lagged far behind their American counterparts in terms of technology and competitiveness.

As China has grown more technologically advanced, its relationship with the U.S. has become increasingly strained. This will only get worse as China's economy develops and its companies compete more with the U.S. and others.

The phase one agreement represents an important step in re-setting the dialogue between the two countries in a positive direction. Whether we see a phase two will depend on open discussion and trust.

Good relations with the U.S. have been one of the foundations of China's successful development and entry into global markets. Chinese leaders are now weighing how much these good relations with the U.S. matter to their future.

---

*Dr. Penelope Prime is the Founding Director of the China Research Center and Managing Editor of China Currents. This article is republished from The Conversation under a Creative Commons license available at https://theconversation.com/us-china-trade-pact-president-trump-just-signed-fails-to-resolve-3-fundamental-issues-130017.*

# China Retail's Newest Inflection Point: From E-commerce to Omni-channel

*Katherine Peavy*
*Vol. 17, No.1*
*2018*

Imagine this: Sitting in your living room in Shanghai or Beijing, you realize that the final Game of Thrones season is a week away. You decide to splurge on upgrading your entertainment system so you can host watching parties every week. You post a request for recommendations on a WeChat music and entertainment forum and narrow down your choices to three brands. Searches on the three brands reveal that two of your favorite musicians and one of your favorite actors recommend each brand. Videos show them listening to music and watching last summer's blockbusters in their decked-out living rooms. You need some face time at an electronics store to help with the decision, so you pop in to the nearest Suning store where a number of brands have set up customer experience centers – soundproofed "living rooms" in the store where you can select a few favorite films and music, dim the lights, recline on the latest ergonomic lounge chair and indulge in snacks while assessing the electronic brands recommended by friends and the famous. Finally, decision made, you scan the QR codes on the equipment with your WeChat app and the order is submitted to the retailer, paid for through your Alipay account and you head off, no bags in hand.

The next day, the doorbell rings and a team of technicians brings in your new equipment, boxed and wrapped. They unwrap your purchases, set up all the electronics, test them, break up the boxes for recycling and clear out after they have shown you how everything works. By the way, when you ordered the entertainment system, you got a coupon via WeChat for the ergonomic lounge chair, and they delivered that as well. You've only lifted a finger and now will be the envy of friends and family.

This is the road China's consumer market is moving down and moving quickly. Consider the sales numbers on Alibaba's platforms Taobao and Tmall on the world's biggest e-commerce shopping day, Singles Day (November 11), in 2016, US$17.79 billion within 24 hours.[1] Online sales figures for big U.S. shopping days such as Black Friday and Prime Day are in the billions, but still in single digits.

According to PwC's Total Retail Report 2017, China's national online retail sales of goods and services for the first quarter of 2017 yielded 1.40 trillion yuan (more than US$200 billion), which was 32.1 percent higher than in 2016.[2]

These numbers show just how dynamic, and potentially competitive, retailing in China is likely to become. After all, the entertainment system example is not yet a reality, but something both online and offline retailers are working toward that will push them into not just online-to-offline (O2O) technology solutions, but omni-channel solutions involving social media, supply chain optimization and efficient fulfillment options. Alexandra Tirado, CEO of Atlanta-based consulting firm Fortuna Holdings International, which includes China e-retailer JD.com as a client, says that this type of "seamless shopping experience and white glove service" will be the key to success for China's online and offline retailers. In the online-to-offline conundrum, China's e-commerce and traditional offline retailers are "looking for ways to connect the online experience to the physical store and figuring out how to blend technology and the online shopping experience," says Tirado.

PwC's Total Retail 2017 report sees the same trends quickly coming to fruition, or "increasing maturity of business in using data analytics and omni-channel technologies to create a seamless customer journey between online and offline channels."

The omni-channel ecosystem, including efficient use of big data, virtual reality and artificial intelligence, dazzles the imagination and the senses. In reality, there are a few hurdles for retailers to overcome, the main one being the competition between the big e-commerce players including Alibaba's Tmall and Taobao and JD.com with the brick-and-mortar stores like Gome Electrical, Suning and others.

Thus far, we have looked primarily at retailers selling electronics and white goods, but the current and pending retail eco-systems can apply to retail ranging from groceries to clothes to services. Most brick-and-mortar retailers are still struggling to adapt to the disruption of their markets over the last 10 years by China's big technology players, commonly called BAT or BAT-J, to refer to Baidu (search engine), Alibaba (retail, fintech, supply chain), Tencent (fintech, social media) and JD.com (retail, fulfillment).

The worldwide focus on the big technology players, with their successes in e-commerce, fintech and social media, tends to cast a lesser light on smaller players, such as micro-retailers and brand-direct e-commerce, as well as traditional brick-and-mortar players. Yet they also play a major role in the world to come. Perhaps recognizing that adapting to the new e-commerce ecosystem was the only way forward – 52 percent of consumers in China prefer to shop online according to PwC, and 80 percent are willing to pay using mobile payments[3] – traditional brick-and-mortar retailers have embraced technology primarily through working with the big tech players, and by developing online retail and finance options of their own.

The major brick-and-mortar appliance retailers, Gome Electrical Appliance Holdings Ltd. and Suning Commerce Group for example, have taken different paths. Yet, consider the range of innovations and investments in the retail sector:

- In 2015, Suning accepted investment from Alibaba of US$4.56 billion and itself invested in Alibaba. The tie-up is widely regarded as part of Alibaba's online-to-offline strategy, and Suning's plan to develop better technology support.
- Gome, meanwhile, prefers to go it alone. The company is developing its online platform in-house. It acquired com in 2012, and integrated it into gome.com.cn for better sharing of back-end systems, and thus better data analysis capabilities.
- Late in 2016, Tencent and Baidu decided not to join shopping mall developer Dalian Wanda on an e-commerce platform, but that is not stopping Wanda from expanding in the internet technology space. Two months later, the company established Wanda Internet Technology Group and in March 2017, announced the division would develop cloud services with IBM.[4]
- Even foreign retailers are trying to stay in the game, sometimes with mixed results. U.S. retailer Walmart sold its China online retailer Yihaodian to JD.com in late 2016 for a five percent stake in JD.com.

Starting in 2016, legacy brick-and-mortar retailers have taken aggressive steps to push omni-channel strategies with and without technology partners. Gome Electrical Appliances set the company strategy for 2016 as "total retail strategy," which the company says includes "fully promoting the integration of online and offline businesses" through technology to support the development of a new retail ecosystem. According to the company's annual report, that strategy allowed Gome Online to increase revenue by 58.8 percent in 2016 and gross merchandise volume (GMV) by 110 percent.[5]

Significant increases in revenue and GMV, such as those posted by Gome, point to the reasons traditional retailers are still in the game despite disruption by the BAT-J companies. China's e-commerce market is primarily driven by consumer preferences. Advertising and brand guru Tom Doctoroff says, "O2O is one of the most dynamic – and, for consumers, satisfying — areas of commercial innovation. Offline and online blend into holistic, rewarding experiences."

Retailers wanting to be at the tip of consumer's fingertips are looking at three aspects of their business:

- Customer engagement
- Experience-led commerce
- Fulfillment

Gome's President Wang Jun Zhou stated in the company annual report: "In the present and future, success in new retail belongs to those who successfully combine strong supply chains, new retail trends and scenarios, seamless integration between online and offline, and technological proficiency."

## Customer engagement: All about ease of connection

Responsiveness to customers is the key to customer engagement for retailers. Both traditional and e-commerce retailers are using technology to reach new markets, employing big data, and enhancing that reach with physical stores.

"Having well-placed physical stores could become an advantage for existing retailers if they are able to integrate an innovative technology play that engages consumers in an attractive way," says retail analyst Mavis Hui of DBS Vickers Securities.

When retailers are able to parse data about customers according to location, income and brand recognition, then link that to an in-store experience, they are engaging customers before they even arrive in the physical store.

Traditional companies have an advantage over pure technology players in that they know their markets and consumers already. By striking out on its own, rather than with a big tech partner, Gome's ambition is to create a retail ecosystem leveraging the company's market knowledge and technology. Apart from expanding into the after-sales service market with an Internet of Things (IoT) strategy geared toward smart homes, Gome also has decided to delve into financing solutions for the upstream supply chain and providing trade support, strategies designed to enhance product quality, delivery and fulfillment speed.

For most traditional players, in-house technology development has not been the preferred strategy, and Gome's new business model is too new to declare it a success or failure.

There are, however, smaller players such as clothing brand Ruhan E-commerce that have used their own technology plays to improve their business. Ruhan created the most prevalent retail trend in 2014, the "Internet star" when the company slashed its marketing and advertising budget and contracted with a young model to influence her followers to purchase their clothes through her posts and videos candidly assessing the clothing and accessories she used. Not only did Ruhan increase sales, but its Internet star also started a trend that other retailers have followed.

### Experience-led commerce: All about new technology

Aside from the phenomenon of Internet stars, other retailers rely on Key Opinion Leaders (KOLs), such as the experts in the WeChat electronics forum mentioned in the example at the beginning of the article. From these initial experiences already in play, companies are developing consumer experience strategies using Virtual Reality (VR) and Artificial Intelligence (AI) to enhance consumer experiences.

A VR experience scenario might involve a consumer wearing a VR headset at home to browse a store. Brands and retailers would then use AI to track where the customer's eyes stopped the longest, or what his or her expression revealed during interactions with products.

PwC noted in its Total Retail 2017 report that Macy's took a step forward in the China retail market on Singles Day 2016, when the U.S. retailer created a virtual tour of the New York flagship store for Chinese consumers.[6]

As always, Alibaba has its eye on the future and what it will mean to consumers. CTO Jeff Zhang says, "Virtual Reality equipment will become the next corner of the consumer market. Once it becomes more realistic, the VR experience will attract more customers to buy online."

### Fulfillment: Technology optimizing the supply chain

Upstream supply chain and last-mile delivery may be the most exciting but least visible impacts technology will have on retail.

DBS Vickers' Hui says fulfillment issues are an area where technology players and traditional retailers have converging strategies "given China's huge land mass and relatively primitive logistics support in many PRC cities. Thus, physical stores could continue to act as merchandise collection points for online orders, or as warehouses or hubs to direct and fulfill last-mile delivery needs."

Smart companies are looking for a quality play, and to most that means developing an ecosystem, which the big tech companies have done through their long list of affiliates. For Tencent that goes from social media to finance to healthcare and retail, and for Alibaba it means going from e-commerce to finance and then delving back into e-commerce and retail via its partnership with Suning, for example.

Gome's new subsidiary Gome Fintech has a different ecosystem in mind, the supply chain. It aims to bring financing solutions to the upstream supply chain, where suppliers of products have difficulty getting financing from state-owned banks, development loans, factoring and trade support – all areas largely ignored by banks. Gome has the expertise to impact the supply chain in these areas, as well as make a difference in streamlining the supply chain through enhancing quality via stable supplier financing and leveraging the company's brick-and-mortar stores for last-mile delivery options or click-and-collect scenarios.

PwC notes another fulfillment issue solved by the use of block-chain data.[7] For many years, luxury goods retailers have struggled with the problem of ensuring products they sell online are authentic. It was one area in which consumers evidenced a lack of trust in purchasing online. However, with block-chain data, products can be tracked from the factory to the consumer's front door, authenticating not just the product, but also the entire supply chain.

### Race to the future

For most retailers, both brick-and-mortar and e-commerce, a key path to the future is through partnering with existing technology companies for the latest in technical advances and for investment. In speeches over the last year, Alibaba's founder Jack Ma has been calling for both technology and traditional companies to improve their research and implementation plays for big data, cloud computing and artificial intelligence.

Players not traditionally in e-commerce or with a strong technology backgrounds have heavy lifting to do in terms of investment, financial as well as talent costs, in making technology aspirations reality. Partnering with one of the existing tech players, or subcontracting to a technology partner (TP) is an attractive proposition for scaling and financial reasons.

But the retail industry has seen advances with privately owned and more innovative players like Gome and Suning making moves in the past 18 months in O2O sales and supply chain financing options.

In a recent speech, Alibaba's Ma predicted that "new technology will become our future product, and service innovation is the most important foundation, and to achieve this online and offline business and consumer experience will be the at the core."

While retail and its supply chain appear to be at a technology inflection point, it is clear that the race to adopt technologies involves identifying the best technology solutions to satisfy customer needs and demands.

### Notes

1   https://techcrunch.com/2016/11/11/alibaba-singles-day-2016/

2   p. 3, *Total Retail 2017: eCommerce in China, the future is already here*; http://www.pwccn. com/en/retail-and-consumer/publications/total-retail-2017-china/total-retail-survey-2017-china-cut.pdf

3   *PwC p. 3 and p. 11 Total Retail 2017.*

4   *https://www.theregister.co.uk/2017/03/20/ibm_wanda_cloud_deal/*

5   *http://www.gome.com.hk/attachment/2017032712491217_en.pdf*

6   *p.15, http://www.pwccn.com/en/retail-and-consumer/publications/total-retail-2017-china/
    total-retail-survey-2017-china-cut.pdf*

7   *p.27, http://www.pwccn.com/en/retail-and-consumer/publications/total-retail-2017-china/
    total-retail-survey-2017-china-cut.pdf*

---

*Currently based in Atlanta, Katherine Peavy spent 15 years in China work-
ing in the risk management field on hundreds of due diligence cases and fraud
investigations. She is a founding partner of the consulting firm Cross Pacific
Partner (www.crosspacificpartner.com).*

# Earth Observing Satellites and Open Data Sharing in China

*Mariel Borowitz*

*Vol. 19, No.1*
*2020*

## Introduction

Over the past decade, governments around the world have begun adopting policies that make data they collect openly available to all users at no cost – notably information from Earth observation satellites.[1] Satellites collect environmental data on a global scale, and the data are directly relevant to understanding and addressing a wide range of global and local challenges.

China, which launched its first Earth observation satellite in 1988, has long been involved in global discussions regarding open access to satellite data and has made a large portion of its data available in line with global norms. Recently, China has announced a number of policies to further increase the availability of its Earth observing satellite data, in line with its Digital Belt and Road (DBAR) initiative. China also seeks to lead in the transition to big data and cloud computing infrastructures that facilitate sharing. This article provides an overview of Chinese Earth observation activities, data sharing policies, and open data initiatives, and discusses potential future developments in this area.

## Satellite Earth Observations in China

China's civilian Earth observation satellite efforts are divided into five programs:

1. Fengyun meteorological satellites
2. China-Brazil Earth Resources Satellite program and Ziyuan resource satellites
3. HaiYang ocean satellites

4. Haunjing environmental and disaster monitoring satellites

5. Gaofen high-resolution imagery satellites. Each of these programs is run by a different organization, and the satellite data have been subject to different data sharing policies.

The Fengyun satellites are operated by the National Satellite Meteorological Center, a unit of the Chinese Meteorological Administration. The Center was established in 1970, and the first satellite in the series was launched in 1988, operating in low Earth orbit and collecting data on a global scale. In 1997, China launched its first geostationary meteorological satellite, which provides coverage of China and the surrounding region. After launching multiple satellites in these first series, in 2008 China started placing its second-generation meteorological satellite series into orbit. These satellites feature capabilities similar to those of the U.S. and European meteorological satellites.[2]

From the beginning of its program, China made its data freely available to other nations in keeping with international norms and coordinated its activities with the World Meteorological Organization. Today, in addition to direct broadcast links, current and archived data can be freely accessed online. China also offers special capabilities to Belt and Road partner countries, allowing them to request dedicated observation services in the case of disasters, such as typhoons, sandstorms, or forest fires.[3]

China's resource satellites, developed by the Chinese Academy of Space Technology, are operated by the Ministry of Natural Resources (originally the National Administration of Surveying, Mapping and Geoinformation).[4] The first of these satellites was the China Brazil Earth Resource Satellite 1 (CBERS-1) in 1999. Additional satellites in the series were launched in 2003, 2007, and 2014. CBERS was a joint project between China and Brazil, developed in response to the increasing costs of satellite remote sensing data in the international market.[5] Although the initial plan was to sell CBERS data on the international market, Brazil and China later chose to provide free access to the data. Data were made available free of charge to Brazilian users in 2004. In 2007, free access was expanded to include African users, and in 2010, the data were made freely available to anyone in the world under an open data policy.[6]

In 2011, China launched the first civilian Ziyuan resource satellite, followed by another in 2012, and a third in 2016. The data from these satellites are primarily used for domestic surveying and mapping. After ZY-3 was launched in 2016, the Satellite Surveying and Mapping Application Center of China's National Administration of Surveying Mapping and Geo-information (later replaced by the Ministry of Natural Resources) made data available on a cloud service platform. Data could be accessed for free by non-profit organizations and domestic educational institutions. Fees were charged for commercial and private access. China also pursued bilateral and multilateral data sharing agreements.[7] As of 2018, China had signed agreements to allow data sharing with 20 countries and was looking to expand these partnerships.[8]

The Ministry of Natural Resources houses the National Satellite Oceanic Application Service, which is responsible for the HaiYang ocean satellite series. The first HY satellite was launched in 2002, followed by additional launches in 2007 and 2011. These satellites were designed to help manage China's marine resources and protect China's marine rights and interests.[9] Data from the HY satellites are available to international users through a tiered system. Researchers or non-commercial organizations that require archived data can fill out a request form online. Organizations that wish to receive large volumes of data in near-real time must pursue a memorandum of understanding or contract the Service. Data on China's exclusive economic zone and sensitive regions are not included in the releases, and data that are provided may not be used for military or commercial purposes.[10]

China launched two Haunjing environment and disaster reduction satellites in 2008. These imaging satellites were joined by a synthetic aperture radar satellite in 2012, providing the ability to make observations regardless of lighting and weather conditions.[11] The Ministry for Ecology and Environment is the primary user of the satellites and is responsible for development of satellite data applications.[12]

In 2011, China announced plans to develop the civilian China High-resolution Earth Observation System (CHEOS). Together with existing satellite systems, CHEOS aimed to provide China with all-weather, 24-hour global Earth observation capabilities.[13] The first Gaofen (GF) satellite was launched in 2013, and 13 additional satellites had been launched by November 2019.[14] For a number of years, China shared data from the GF satellites on an ad hoc basis with selected partners or to support natural disaster recovery efforts. In November 2019, China announced that it would make 16-meter resolution imagery from GF-1 and GF-6 satellites openly available to users around the world. Ms. Wenbo Zhao, Deputy Director of Earth Observation System and Data Centre, China National Space Administration, stated that China had "just started the journey of open data," suggesting more steps in this direction may come in the future.[15]

### Earth Observations in Regional and Global Initiatives

Although China's Earth observation satellite programs focus on different application areas and are operated by a variety of agencies, there has been an effort to also consider their potential benefits as a whole, both for domestic applications and for strategic value. In 1999, China initiated the first International Symposium on Digital Earth, bringing together 500 delegates from China and abroad. The resulting Beijing Declaration on Digital Earth identified the importance of integrated Earth observations for addressing major global challenges, such as environmental degradation and natural resource depletion.[16]

In 2007, China formed the Center for Earth Observation and Digital Earth within the Chinese Academy of Sciences. The organization focused on exploration of cutting-edge Earth observation technologies and applications.[17] In 2011, the Center announced the Earth Observation Data Sharing Project, which would make data from international Earth observation satellites, such as the U.S. Landsat system, openly available to domestic Chinese users. Leaders identified data sharing as a necessary and important component of promoting innovation in environmental sciences.[18]

Three years after Xi Jinping announced the Belt and Road Initiative to provide $1 trillion of investment in more than 60 countries, the Chinese Academy of Science initiated the Digital Belt and Road Program. The aim of the program is to improve environmental monitoring, promote data sharing, and support policymaking using big data on Earth observations. The program involves more than making Chinese data available to others; it also aims to address the digital divide, raise awareness of the potential benefits of Earth observations, and increase international collaboration.[19]

In response to the rapidly growing volume of Earth observation data, the Chinese Academy of Sciences launched its Big Earth Data Science Engineering (CASEarth) program in 2018. CASEarth aims to establish an international center for big data and Earth science. It includes the development of an advanced cloud service platform to enable data access and analysis. It is expected to incorporate the Digital Earth Science Platform to provide information and visualizations to aid decision-making. It will also provide capabilities to promote sustainable development in support of the Belt and Road Initiative. CASEarth is expected to "break through the bottleneck of open data and data sharing" and produce a platform "with global influence."[20]

China has already put an emphasis on using Earth observation satellite data to contribute to major international efforts. China became a member of the Group on Earth observations in 2009, participating in international meetings to identify opportunities for international collaboration. China has used satellite data to monitor climate change, in support of the Paris Climate Agreement. In support of the Sendai Framework for Disaster Risk Reduction, China distributes satellite data to enable disaster response. China also completed the world's first comprehensive measurement of progress toward the United Nations Sustainable Development Goals by combining Earth observations with statistical data.[21]

China's efforts to leverage open data sharing with respect to Earth observation satellite data fit within a broader move toward open data sharing. The Chinese Ministry of Science and Technology launched the Scientific Data Sharing Program in 2002, to make scientific data collected by national research projects more accessible in order to promote scientific and technical innovation.[22]

In September 2019, the International Science Council Committee on Data, with support from Chinese Academy of Sciences, organized the International Workshop on Open Research Data Policy and Practice in Beijing. At the conclusion of the workshop, attendees released the Beijing Declaration on Research Data, which called for global cooperation in making public research data as open as possible on a global basis.[23]

## Conclusion

Over the last 30 years, China has developed a large and advanced Earth observation satellite program capable of collecting high-quality data for a wide variety of applications. While many of these programs have involved international collaboration and data sharing from early in their development, in recent years there has been a concerted effort to leverage China's advanced capabilities on the global stage.

This is seen in the large-scale efforts to open access to Earth observation data and to develop platforms open to a wide range of users. China is using its Earth observation data to contribute to major international efforts, increasing its stature and role in these efforts, and setting precedents with regard to how data may be used. Data sharing is directly contributing to its Belt and Road Initiative, strengthening ties with other nations in the region.

Open data efforts in other nations have demonstrated that open access to scientific data has significant benefits, enhancing scientific research and development of new applications. As China continues to increase the amount of data made openly available on the global level, its significant investments in data collection systems – including expensive Earth observation satellite systems – should generate social benefits on a global scale.

## *Notes*

1   Zhang, Y., W. Hua and S. Yuan (2018). "Mapping the scientific research on open data: A bibliometric review." *Learned Publishing* 31(2): 95-106.

2   Yang, J., P. Zhang, N. Lu, Z. Yang, J. Shi and C. Dong (2012). "Improvements on global meteorological observations from the current Fengyun 3 satellites and beyond." *International Journal of Digital Earth* 5(3): 251-265.

3   Peng, Z., C. Lin, X. Di and X. Zhe (2018). "Recent progress of Fengyun meteorology satellites." 空间科学学报 38(5): 788-796.

4   Jones, A. (2016). China launches Ziyuan-3 remote sensing satellite and Argentina's Aleph-1. GB Times (2016). China's New Satellite for Civilian 3D Mapping in Business Operation. Beijing Review.

5   Lino, C. D. O., M. G. R. Lima and G. L. Hubscher (2000). "CBERS—An international space cooperation program." *Acta Astronautica* 47(2): 559-564.

6   Nascimento, H. F. (2019). *The diversity of applications in free use of CBERS series satellite images for local problem solving in Brazil. United Nations/Austria Symposium Space: a Tool for Accessibility, Diplomacy and Cooperation.* Graz, Austria.

7   Tang, X. (2017). *China's SASMAC advances regional cooperation on Earth observations. Group on Earth Observations Blog. 2019.*

8   Xinming, T. (2018). *International Service and Application: China's Ziyuan and Surveying and Mapping Satellites. GEO Week 2018: Asia-Oceania Day.* Kyoto, Japan.

9   Guo, H., W. Fu and G. Liu (2019). *Chinese Earth Observation Satellites. Scientific Satellite and Moon-Based Earth Observation for Global Change,* Springer: 189-243.

10  (NSOAS), C. N. S. O. A. S. (2016). *"Distribution Policy: HY-1B satellite, HY-2 satellite data product international user releasing policy and guide."* Retrieved 6 July 2016, from *http://www.nsoas.gov.cn/NSOAS_En/Products/3.html.*

11  Guo, H., W. Fu and G. Liu (2019). *Chinese Earth Observation Satellites. Scientific Satellite and Moon-Based Earth Observation for Global Change,* Springer: 189-243.

12  (2017). *"Ministry of Ecology and Environment Center for Satellite Application on Ecology and Environment: Main Duty."* 2019, from *http://www.secmep.cn/zxjj/zyzz/201103/t20110308_562012.shtml.*

13  Guo, H., W. Fu and G. Liu (2019). *Chinese Earth Observation Satellites. Scientific Satellite and Moon-Based Earth Observation for Global Change,* Springer: 189-243.

14  Jones, A. (2019). *China tests grid fins with launch of Gaofen-7 imaging satellite. Space News.*

15  Observations, G. o. E. (2019). *China announces open sharing of Gaofen data.*

16  (1999). *Beijing Declaration on Digital Earth. International Symposium on Digital Earth.* Beijing, China.

17  (2019). *"About CEODE: Brief Introduction."*

18  Qing, G. (2011). *Implementation of Medium-Resolution Earth Observation Data Sharing by CEODE. C. A. o. Sciences.*

19  Huadong, G. (2018). *Steps to the digital Silk Road, Nature Publishing Group.*

20  Guo, H. (2017). *"Big Earth data: A new frontier in Earth and information sciences."* Big Earth Data 1(1-2): 4-20.

21  West, M. (2019). *Member spotlight: China. Group on Earth Observations. 2019.*

22  Xu, G.-H. (2007). *"Open access to scientific data: Promoting science and innovation."* Data Science Journal 6: OD21-OD25.

23  (2019). *The Beijing Declaration on Research Data. International Workshop on Open Research Data Policy and Practice. I. S. C. o. Data.* Beijing, China.

*Dr. Mariel Borowitz is Assistant Professor at the Sam Nunn School of International Affairs, Georgia Institute of Technology, and author of Open Space: The Global Effort for Open Access to Environmental Satellite Data (MIT Press, 2017).*

# How United Hospitals Continues to Lead in China: Reflections from the Founding Executives

*Michael Wenderoth*
*Vol. 15, No.1*
*2016*

In an earlier article I interviewed Roberta Lipson, CEO and Chair of United Family Hospitals (UFH). (See article at China Currents, Vol.17, No.2, 2017.) To learn more about the premium healthcare network, I visited the headquarters of UFH in Beijing and spoke to the core team of executives, Western and Chinese, who established UFH. They reflected on their challenges and success, how China has changed, and what westerners don't fully appreciate about doing business in China.

These executives included:

- Robert C. Goodwin, Jr. – EVP and General Counsel, Chindex[1] (1984- 2005); currently Professor and Vice Dean, University of Maryland
- Ming Xie – VP of Business Development, Chindex/UFH (1993- present)
- Zhongying Pan (Sylvia Pan) – Project Assistant, Chindex who joined in 1995 and later became VP and General Manager of Beijing United Hospital (2008- present)
- Xuming Bian – Obstetrician and Consultant to Chindex/UFH (1994- present)
- David Hofmann – Administrative Director, Chindex (1993- 2005); currently China consultant, Hofmann Advising
- Judy Zakreski – VP U.S. Operations, Chindex (1994- 2015); currently Executive Vice President, EkPac China Inc.

## Have Vision, Perseverance and Adaptability

In the early 1990s, most observers dismissed Chindex International's efforts to establish UFH as a radical, impossible dream. A private, foreign-invested western hospital in China had no precedent, and lacked a clear path to approval.

The core team of UFH executives I spoke to unanimously agreed that in these early years, Roberta Lipson's vision – and the "can-do" spirit she infused in those around her – carried the organization.

"[Setting up Beijing United Hospital] was truly unique and is directly related to Roberta's perseverance," said Robert Goodwin, EVP and General Counsel.

"We simply refused to take no for an answer every time we hit a stumbling block," added Judy Zakreski, who managed relationships with western suppliers and advisors. "Our [goal] was to make sure that [the hospital got] established and operating in full compliance with all of the laws and regulations, no matter how long it took."

Ming Xie, VP of Business Development, praised Lipson for her boldness. "There was a lot of 'feeling the stones while crossing the river,' because we needed to convince and change the minds of a lot of authorities in the Ministry of Health and other regulatory bodies," he said. "Maybe because some on the team were foreigners, they failed to appreciate the size of the task, enabling us to dare to go forward."

In fact, the team originally received approval for a birthing center, focused on serving expatriates – a deliberate strategy to start small and build trust in China, before expanding the scope. As UFH established a track record and market demands evolved, the center became a women and children's hospital, and subsequently grew to a network providing a full range of healthcare services.

## Admit when you are wrong

No one on the core team imagined UFH would be as big or successful as it has become today. While China's growth did not surprise them, the velocity and scale of the country's economic transformation caught them all off guard.

For example, more than half the patients today are Chinese, said Sylvia Pan, the GM of Beijing United Hospital, the UFH network's flagship center. "I don't think any of us could have ever anticipated that! It has pushed us to respond quickly to our rapidly changing patient base."

The willingness to show humility and admit they didn't see what was coming, the executives all stressed, should be a requisite for any westerner who plans to work in China.

"It's important to accept up front that market access in China is difficult, that nothing is really simple, and that regulations are always changing. In this way, nothing can truly surprise you," said Zakreski. She brings that philosophy to many of the western clients she works with. "[You need to] deflate the ego, be constantly willing to learn, and [have] an open mind to consider – not necessarily accept – different approaches to addressing a challenge."

All credit those early years, and doing business in China, for making them nimble, resolute and creative in conducting business – key skills to surviving and thriving in their careers since.

## Think long, but focus short

In the early 1990s when Chindex raised financing, the company declared its goal was to create a multi-hospital network. While that was known by the core team, they admitted to a maniacal short-term focus on getting the first hospital in Beijing up and running.

"I always assumed BJ United would be successful. Not only was that the Chindex mindset but I couldn't imagine not meeting our publicly announced plans," said Goodwin.

Fostering a strong partnership and agreement with their joint venture partner, Chinese Academy of Medical Sciences, took close to a year. Ensuring Chinese approval authorities understood how the hospital would fit into China's healthcare system – and getting approval – took close to two years. And making sure the right steps were taken to design and build a world-class healthcare facility spanned close to three.

Several observed that this "short-term" focus helped Chindex and UFH avoid the trap many multinationals fell into at the time and still fall into today: Perpetually labeling China a long-term market becomes a handy rationale for letting losses pile up or clinging to a business model or strategy that isn't working.

Lacking deep financial resources, they reflected, forced the team to be incredibly resourceful. For example, they did not use an army of highly paid consultants or intermediaries. Conducting much of the fieldwork themselves gave them direct exposure to market realities, enabling them to make decisions more rapidly.

Understand how you fit into China's "system"

Goodwin, Xie and Zakreski firmly believed that the hospital's strong foundation was due to establishing a strong joint venture partnership and securing the early licenses and government approvals.

"There were a continuing series of challenges to be solved on a regular basis but, to my mind, none of them was unusual in a project of this nature," said Goodwin. What helped the most, he reflected, was Lipson's and Chindex's reputation within the Chinese medical community.

At the time of UFH's founding, Chindex had been operating almost 15 years in China, providing medical equipment to China's top hospitals and having established a formidable track record of honesty and genuine concern for improving healthcare in China.

"Chindex was always unique in approaching the market from the perspective of how can we help China do what they currently do better," said David Hofmann, Administrative Director at the time. The early work was making sure the Chinese authorities understood how UFH would fit into the Chinese healthcare system, and what role it would serve.

"In terms of making things work, it is essential that you have a story as to why your proposal or project is of benefit to China," advised Goodwin. "Approval authorities are not impressed that your venture will help make money for your organization. They may be impressed if you can show how many employees you will train, or how the local population will benefit from [your] services."

Of course, not every western company enters China with 15 years of relationships under its belt. Xie, the VP of Business Development, is highly skeptical of how westerners approach China, which he feels is based solely on reading the relevant rules and regulations. He advises newcomers to take more time to determine what national or regional authorities want out of a relationship. He himself spends significant time cross-referencing information with people in the know.

"If one's partner is a public hospital, [that partner's] interests will diverge dramatically from a small, private one," Xie said. "Too many western companies fail to appreciate the Chinese history, politics and ecosystem."

"My basic advice would be to take it slow and forget the approaches that you took in the U.S. or other countries," commented Goodwin. "You need to listen to the interests and concerns of your Chinese counterpart and see what you can do to create a win-win situation."

Zakreski, who now advises companies that face complex regulatory needs, concurred. She recommends having someone on the ground in China engaging key stakeholders, which is hard do from one's home country. She added that having some level of guanxi (relationships) is important, because it allows a constant flow of nonmarket information.

## Manage Those Relationships

Hofmann emphasized that the goal setting up Beijing United Hospital was not to stand out; it was to build lasting relationships, something that Pan, the current GM, and Xie agreed with.

Goodwin, the lawyer, said it best: "Savvy investors learn that relationships with party officials are equally as important as legal arguments, and they develop an approach that covers all the levels of the decision-making apparatus. My belief is that the future will not change much so long as the judiciary is not independent."

They all emphasized the need to have continuous efforts placed on managing key relationships, citing how many western organizations make the mistake of focusing solely on the setup phase. After Beijing United opened in 1997, Pan's work, for example, began in earnest: She kept in constant contact with local authorities to understand their points of view, their concerns and to seek advice.

Forming industry groups and staying in touch with the American Chamber of Commerce enabled the team to influence policy direction on a larger scale between the U.S. and Chinese governments. It's no coincidence that Lipson, Goodwin, Hofmann and Zakreski have held a variety of roles over the past 30 years with the U.S.-China Business Council, the American Chamber of Commerce, or interest groups based in Washington, D.C.

On the China side, Pan serves as the only Chinese representative on the JCO, the top international hospital accreditation commission, which helps set international healthcare and hospital management standards. And she, Lipson and other UFH hospital leaders are increasingly sought after by Chinese healthcare officials for their advice on improving China's healthcare system.

### Shatter the cross-cultural divide

The executives I spoke to average 25 years of doing business in China, but they surprisingly shied away from making any blanket statements on how Chinese culture operates.

"When you look at case studies of Chinese companies you see that, like western companies, they are all over the lot in terms of management style," said Goodwin. "But there is a consistency in that all of them function within a Chinese cultural framework."

To understand that Chinese cultural framework, the executives were critical of many "cross-cultural" training, finding it shallow, or downright dangerous in the stereotypes people came away with.

"Learning how to use chopsticks and exchange business cards properly is fine but the real issue is whether you can figure out how someone from another culture thinks, what is important to them and why," he added. "You'll never get everything right but at least you'll be asking the right questions if you approach it that way."

They stressed that relationships between and among people play a larger role in China than in the U.S. and Europe, which tend to be more "legalistic" societies where rules assume more importance.

To break down cultural barriers, Goodwin puts many of his executives and students through simulations and negotiations, to help them see what their Chinese counterparts may be facing. Xie encourages executives to talk to people on the ground to get multiple reference points.

Hofmann highlighted the need to recruit people with a more global mindset, and to foster more cross-border exchanges. Early on, UFH's Chinese partner, the Chinese Academy of Medical Sciences, sent its representative, Dr. Zeng Su, to visit the U.S. to better understand the UFH vision and model. Dr. Bian, having spent time in the U.S., also helped bridge the two healthcare systems. Hofmann and the team also brought western doctors to China.

To accelerate "acculturation," Pan, the Beijing United Hospital GM, gets new UFH employees out of the classroom and into Chinese hospitals. She wants her western employees to see more of China's healthcare system, so sends them to VIP wards, Tier II and Tier III hospitals, so they can experience firsthand the top and bottom of the Chinese healthcare system.

"They realize China is complex and there are many Chinas," she said, noting that they come away better understanding the attitudes of Chinese patients. "For instance, Chinese place more emphasis on family ties in decision-making than westerners do, and Chinese patients question their doctors much more than their western counterparts do."

As the patient base at UFH has become increasingly Chinese, she added, it has become increasingly imperative to train UFH staff in this way. For example, elderly Chinese are much more inclined to want their daughters to schedule C-sections, which often runs counter to the desires of their western-influenced children.

"As the healthcare provider, we need to understand and be prepared to manage this dynamic."

**Localize by teaching the "why"**

Across industries, western executives struggle with how to best segment the Chinese consumer market, maintain their brands and meet local needs. Americans, reflected Goodwin, do not appreciate the speed of change that has occurred in a generation in China, and therefore find this challenge to understand Chinese attitudes incredibly difficult.

"All our patients are well-off and regional differences not so stark," said Pan. "But in general, we see the biggest divide among generations, and between those who have a more international outlook versus those who have never left China." Training their doctors to manage these differing expectations has been critical to ensuring patient satisfaction.

Differences in their Chinese patient base can be seen, for instance, in attitudes toward antibiotics. "Many Chinese patients who are accustomed to Chinese hospitals, feel if they don't get a prescription, then why are they paying high fees to visit the doctors?" Pan said, emphasizing that UFH does not prescribe antibiotics at the same rate as Chinese hospitals. "One local patient, after seeing our price list (among the highest in Asia), half-jokingly asked if the staff kneeled when serving them!"

"To be able to explain why to customers, you need to first explain why to your own employees," she said. "Teaching them the WHY is actually more important than the HOW."

To fully prepare staff, UFH created an academy, a prestigious yearlong program for registered nurses, to instill and practice the network's ICARE values. During my visit, I attended the graduation of more than 20 nurses, their largest group to date. The curriculum was designed by a blend of western and Chinese nursing professionals. Without this academy, UFH could not find the right talent and skill in the marketplace, Pan commented.

Hofmann, now based in Washington, D.C., remains surprised how many westerners continue to believe China is the land of cheap labor and is backward in terms of technology, when in fact the opposite is truer, particularly in Tier I and Tier II cities. Pan said wage differentials between her top western and Chinese staff no longer exist. In fact, some of her top Chinese get paid more.

Pan also attacked the myth that Chinese millennials are selfish and lack drive.

"Nothing could be further from the truth," she said. "You can't generalize. The employees we have are driven, want to learn, need a sense of achievement, and – perhaps more than any generation – want a sense of purpose. Volunteering is much higher than in the past."

To stay in touch with that generation born after 1990, she conducts lunches with many employees, and is highly active on Weibo, the Chinese social media equivalent to Twitter.

## Hold firm on non-negotiables

At the same time, they all agreed, one can be too culturally sensitive. They all attacked a common sentiment that you cannot be direct in China, and that certain topics are taboo. Goodwin, the lawyer, warned: "You just need to do [be direct] in the right context." Zakreski urges all clients to determine "non-negotiables" and stick to them.

"When I was handling a particularly tricky legal case in China back in the mid-1980s the common wisdom of 'China experts' was that you had to be careful not to address certain subjects or disagree with those officials you were interfacing with," Goodwin said. "While there were indeed some subjects that were best avoided, that list was fairly short and the notion that you had to agree with a particular approach in a negotiation for fear of offending your hosts was just nonsense. The real issue is that you need to display genuine respect for the people with whom you are interfacing, and if you do that you can be quite frank in your expression of disagreement."

## Reconsider your competition

On the subject of competition, all noted that while the number of competitors has heated up, the market has also grown considerably, and the level of sophistication varies. Well-heeled western firms are the most direct competitors, but UFH recently went private and raised additional investment from the private equity group TPG. They believe UFH can remain the market leader if it continues to deliver quality care and attract the right talent.

They believe the threat of domestic private competitors is overblown, and that UFH competes in very select, high-end healthcare, a space where local firms have not shown they can go – yet.

Xie, VP of Business Development, said: "Domestically invested medical bodies are very different than UFH, many of them hope to make 'quick money,' raise capital and they 'advertise' to bring in patients. This is not the greatest in terms of word-of-mouth reputation."

The more serious threat, said Pan, is the rise of China's state-owned public hospitals, and Xie added the Chinese government has gotten very serious about addressing the country's healthcare needs.

"It's not that [state-owned public hospitals] have a lot of money (although they do). It's more that they can make big changes quickly, if they want. They have the advantage of a top-down hierarchy – we western firms can actually be very slow," said Pan. "Many westerners consider the public hospital system here outdated, but that belief itself is becoming outdated. Many of the new hospital leaders there are quite brilliant and ambitious. For UFH, we see these as opportunities, or imperatives, to cooperate or partner."

### Look forward: The next 20 years

Everyone agreed that doing business in China remains complex. Managing this requires talent. On the bright side, they observed that there has been an increase in western executives who have a better understanding of China, as well as firms that have almost entirely localized their China offices.

But a rapidly evolving China, Pan said, has really forced westerns to rethink their place in the new world order. "Honestly, I think some westerns are lost. There used to be a feeling of superiority, and when they come here, they are no longer the top, and they no longer have the top salaries."

No one wanted to predict China's future. The irony, said Zakreski, is that the reduction of tariffs and "openness" that came with China's entry into world bodies has largely felt like it has been accompanied by an increase in regulatory hurdles.

"This doesn't mean that there isn't opportunity for western companies in China. It just means that there is no longer a default approach of finding a distributor and exporting your product to China," she said, citing licensing technology as one alternative.

Overall, the executives voiced concern with the increased nationalism and growing restrictions, but also said that every period of China's past 30 years has been filled with concerns! They believed staying to a core mission, being persistent and adaptable, and fostering talent – the same things that got them to where they are now – are the best ways to manage future change and deepen UFH's premium service and established brand.

"There is a lot of money in China right now," they all said. "People think healthcare is easy. It is not."

## Notes

1   Note that I served as Project Manager at Chindex from 1994-98
    Chindex was previously parent company of UFH

*Michael C. Wenderoth is an Executive Coach and a professor at IE Business School in Madrid, Spain.*

## Commentary: Making China Great Again

*C. Donald Johnson*
*Vol. 17, No.2*
*2018*

Centuries before President Donald Trump began withdrawing from multi-lateral trade agreements and retreating from international leadership roles, while promising to build a "big, beautiful wall," there was another great world power that chose to abandon global engagement and seek chauvinistic refuge behind a Great Wall. It involves a critical period of Chinese history that offers some insight into the politics of trade wars emerging today.

### The Fall of a Great Power

During the reign of Zhu Di, who became Yongle, the third emperor of the Ming Dynasty in 1402, the sphere of Chinese culture and influence expanded far beyond its traditional territories. Although Zhu Di's tactics were often ruthless, his reign is considered one of the most brilliant in Chinese history. He moved the capital permanently to Beijing from Nanjing, reconstructing the 2,000-mile Grand Canal to transport grain from the fertile Yangtze River valley in the south to Beijing and building the majestic monuments known to most tourists visiting China today, including the imperial palace of the Forbidden City, the Temple of Heaven, and the palatial Ming Tombs. Zhu Di personally led five successful military campaigns north of the Great Wall against the Mongols, who had ruled China for the century preceding Ming rule under the Yuan Dynasty beginning under Kublai Khan. He fought the Mongols his entire life as they continued to be the greatest threat to Ming rule.

One of the premier achievements of his reign was the expansion of the Ming naval fleet under admiral Zheng He and the historic maritime empire created through Zheng's expeditions.  Ironically, Zheng He was the son of a devout Muslim of Mongol extraction who was killed in battle while fighting with Mongol rebels against the Ming army. The Ming soldiers captured the 10-year-old Zheng, castrated him, and gave him as a servant to Zhu Di, a prince and prominent young army officer at the time.  Although eunuchs had not often been trusted with political or military assignments during the reigns of Zhu Di's predecessors, Zheng became a valued confidante to Zhu throughout his military campaigns, including the rebellion Zhu led to take the throne from his nephew not long after the death of Zhu Di's father, emperor Hong Wu.  Shortly after becoming emperor, Zhu Di placed Zheng in charge of the Chinese naval fleet.

Chinese vessels and sea charts had led the world for several centuries, but Zheng He expanded the capacity and reach of China's navy exponentially.  His lead vessels, called "treasure ships," were enormous for the age (at least five times the size of the vessels sailed by Christopher Columbus 90 years later). Each of these ships, which numbered more than 60 on the first voyage, carried at least 500 sailors and treasures of Chinese porcelain, silk goods, iron implements, and silver coins. The entire fleet of more than 300 assorted ships carried horses, weaponry, grain, and a crew of around 28,000 men.

From 1405 to 1433, Zheng led seven voyages, lasting two years each, to more than 30 countries throughout Asia, the Middle East, and Africa.  His plan under Zhu Di's direction was to chart the entire world carrying thousands of tons of treasure and a military force to promote the power and influence of the Ming dynasty and build a great empire through gifts, trade, and foreign domination.  Using his military and diplomatic skills, Zheng founded numerous colonies during these voyages and brought many of the kingdoms he visited within the Chinese tribute system.  Zheng spread Chinese culture and influence throughout the regions he traveled, which can be traced centuries after his expeditions ended, as temples were constructed in his honor.

After Zhu Di died in 1424, the imperial power and influence of the Chinese navy soon ended.  Much like President Trump's abandonment of the international trading system created and maintained by his predecessors for seven decades since the Second World War, the emperors who succeeded Zhu Di failed to see value in maintaining alliances beyond its borders.

Subsequent Ming ruler allowed its ocean-going vessels to deteriorate and withdrew behind the Great Wall in the grand sanctity of the "Middle Kingdom."  In an ancient version of "China First" policies, the kingdom closed its ports to foreign ships, which succeeding rulers believed only carried barbarians, in their xenophobic view of the outside world.  This policy continued into the Qing dynasty and ultimately led to disastrous, humiliating consequences in the last century of the empire.  In the nineteenth century, the Opium Wars, the territorial concessions taken by the Western powers, and the ravaging abuses inflicted by Japanese militarism have all instilled a lasting national resentment that plays a significant role in Chinese policy to this day.

## A Great Rejuvenation

The current leader of the Chinese Communist Party, Xi Jinping, who has become the most powerful Chinese ruler at least since Deng Xiaoping (and likely will become the most powerful since Mao Zedong now that Xi's term is unlimited), invoked the slogan, the "Chinese Dream," as the guiding creed for his regime soon after he became president of the People's Republic of China in 2012. At first, many observers likened the phrase to a meaning similar to the "American dream" of individual economic prosperity, especially in view of the rising wealth of China as much of its population emerged from poverty under the economic reforms implemented during Deng's rule. But Xi's use of the slogan offered a much broader theme: the dream he proposed was a nationalistic call for "a great rejuvenation of the Chinese nation." Frankly, the message could be made into an American baseball cap with the slogan, "Make China Great Again." But unlike the Trump slogan, Xi's includes a well-crafted strategy of revival and a true reference point to a time when China actually fell from a pedestal as the single most powerful nation on Earth.

President Xi cited the Chinese dream for a national rejuvenation in a speech given at the National Museum of China commending an exhibition called "Road to Revival," which juxtaposed the achievements of ancient imperial China in the permanent exhibit against the spectacle of national humiliation that followed the penetration of European imperialists into the isolated Middle Kingdom and ended with what the Chinese call the "Second Sino-Japanese War" from 1931 to 1945. The exhibition presented a sanitized version of the progress made since the Communist "liberation" of China in 1949 on the road to the current "socialist market economy," or what Deng Xiaoping called "socialism with Chinese characteristics." Of course, the exhibits gave no hint of the 1989 massacre that occurred in front of the museum on Tiananmen Square, downplayed the chaotic destruction of the Cultural Revolution, and largely ignored China's other self-inflicted disasters occurring during the rule of the charismatic Mao Zedong. It was against this backdrop that Xi urged national unity in the effort to revive the pride and greatness of China.

The memory of Zheng's powerful navy was revived in the early twentieth century as the new Chinese republic began building a navy to defend against the imperial Japanese incursions. More recently in the current century his diplomatic successes are being honored by recalling his exploits as a national hero and by imitation, especially in the use of soft power to extend Chinese influence. As China has risen to become the second largest economy in the world behind the United States, President Xi has taken modern version of treasure ships abroad to welcoming countries and invested in infrastructure and established trade relationships.

While fulfilling the "Chinese dream of a great rejuvenation of the Chinese nation," Xi's plans include the construction of a land-based Silk Road Economic Belt and the Maritime Silk Road tying Asia to Europe, the Middle East, and Africa (known in a characteristically Chinese expression as "One Belt, One Road") running along the path of the historic Silk Road and the maritime voyages of admiral Zheng He in the early fifteenth century. The One Belt, One Road project is not just a transportation project. China says it is committing more than $1 trillion for infrastructure projects in over 60 countries, spreading its soft power to win friends and expand its orbit of influence, presumably to "Make China Great Again."

On November 15, 2016, a week after the U.S. presidential election, the Chinese government's English language newspaper, China Daily USA, ran a large editorial cartoon depicting President Barrack Obama diving off the bow of a large container ship, named "TPP" (for Obama's 11-nation trade agreement initiative, the Trans-Pacific Partnership), depicted stuck in the desert surrounded by cacti, sand dunes, and cattle skulls. A long editorial described Beijing's relief that "TPP is looking ever less likely to materialize by the day. After all, the trade grouping has been essentially . . . meant to counter China's economic influence in the Asia-Pacific." The piece described Chinese President Xi Jinping and President Trump's phone call exchanging good wishes for the "Trump era."

Strategically, President Trump's withdrawal from the TPP three days after his inauguration was a major win for President Xi in reaching his goal to make China great again. As President Trump withdraws the United States from world leadership roles built over the last century (including his expressed desire to abandon the World Trade Organization), he gives an assist to President Xi as China attempts to transform into a global leader based on a strong economy, transformational infrastructure projects, a strong defense, and extensive international application of soft power projects.

### Trump Retreats to Mercantilism and Trade Wars

Like the Ming emperors who withdrew behind the Great Wall and let their great ships rot in the docks to keep barbarians from entering the Middle Kingdom, President Trump is trying to build tariff walls (not to mention the campaign border wall) to withstand intrusion by foreign barbarians while withdrawing from world leadership under the illusion of America First economic nationalism. Three days before the Trump inauguration, President Xi appeared for the first time to reach out to the global elites with a free-trade message at the World Economic

Forum in Davos, Switzerland, as if to offer himself in a debut role as the unlikely new champion of the liberal world economic order.

From the outset of his entry in public affairs, President Trump has revealed a dangerous degree of naiveté, to put it kindly, on international trade policy. He thinks, for example, that unilaterally raising tariffs to trade war levels will force China to protect U.S. intellectual property rights and eliminate the trade deficit. Before taking office, Trump's ignorance of the U.S.-China bilateral history seriously undermined the relationship, as he threatened to terminate the all-important "One China" policy and proposed to give U.S. debt obligations to China a "haircut," as if these debts deserved no more respect than a fee owed to one of his obsequious lawyers. Now in his second year in office, the president has begun a full out trade war with China, America's single largest trading partner, using Art of the Deal bully tactics, apparently thinking that he has leverage to bluff his way to victory. It is a war he wages in the face of opposition from a majority of the American business community, at least a plurality of Congress, and growing public sentiment. To date, the Chinese are not only refusing to capitulate, they are refusing to come back to the table.

With its large import market, the United States has some economic leverage, but China's exports to the United States represent only four percent of its GDP, which continues to grow at six-point-six percent per year. President Xi, who is trying to convert the Chinese economy away from being export driven now has an unlimited term of office, may be putting more stock in his political leverage, as he strives for a return to the greatness of China. Meanwhile, President Trump's political stock is down.

This trade war will likely have no winners in the short run, but may determine which leader's slogan prevails in the long run. President Xi has the obvious edge.

---

*C. Donald Johnson is Director Emeritus, Dean Rusk International Law Center, University of Georgia School of Law; a former U.S. Ambassador in Office of U.S. Trade Representative; a former Member U.S. Congress; and author of The Wealth of a Nation: A History of Trade Politics in America (Oxford University Press, May 2018), from which this essay is partially derived.*

*Economy and Business*

# Discussion with Economist Barry Naughton, January 24, 2020

*Li Qi and Penelope Prime*

*Vol. 15, No.1*
*2016*

*Editor's note: Dr. Barry Naughton, the China Research Center's 2020 annual lecturer, sat down for a wide-ranging interview with China Currents Managing Editor Penelope Prime and Center associates John Garver, Georgia Tech professor emeritus, and Li Qi, professor at Agnes Scott College, on January 24, before the devastating impact of the coronavirus was widely known. Dr. Prime followed up by email with Dr. Naughton with a question about the pandemic on May 9. Below is the January interview followed by the May 9 question and answer.*

*Dr. Barry Naughton is the So Kwanlok Professor at the School of Global Policy and Strategy, University of California, San Diego. Naughton's work on the Chinese economy focuses on market transition; industry and technology; foreign trade; and political economy. His first book, Growing Out of the Plan, won the Ohira Prize in 1996, and a new edition of his popular survey and textbook, The Chinese Economy: Adaptation and Growth, appeared in 2018.*

**Penelope Prime: Dr. Barry Naughton is the China Research Center's 2020 Annual Lecturer. We are very pleased to have him here today. Dr. Li Qi from Agnes Scott College and Dr. John Garver from Georgia Tech are also joining us.**

*Dr. Naughton, what inspired you to earn a Ph.D. in economics and how did you come about your interest in China?*

Dr. Barry Naughton: My interest in China came about first, unlike probably a lot of economists who study China. I became very interested in China and Chinese language in the 1970s for a lot of the wrong reasons really. I had romantic illusions, both about the nature of Mao's socialism in China and about the idea that China could present an alternative way of thinking. So, I like to say I was attracted to both Maoism and Taoism at the same time.

*PP: Interesting, and why Economics?*

BN: In some sense econ had always seemed like a powerful way to look at the world and so once I decided to get serious about studying China, for me it was natural to go do further study in economics.

*PP: What have been the most significant changes you have seen in Chinese society going back to your first visit?*

BN: My first visit was in 1982 and of course, tremendous differences in all areas, but I guess two dimensions seem most significant to me. One is just the level of human capital and awareness and skills–at that time China was still so far behind the world in everything and now it's caught up in most things. But the other thing that was most striking to me when I first arrived in China was it became clear pretty quickly that people were still scared, that they had to watch carefully what they said and their interactions with foreigners. And that surprised me: not the fact of it, but how clear and palpable it was. And then in the 20 years after that, you saw that fear disappear and young people in particular became self-confident, interested, open-minded, exploring and it was such a wonderful change to see and I hope we don't lose that. I don't think we've lost it yet but there has been some regression lately in the ability of the Chinese government and society to tolerate open-minded free thinking.

*PP: Your topic today at the annual lecture focused on innovation and technological change in China. What drew you to this topic and what have been the big takeaways?*

BN: Well, I've always been interested in the interaction between the government and the market in China and, of course, for so many decades that movement was toward more market and less government. Then about 10 years ago the pendulum started to swing the other direction as the government found new instruments for intervening in the market and a new desire to shape China's development in more of a high-tech direction. So in some ways it was just a continuation of what I've always been interested in. But in addition, I was really struck by the fact that the image of a high-tech China had become the driving force that motivated so much of government policymaking not only in economic realms but also in international and strategic affairs and everything else. It really seemed this was a key piece and we needed to understand it better, or at least I needed to understand it better.

**PP: *What do you think caused that pendulum to swing back? I think it was under Hu Jintao really, not President Xi and it seems in hindsight somewhat stark that change and unexpected from our point of view. So how do you read that?***

BN: Let me say as a prelude, one of the striking things is there is no abrupt turning point. We see in so many different dimensions policy gradually stalling out and then very, very slowly moving in the reverse direction. So, it's really hard to call a turning point. From a purely economic standpoint, I think the most powerful explanatory factor is reform is costly and scary and so people don't do it unless they have some kind of crisis, some kind of challenge. And it's easy to see in China from the '70s through the '90s the nature of the crises and how the government responded to it. So, I think one part of the answer is there were no crises in the early 2000's and economic growth actually accelerated after China's entry into the World Trade Organization, and everything seemed fine, so why take chances, why take risk, why reform?

But I don't think that's enough of an explanation. I mean that helps, but I think there are a lot of things we don't quite understand. Clearly part of it has to do with forces in the Communist Party who always felt that the party needed to reinvigorate its mission and consolidate its power, and it's funny, a lot of things that Hu Jintao did back then which seemed kind of romantic and backward looking but not very important now seem surprisingly important and foretelling, things that Xi Jinping has done much more intensively. So, I think a lot of it is the nature of Communist Party governance and aspects of that that we underestimated.

**PP: *Would you tie that into the current administration's approach of cracking down on liberalization and information as maybe the party feeling we have to be in control or we're going to lose control?***

BN: I wonder. It seems plausible, but first of all I have to say I don't know. And the second thing is it seems that often when people go too quickly to the need to preserve power as an explanation, it gets a little—it starts to become making excuses for people.  I don't feel at all like the fact that Xi Jinping, or Hu Jintao before him, think that they need to crack down in order to maintain social stability is either a good explanation or in any case an exculpatory factor. We could just as well say look at this society, it's the most successful society by many metrics in the history of the world and the people on top of it say, oh we're afraid that we're going to be overthrown if we allow basic freedoms to people?  To me that is just such a weak argument.

*Li Qi:  In terms of balancing market and government power, is it fair to say that recent economic events in western economies (such as the subprime loan crisis back in 2008) did not inspire confidence and aspiration in the typical market- dominated model, as China evaluates its own system that produced its proud achievements?*

BN: Sure, that's totally fair, in terms of both a sense of pride, and the real things China has accomplished. And a sense of disappointment at the U.S. in the 21st century, because even before the global financial crisis, there was the Iraq War (in 2003) where U.S. acted as the sole world superpower. In the end, even the economic cost-benefit calculation could not justify that decision for the US to intervene in Iraq. And it certainly showed the U.S. as an actor who is not committed to a rule-based global system.

*LQ:  The doubt in the western model and system does not seem to come from only the top leaders, but is more widely shared now even among average citizens. I felt in the '80s and '90s, Chinese people generally and genuinely wanted to learn everything from the West because that represented higher productivity, more wealth and better ways of doing things. But now, even if we acknowledge that people's views can be influenced by propaganda, there is this suspicion that American society and the way things are done there are not necessarily better anymore.*

BN: Who wants to be like Trump's America?  Nobody in particular looks at Trump's America and says I want our country to be like that.  Maybe some leaders in various places say I can adapt some of those techniques of leadership.

But I guess what's funny about it is that there are lags in how anybody perceives their experience. Let's say we pause in 2005 and we're in China. First of all, we've accomplished so much in terms of economics, and we paid prices for it too (for example, we paid a big unemployment price and other dislocations). But we got the payoff in terms of growth. So, you would think that that leads people to say, "the reforms were good, and the price paid was worth it." But generally speaking, that's not the conclusion people came to. They came to the conclusion that, as you said, therefore there's a China way and it's not the U.S. way, and it's different and we should be proud of that. Well, that's true but there's a subtlety there and part of that conclusion should have been that Zhu Rongji took some big risks and they paid off.

Another thing about 2005 is that Chinese society at that time was completely acceptable from a foreigner's standpoint. In other words, the criticism of China and human rights had pretty much disappeared, because I think Americans could look at China and say this is certainly not a democracy and it's certainly not free speech, but there is this area that's been carved out and everybody knows where the red lines are and within that area you can say a lot of different things and have a lot of different discussions, and who are we to pass any kind of judgment about that system? A system that seems perfectly fine, and they start to move away from it!

*PP: Yes, but they talk a lot every year about what reforms are going to do. So, the rhetoric about reforms hasn't gone away, but not that much has happened. Can you talk about that a little bit given the failure of the financial reforms, for example, which seems to be something they really do want to do but it hasn't succeeded?*

BN: Yes, it certainly hasn't succeeded. On the other hand, they really seem to be trying to restart the financial reforms again now. So, I think, you know, maybe the best thing that could be said about the trade war is it does seem to be creating a source of external pressure that maybe is substituting for that sense of economic crisis that was a reform driver before. So, they do seem to be doing some things. Now, the reforms are limited and uncertain and we'll see what happens but at least there's a feeling of movement again and so that helps. Of course, whether economic reform without political liberalization, without serious openness to the outside world can work, that's a whole new set of issues way too complicated to address here.

*LQ: You had translated a lot of Wu Jinglian's work. It was so interesting to me because there is always this fascination and eagerness (at least from the China side) to learn about what American scholars are saying about*

*China's economy.    But we rarely see the same level of interests here in the U.S. to find out what Chinese economists were saying or their schools of thought about the whole economic system and the reform path.  Can you tell us a little bit more about your decision to translate Wu Jinglian's work?*

BN: Sure. I'm delighted that you asked this. To me it just seemed natural because he's somebody whose thinking is interesting and whose personal role in trying to influence the policy process is really, really important.  He is not always right, of course.  There were so many different and contending ideas, but he was just there from the late '70s until very recently being super knowledgeable about what the existing policy and political context was and pushing and pushing and pushing.  How can somebody do that for 40 years without just making you have an enormous respect for them?  I do think there is a revival of interest especially in the '80s when it was so open and there were so many people and debates, some were really intense and involved actual bad feeling, but now a lot of people seem to want to retrieve their role and claim some credit for all the good things that happened.  At the time the key thing was the focus on moving forward.  But now looking back on it, we saw so many different dimensions, different views and realities.

*PP:  Not top down.*

BN: Yes, that's right.

*PP:  Coming back to innovation, China is really focusing on this right now as are many countries, but they don't talk about innovation in terms of reforms, so there seems to be a distinction.  Can you talk about that?*

BN: That's a really, really important observation.  I mean it's funny, when you go back to the 2006 Long Term Plan on Science and Technology, which in retrospect we can see was very clearly the beginning of this accelerating industrial policy push, but when you look at the document and when you look at how Westerners interpreted it at the time, it actually seemed to be pretty reformist. It was as much about creating a richer innovation ecosystem supporting intellectual property rights to a certain extent.  Remember they were much worse off then, overall, with respect to funding, research and development, and innovation outcomes.  So, a lot of that has been achieved but what hasn't been achieved is creating a more competitive, open environment for innovation.

Look at the tech giants like Alibaba and Tencent that were formed in the 1990s through international capital markets. They're not industrial policy products at all and so, yes, it's been very disappointing to see the inevitable erosion of market forces in the innovative sectors because of this bigger state presence. Even when people still want to participate in certain innovative sectors within China, they find, well, I have to compete with the government who has very, very deep pockets. I saw a result that I haven't been able to trace so I'm not 100 percent sure it's right: the government share of the venture capital market in China declined until 2014 and then turned around and started to increase significantly since then. So absolutely there is a reversal happening where the government is squeezing out certain types of innovators and squeezing out market forces from the high-tech sector.

***John Garver: Is there still a voice for market-based reform that argue trends like these are bad?***

BN: Oh, definitely there's a voice but it's muted. You don't see it trumpeted in the official media and therefore in the public discourse. There are lots of people who feel this way but, of course, those people have to be careful because they probably have some investments of their own and in this environment, you have to have a government partner so the voices aren't heard as clearly and coherently as they should be.

It's more intimidation that they are careful to modulate the way they express their views. I think if you get together a couple of people from high tech sectors and banking sectors after dinner having a couple of drinks, they'll be very, very critical, but you're not going to see a really coherent article in the press.

***LQ: In reflecting on 40 years of reform, what is still the weakest link? You can argue, for example, some of the product markets are very market driven and competitive. Would you say the financial decision-making and the allocation of resources is still the weakest link?***

BN: Yeah, definitely. Not just the financial sector but the banking sector in particular. You can't help but notice that in the last year-and-a-half there's been progress in the financial sector liberalization but not so much in the banking sector.

**PP:** *It is striking that investment hasn't fallen which was one of the goals in terms of a share of GDP. It's actually risen and as it's risen, growth has slowed. So just simple macro math says efficiencies have gotten worse and worse, so how can any economy sustain that or for how long?*

BN: Well, it depends how they handle debt, right? I mean you can sustain— I mean, again, sort of the Iraq War, what did we spend, $2 trillion on the Iraq War? What did it get us? Nothing. Does that mean our economy will collapse? No. It just means we're worse off because that money was raised through taxes and to a certain extent through national debt. So as long as those markets are healthy you can do that for a long time.

**LQ:** *In terms of misallocation of resources, why not invest more resources on Chinese people and public services (such as public health and education)? Penny and I had a paper that showed, rather than always boosting GDP via investment, there were important benefits of investing more in public services. You also mentioned that total factor productivity had been declining or disappeared, why not invest more in public services?*

BN: The basic premise of economics is that there are trade-offs for everything and that implies that you're operating efficiently when the marginal return is the same across different sectors. But that doesn't seem to be at all true in China right now. It seems that the marginal return to government investment in health care and elementary education will be far higher than the marginal return to semiconductor labs and other kinds of industrial policy. So absolutely I think there is a clear evidence of misallocation.

**PP:** *Barry, from your vantage point, how do you see U.S.-China relations today and going forward?*

BN: Well, I think there's no question that relations are getting worse and I think they'll continue to get worse. I mean the first phase of the trade agreement is interesting because it does give us a pause maybe for a year or a year-and-a-half. We're in this ironic situation where if China follows through with this commitment to buy $200 billion incremental goods by 2021, even though there's some decoupling going on, this means there actually would be a certain amount of goods recoupling. And, you know, there's this discussion about can the U.S. economy provide $200 billion goods to China and, of course, the answer to that I think is we can if the businesses that provide those goods have confidence that the market is stable so that they are willing to reallocate resources in a way that supports that supply. But then when we say that, we realize, no, of course they don't have that kind of confidence.

**PP: *Given all of the sensitive issues and the changes that have happened, what advice would you give young scholars who are thinking about doing China studies and research on China?***

BN: Great question. I'd say dive into it. It's more fascinating than ever. Although we've got some really serious problems and you can't even rule out overt conflict between the countries, but the interaction between the incredible dynamism of Chinese society and the Chinese economy and just the dynamism of this gigantic generation of people especially in their 20s and 30s who are going to be on some level the main drivers of world history. Chinese people in their 20s and 30s will determine everything. If we can understand them, if we can influence them, if we can cooperate with them, it's the most interesting, the most exciting thing in the world. So, I hope we get more young scholars to study this process.

———————

*May 9 email exchange between Dr. Prime and Dr. Naughton:*

**PP: *Since we met in January, the coronavirus has struck. What are your views now on the steps that China's leaders took in response and the evolving U.S.-China relationship?***

BN: The initial instincts and responses of the Chinese government in the face of the coronavirus were damaging and increased the threat to the world, there's no question about that. They suppressed information about the virus and still haven't provided the opportunity for a thorough and transparent examination of the source of the virus.

But it also produced heroic responses among Chinese doctors, scientists and frontline health care providers, and an individual hero, the late Li Wenliang. Li's simple statement "a healthy society should have more than one voice (健康的社会，应该有多个声音)" is something that won't ever be forgotten. We should also remember that Chinese scientists posted the genome sequence of the virus on January 11, 2020. We in the U.S. had two months to mobilize a response, and, generally speaking, we wasted it. The Chinese response, on the other hand, has been crude but effective. Since their nationwide lockdown went into effect on January 23, they have gradually throttled the virus and appear to have stopped its spread.

The U.S.-China relationship, in the course of all this, has gone from bad to worse. Mutual recrimination has become the main content of the relationship. In both countries, the top leaders are desperate to avoid being blamed by their own people, and eager to put the blame on foreign countries. It's hard to be optimistic in this context.

# Exe-Xi-sis on Making China Great Again

*Stephen Herschler*

*Vol. 17, No.1*
*2018*

Just after the 19th Party Congress in October, when a second volume of Xi Jinping's Thoughts was published, I quickly moved to order my own copy through Amazon. Weeks later, still no anticipated delivery date. If I am to believe the website Stalin's Moustache, that's because Chinese citizens are voraciously buying up books by and about Xi Jinping Thought.

The recent 19th Party Congress may well require revising many previous publications. At the Congress, Xi followed Communist Party of China (CPC) tradition in presenting a Report (报告baogao) to the 2,200-odd delegates assembled and to the nearly 1.4 billion Chinese citizens more generally. One thing that broke with tradition was the sheer length of his speech: 3 ½ hours. The length resulted in part from the CPC's comprehensive governance – implicating all facets of Chinese society. That's lots of ground for a speech – and the Party – to cover. Xi clearly felt comfortable claiming the verbal space, using it to map out a path to Make China Great Again.

Western press reports framed the event as Xi's fast-track enshrinement among the pantheon of great Chinese Communist leaders. The report championed the leader's trademark ideology, Xi Jinping Thought on Socialism with Chinese Special Characteristics, which has already been ensconced in the Chinese Constitution. This is notable as his predecessors, Jiang Zemin and Hu Jintao, were inscribed only toward the end of their ten-year tenures, not mid-term.

More specific policy details will appear late 2018, at the 3rd Plenum of the 19th Party Congress. What the Report does, however, is set forth a general ideological framework legitimizing the policies to be followed over the next 5 years.

That being the case, it is well worth our while to see what sort of leadership powers and prerogatives the Report confers upon Xi.

## Measuring the dimensions of Xi's Authority

*Its height:*

Xi not only has some good ideas; he already has "thought," which, in the CPC's carefully crafted lexicon means a higher, longer lasting active status in the hierarchy of Communist philosopher-leaders. Marx and Lenin get highest and longest lasting honors; they're "isms" (主义 zhuyi) as in Marxism and Leninism. Mao and apparently now Xi are just one step below, being "thought" (思想 sixiang). While Deng is officially only "theory" (理论 lilun), I'd still place Deng among the Chinese Communist demi-gods, for reasons explained below. Below them would be Jiang Zemin (even though he has "important thought") and Hu Jintao. Hence the authority denoted by the term Xi Jinping Thought.

*Its length:*

The relative authority of isms, thoughts, and subsidiary forms of thinking is determined by the scope of time and space the ideas cover. Marxism covers all time and space; Socialism with Chinese Special Characteristics primarily covers China after the founding of the CPC. Within Socialism with Chinese Special Characteristics, one finds more Communist Party guiding concepts deemed authoritative for some particular segment of time.

Accordingly, each Party congress report presents some clear marker of change, usually depicted in new slogans, which are tied to particular eras much as hit songs evoke distinct periods of one's life. Some such past "hits" include: Deng's Reform and Opening to the Outside World, Jiang's Three Represents, and Hu's Harmonious Socialist Society. Attaching Xi Thought to a new era (新时代 xin shidai) affirms its long-lasting importance. More than just this season's hit, it's hoped that upon hearing Xi's new tune, generations of Chinese will exclaim, "Honey, they're playing our song!"

*Its depth:*

Undergirding all these isms, thoughts, and theories is a notion of progress, or rather of development (发展 fazhan). Indeed, the word pervades the 19th Party Congress Report, which flatly declares at one point: "Development is the Party's primary task" – echoing Deng Xiaoping's adage that "only development is firm reason" (发展才是硬道理 fazhan cai shi ying dali.) Perhaps to state the obvious, development is understood as moving forward along the socialist path, stage by stage, towards some better place. Progress is marked by reaching various "landmarks" along the way. The ultimate destination, communism, is some ways off. Better keep those seatbelts fastened as officially we're still only in the Primary Stage of Socialism which, according to Deng Xiaoping Theory, will last about

100 years.

The nature of movement along this developmental path differs depending on whether one is moving from phase to phase or from stage to stage. Phase-to-phase, denoting more minor forms of progress, can be characterized as predominantly quantitative change, that is, involving persistent incremental improvements over time. (Think Adam Smith: "the division of labor is limited by the extent of the market.") Stage-to-stage, however, involves a qualitative change, reflecting categorical transformations between epochs. (Think Karl Marx: feudalism replaces slavery, capitalism replaces feudalism, communism replaces capitalism – all through revolution.)

Xi's new era denotes that qualitative changes are required, not just more of the same. More specifically, key elements of Deng Xiaoping Theory can be set aside, not as illegitimate but rather as inappropriate for this new stage in history. As the CPC discourse puts it, a new era and its new goal bring with them a new primary contradiction, which means new struggles for the Party and the people.

It's all so new, and yet....

## Two-timing and two-stepping in Xi's New Era

There's something distinctive about Xi's Report to the 19th Party Congress from the very start. At first, the official title fits firmly in the Party's standard framework:

- Secure a Decisive Victory in Building a Moderately Prosperous Society
- Strive for the Great Success of Socialism with Chinese Special Characteristics.

But then the Report's opening immediately reframes the goal as:

Struggle Tirelessly to Achieve the Chinese Dream of the Glorious Revival of the Chinese Nation (中华民族伟大复兴的中国梦 Zhonghua minzu weida fuxing de Zhongguo meng).

The Report, thus, presents two goals, denoting two framings that coexist throughout. The first goal focuses attention on the future, a socialist future. The second goal focuses attention on the past, a civilizational past. Xi's not just giving a Report to the Party Congress, he's leading a revival meeting.

Indeed, the Report lays out not one but two concurrent timelines: one of the Chinese people and the other of the Chinese nation. Xi's great power derives from him occupying a critical strategic position in effecting progress toward longstanding historical goals for both China as state and as nation.

## The Where, Who, and What of Xi's New Era

A new era denotes Xi's movement toward the status of Mao and Deng, each of whom is lauded as a progenitor of particular stages of history. Mao proposed the right guiding thought for an era of war and revolution; Deng proposed the right guiding thought for an era of peace and development. (Mao's "tragedy" according to the definitive Party account of the Mao Era, the 1981 Resolution on Some Problems of Party History, is that he failed to realize that war and revolution had given way to peace and development.)

This new era, says the 19th Party Congress Report, is still a time of peace and development. Xi doesn't break completely with Deng, as Deng did with Mao. Moreover, China is still firmly embedded in the Primary Stage of Socialism; it's still a developing country. The 19th Party Congress era (2017-2022) spans a 5-year period bracketed by centennial anniversaries of key Communist historical "landmarks" that will help frame stages and their significance in ways that tug at Chinese Communist civic heartstrings.

It is bracketed by, on the one hand, the centenary of the Russian October Revolution (1917) and, on the other, by the centenary of the founding of the Chinese Communist Party (1921). The centenary of the founding of the CPC coincides with the achievement of xiaokang, the concrete goal Deng set forth several decades ago: achieving a moderately well-off society (小康社会xiaokang shehui), a developmental landmark declared by Jiang in 2002 as a goal to be reached in 2020. This goal shaped the polity's marching orders in the 16th, 17th and 18th Party Congress reports, framing the endeavors of both Jiang and Hu's rule as well as Xi's first term.

Now, however, xiaokang is so, well, last stage.

Xi's new era (新时代 xin shidai) is bounded on its outer limits by another centenary, 2049: the 100-year anniversary of the founding of the People's Republic of China. What will China find when it gets there? This is part of Xi's power: the ability to set forth an agenda for the next 30 years.

**A New Goal for A New Era**

The goal, as trumpeted in the Report's title Great Success of Socialism with Chinese Special Characteristics, cannot be reached in a single bound. Rather, it requires an intermediary goal, each one separated by a distance of 15 years. Thus, on his big stage of history, Xi performs a 2-step dance: first, from 2020 to 2035, China basically achieves socialist modernization (社会主义现代化 shehuizhuyi xiandaihua); next, by 2050 for China becomes a socialist modernized strong country (社会主义现代化强国 shehuizhuyi xiandaihuaqiangguo).

Both goals fit firmly within the logic of CPC developmental stages. A closer look, however, shows that the second melds with a goal that has saturated the Chinese psyche since well before Marx was even a twinkle in Chinese eyes, much less the inspiration for the CPC. This resonance comes forth in a full description of the final goal: a powerful socialist modern country that is wealthy and strong, democratic, civilized, harmonious, and beautiful.

## Make that an Old Goal for A New Era

The phrase "wealthy & strong country" (富强国 fuqiangguo) has been around a long time, wailed by Qing Dynasty scholar-gentry seeking to save the country (救国 jiuguo) from colonialism and imperialism of Japan and Western countries. Over 50 years ago, Benjamin Schwartz titled his book on Yan Fu, the Qing Dynasty official who introduced Spencer's Social Darwinism to China in the aftermath of the Sino-Japanese War, In Search of Wealth and Power. Just recently, Orville Schell and John Delury saw fit to name their history Wealth and Power: China's Long March to the Twenty First Century.

What we have here, then, is not a purely Chinese Communist goal. Rather, it's a goal that hearkens back to China's initial encounters with Western notions of progress in late 19th century Qing Dynasty, when China was gripped with fear of civilizational decline that in time gave way to concerns about national sovereignty as Chinese worked to reimagine their polity, as Wang Hui expresses it, in From Empire to Nation-State.

This is where Xi's speech sounds off-key if listened to expecting a pure Marxist dialect. Terms like "Chinese Dream" and "Revival of the Chinese Nation" just don't fit with historical materialism, either in tone or substance.

But then the end of the new era comes in 2049, the centenary of the founding of the PRC in 1949, and that immediately evokes what 1949 marked: the centenary of: the commencement of the "century of shame and humiliation" suffered under imperialism and colonialism. This is referenced throughout the Report and evoked by the 2049 goal of building a 近代 (jindai) rather than a现代(xiandai) historical aspiration. Both terms mean "modern," but each has significantly different connotations. Generally speaking, for Chinese historians, the jindai stage of history starts with the Opium Wars while the xiandai stage starts with the May 4th Movement in 1919. A jindai aspiration is a civilizational aspiration, a xiandai aspiration is a nationalist one.

## Xi's Creole Marxism: tradition, the people, and dreams

The phrase, "great restoration of the Chinese nation," rings odd relative to traditional Marxism in several respects. First is the very idea of China's feudal past having anything worthy of reviving. Marxist history finds resolutions to present conflicts in the future, not the past. Under Mao, anything associated with the Four Olds of Feudal China (old customs, old culture, old habits, old ideas) was excoriated, even becoming the object of violent political struggle. Before he helped found the Chinese Communist Party, Chen Duxiu spoke for a generation of New Youth in his eponymously named journal when he railed against Chinese traditional culture.

Yet in the 19th Party Congress Report, we read of the wonderful things in China's traditional culture:

"With a history of more than 5,000 years, the Chinese nation created a brilliant civilization, making remarkable contributions to humanity, and became one of the world's great nations." These too become part of the repertoire of resources for the CPC to draw upon, a part of Socialism with Chinese Special Characteristics. When saying this phrase in the Xi Jinping dialect (习近平话 Xi Jinpinghua), not to be confused with Xi Jinping Thought, remember the stress falls more on "Chinese Special Characteristics" than on "Socialism."

What one sees encoded in the Report is China's new nationalism, perhaps most clearly connoted in the double ways of referring to "the people." The term "renmin" (中国人民 Zhongguo renmin) takes on a more civic connotation. When Mao Zedong stood on the podium at Tiananmen Square in 1949 to proclaim the founding of the PRC, he used this term when uttering the famous phrase, "The Chinese people have stood up." ("中国人民站起来了Zhongguo renmin zhanqilai le. ") While Xi references a civic notion of "the people" throughout the Report, the term used in conjunction with past and future is (中华民族Zhonghua minzu), which can mean Chinese nation and also Chinese ethnicity. Xi's speech denotes a nationalism that is both civic and ethnic.

This brings us to a third word that has no place in conventional Marxist lingo: dream, as in China dream (中国梦Zhongguo meng). Historical materialists don't generally have dreams; they have plans. "Dream" brings to mind pejorative declamations from Marx like: "Religion is the opiate of the masses."

This dream, however, has two reference points, one historical the other contemporary. The first is a 19th Century China debilitated by the scourge of imperialism and opium addiction. The second reference point: another dream that's out there – the American Dream.

### 复兴Fuxing: A Middle Kingdom once more

While a rich and strong country has been a dream for some time, this dream now seems close to becoming a reality. Accordingly, Xi's speech begins to revise China's spatial imagining. As noted above, China officially considers itself a developing country. Much of Deng's agenda was about development – again, "only development is firm logic" – but a development that was calibrated relative to other, more advanced (发达 fada) countries. China needed to develop at breakneck speed to catch up with (赶上 ganshang) the more advanced countries.

In Xi's new era, the dynamic changes. Deng broke down Maoist autarchy when he called for learning from more economically advanced countries, including capitalist countries. His formulation placed China in apprenticeship to those countries' practices. Xi's Report affirms that in contrast to the former era's focus on high-speed development, this new era will be about high-quality development. Previously, Deng emphasized developmental "initiative" (积极性 jijixing). Now, the emphasis is on developmental "innovation, creativity" (创新性 chuangxinxing).

Thus, development involves both the tangible and the intangible. On the one hand, the degree to which China is a "strong country" is readily measured through standardized criteria associated with "comprehensive national power," criteria that distill down to hard power, good old realpolitik. On the other hand, part of being a "strong country" in this new era places added emphasis on intangible factors. Among those highlighted in the Report are civilizational strength as well as international influence, by which is meant not just diplomacy but the effective spreading and inculcating of ideas, such as creating philosophy and social sciences with Chinese special characteristics.

All of this requires the dogged, determined oversight and guidance of the Party in all domains of the polity. Nothing is to be free of the Party's influence, even the Party itself – which Xi presents as critical to the success or failure of this historic, and historical, mission.

The 2050 goal is presented as aspiration not just for China but for humanity: "The era of striving to achieve the Chinese nation's dream of China's restoration, is an era of our country moving closer to the world's center stage, an era of incessantly greater contributions to humanity."

What Xi is setting up in the China Dream is an alternative to the American Dream. It is a move to present, if not a challenge then at least a clear alternative to the previous U.S. hegemony in the economic and ideological realm. In part the alternative presented is one of systems – a socialist market economy as a coherent system, an organism distinct from – not subordinate to nor a perversion of – a capitalist market economy. One thinks back to Deng's adage that both socialism and capitalism have markets. In part, though, it is presented as a civilizational difference, one rooted deeply in the past yet creatively competing for more market share in the future. In 2050, then, China resumes a version of its proper historical position, if not as the Middle Kingdom than certainly as a Middle Kingdom.

## Xi-ing Double

Xi Jinping's speech refracts in two ways, much like those 3D lenticular postcards – a.k.a. wiggle pictures – I loved as a kid. (You know the ones: at first look there's the Cheshire Cat but shift your gaze just slightly and you see only its grin.) The 19th Party Congress Report, looked at one way, manifests a great Communist leader – a Mao or a Deng. Of course, we're talking about the "good" Mao not the "bad" Mao. The Mao of Mao Zedong Thought, who proclaimed in 1949 atop

Tiananmen Square: "the Chinese People Have Stood Up." Not the Mao of the subsequent "20 wasted years," in Deng's blunt assessment.

But tilt the card just slightly and another image of Xi appears: Xi as the latest of a line of great Chinese emperors, concurrently advancing civilization and keeping the barbarians in their place. As used with images, the process is called Xography. As used in reference to the text of the 19th Party Congress Report, let's call it Xigraphy.

The CPC worked hard for much of the past century to keep these two images of Chinese leadership on two separate cards. Not always successfully, as I know from personal experience. Some 20 years ago, a grassroots official proudly told me that China had two peasant emperors. One hailed from his district: the founder of the Han Dynasty, Liu Bang. The other? Mao Zedong. At that time, his utterance produced a wave of angst amongst the other officials present, who were quick to interject that Mao wasn't an emperor. Twenty years later, I doubt they'd be so concerned.

Indeed, Xi's Report repeatedly calls not just for confidence (自信 zixin) in China's current system but also in traditional culture. This is a China that, after nearly breaking its national neck when attempting The Great Leap Forward some 60 years again, now not only speaks of catching up in great strides (大踏步赶上 databu ganshang) but even of taking flying leaps towards glory, wealth and power (向繁荣富强的伟大飞跃 xiang fanrong fuqiang de weida feiyue).

Xi is known as a big fan of Chinese traditional philosophy, and in the Report's conclusion, he sums up Chinese Communist and Chinese civilizational aspirations through a phrase known to most any student of Chinese history:

大道之行，天下为公

Where the "Great Way" (大道) prevails "all under heaven" (天下) is one community.

These words, from one of the four Confucian classics, the Book of Rites (礼记 Liji), and inscribed on Sun Yatsen's mausoleum, can be found in traditional centers of Chinese communities around the globe. For them to be accorded a place of prominence in a Party Congress report – indeed, not just the final word but a final proverb! – creates conceptually a political dish that is strikingly retro nouveau.

In *Confucian China and its Modern Fate*, Joseph Levenson wrote of a China that, having failed as an empire, sought to reclaim victory as a country. It is said that reversal is the essence of the Dao. Flash forward almost exactly 100 years from Yuan Shikai's farcical attempt at dynastic restoration in the Republican Era. Now we see China as country, seeking to reclaim a status as empire. This time, the Great Way refers not to a Confucian Way (儒道 Ru dao) but rather the Socialist Path (社会主义道路 shehuizhuyi daolu) with Chinese Special Characteristics.

Guiding China as nation state along the correct path through this new era: Xi Jinping Thought.

### 'Making Great Again' – what's lost in translation

Xi is far from only state leader pushing a mission of national revival. Across the Pacific, Donald Trump came to power on the phrase "Make America Great Again." There are resonances between their respective aspirations. Both evoke nationalist sentiments that are more ethnic than civic. Both forms of nationalist sentiments evince protracted conscious framing efforts made more impactful through strategic deployment of media resources. Both see restoring greatness as a fraught process, occurring in an international environment filled with grave threats as well as tremendous opportunities.

But one also finds striking differences in their respective formulas on how to make their countries great again:

- One views the goal largely proactively, from the perspective of centuries.
- The other views the goal largely reactively, from the perspective of only a decade, maybe two.
- One vision upholds a unified nation by obscuring differences and repressing dissent.
- The other vision asserts one nation over others by accentuating differences and demonizing dissent.
- One Party declares it best can "serve the people" through state-led economic redistribution policies.
- The other party avows people are best left to serve themselves, promoting laissez-faire and trickle-down policies.
- One leader affirms government as a critical part of the solution.
- The other leader attacks government as a critical part of the problem.

To paraphrase Mao, what we have here is a whopping contradiction.

Another difference, of course, are their histories and the distinctive flavors of cultural nationalism each can impart. In their efforts to define "great," each leader has a different pantry of cultural resources to complement the various kinds of civic and ethnic nationalism they're dishing. Whatever "nouveau retro" cuisine Trump may be serving up, I'm sure the list of ingredients doesn't include four Confucian classics, Maoist contradiction, or dragon tales.

All joking aside, as Xi and Trump would both agree, we see before us two very different recipes for becoming great again. Beyond simply affirming systemic differences, each intends to cultivate – even entrench – civilizational differences. More work needs to be done to compare and contrast their respective logics.

Fortunately, this being an exi-Xi-sis, not an exi-Trump-sis, I can keep this point provocatively evocative. Besides, key pieces of information – ingredients – have yet to be assembled. Trump's recently released National Security Policy (December 18, 2017) on Making America Great Again has brought his vision into greater focus through some policy specifics, much as the Report to the 19th Party Congress' 3rd Plenum fall 2018 will do for Xi's agenda.

In the meantime, if anyone's got an extra ticket to Xi's show at the 19th 3rd this coming fall, I'll trade you a Xi Jinping chairman-emperor wiggle picture for it.

*Dr. Stephen B. Herschler is Professor of Politics at Oglethorpe University and an Associate of the China Research Center.*

# Squeezing the Same Old Stone: Suing the Rural Chinese State and the Shift from Tax Reform to Land Seizures

*John Givens and Andrew MacDonald*
Vol. 17, No.2
2018

## Introduction

Beginning in the 1990s, both scholars and central officials repeatedly suggested that taxes and fees imposed on peasants[1] by local governments were the biggest source of discontent and protest in China.[2] Although higher levels of the Chinese government frequently urged lower levels to "reduce peasant burdens," little changed in the countryside until the central government rolled out tax-for-fee reforms (TFR), first in Anhui province in 2000 and then throughout most of the rest of the country in 2002.[3] TFR was a program designed by the central government to reduce and rationalize local governments' extraction from peasants by replacing a wide range of taxes and fees that officials abused with one low agricultural tax. Going even further, the central government mandated that local governments phase out even this agricultural tax completely by 2006.[4] Over a period of a few years this freed China's peasants from a tax they had paid for over two millennia. Yet, despite this decrease in what was likely the largest source of unrest, the number of protests (euphemistically termed "mass incidents") increased dramatically (Graph 1) during this period and probably since, although no official data has been released since the mid-2000s. While a wide variety of factors are surely at play, the simplest explanation is that officials in rural areas continued to rely on rural residents as their primary source of revenue. Specifically, rural governments shifted from taxing rural residents to taking their land. We demonstrate this by showing that in this period the number of administrative lawsuits related to taxation decreased while the number of land cases increased dramatically.

*Graph 1: Number of "Mass Incidents" in China 1993-2009[5]*

**Number of "Mass Incidents"**

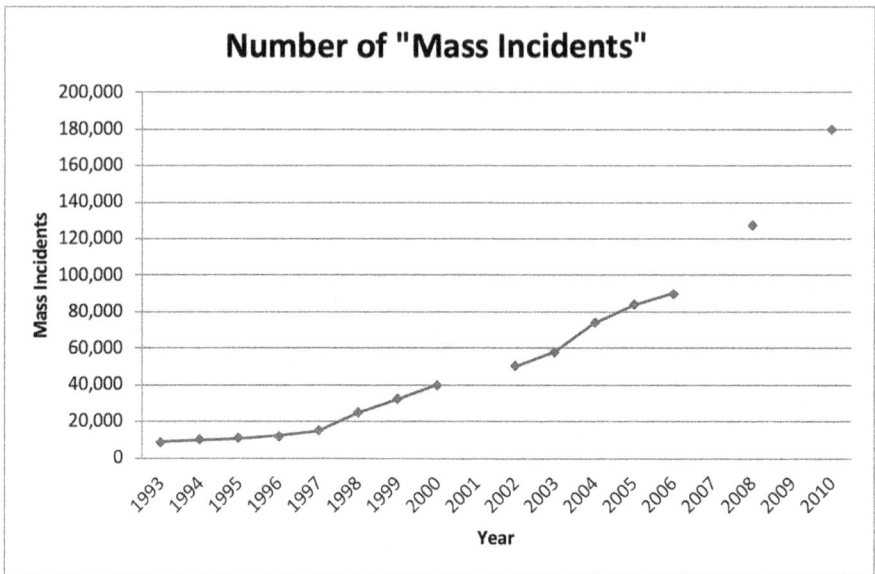

While this shift may seem dated in a country changing as rapidly as the People's Republic of China (PRC), it illuminates an underlying dilemma that has still not been solved by the central Chinese state: the lack of an appropriate funding mechanism for poorer local governments (still not resolved even after the 2015 fiscal reforms) and the resulting Hobson's choice for local officials of imposing a heavy and unfair tax burden on residents of poorer areas or simply underfunding services and development. Our results suggest that if the central government insists on unfunded social spending mandates for programs such as rural health insurance, subsistence income subsidies (the dibaoprogram), and basic retirement pensions, officials in poorer areas will continue to grab resources from poorer and less politically connected residents via whatever means available.[6] These actions are the local officials' attempt to square a circle and therefore occur regardless of how many circulars the central government distributes prohibiting the conduct or how often the central leadership harangues local officials to discontinue extraction from residents. This pressure dynamic is the fundamental driver of continuing unrest in rural areas and contributes to migration to China's cities.

**Background**

Our point of departure is the 2005 agricultural tax reform structure. When the central government eliminated the tax, the shortfall was supposed to be made up for by a combination of more efficient local government spending and transfers from the central government. In most cases, however, this combination proved insufficient to compensate for the loss of revenue. Officials pursued various strategies: finding alternate sources of revenues, reducing the provision of services, and the borrowing that has put local governments in their current perilous financial state, with debts exceeding US$2.5 trillion.[7] Here we present data to show that one of the major responses was simply switching the basis of extraction from taxing rural residents to the less-sustainable practice of appropriating and repurposing their land.

Tax reforms seem to have been a way for the central officials to have their cake and eat it too. By eliminating widely disliked taxes and fees, Beijing could appear to be doing its best on behalf of disadvantaged peasants, force local governments to use funds more responsibly, and only have to foot a relatively small portion of the bill. Without larger fiscal transfers, however, many local governments have been left in a tenuous funding situation – particularly the governments that relied most heavily on agricultural and other ancillary taxes. Evidence also suggests that these reductions in income have resulted in skyrocketing local government debt, with township governments facing dire budget deficits and debt amounting to twice their annual income.[8] Yet the central government seems reluctant to increase taxes on China's wealthier populations and implement the massive transfers that would fully fund their reforms and help address the country's widening rural-urban income gap. This again echoes the problems of imperial China, when efforts to pacify the gentry by exempting them from taxes ended up bankrupting the Ming government.

Existing qualitative research already suggests that many localities made up for the loss of the agricultural tax by appropriating land previously allocated to peasants. Takeuchi's ethnographic work found that township officials explicitly considered and then implemented a shift from tax to land extraction. Yep also notes this likely change in local government extraction practices, and Oi and Zhao found in interviews with township officials that, after the tax and fee reforms, many considered turning to illegal land sales.

It is relatively easy for local governments to seize peasants' land because it is allocated to peasants for 30-year terms rather than owned outright. While many peasants were unwilling to give up land they had been allocated during post-Mao decollectivization, in most cases officials did not even wait until the 30-year terms were up. Instead, they used a variety of tactics to pressure peasants into signing over their land-use-rights for relatively minimal compensation that often never materialized. One common tactics in more extreme cases was for officials, often working with the future developers of the land, to bulldoze peasants' farms and homes, leaving them with few reasons or resources to continue to resist. Land takings became common in the reform era, but evidence suggests that they gained prominence in the early 2000s. A 2005 survey found that land takings had grown by a factor of 15 in a decade.[9] The land can be used to make up for budget short-falls by selling it to developers, "re-contracting" collective agricultural land to non-villagers, and/or creating a tax base via the development of commercial agri-culture or industry, yet all end in the expropriation of farmers' land and meagre compensation.

Whatever the ultimate use of the land, cash-strapped officials often attempt to minimize the compensation paid to peasants for their land, both for reasons of corruption and to maximize the amount of money available to meet other spending priorities. "Villagers complained about low compensation when local governments expropriated their land for building an industrial zone or a freeway. They also complained that local governments then sold the confiscated land to developers at a much higher price, so that local cadres could cover the funding shortage."[10] Cadres sometimes employ harsh methods not only to force holdouts to leave their land, but also to pressure farmers to reduce the value of their land (by cutting down fruit trees, for example), and hence the required compensa-tion. Village collectives receive and keep the largest portion of compensation with farmers getting a small fraction of market value. Not only are peasants gener-ally dissatisfied with the amount of compensation, but such payments may leave farmers without a livelihood once the money runs out or fails to materialize.[11] This has continued in spite of increasingly strident instructions from the central government to ensure proper compensation is paid for land takings.

The harsh tactics, while generating significant revenue, unsurprisingly stoke peasant unrest. Evidence strongly suggests that the importance of land seizures has increased dramatically since the mid-2000s. Yu Jianrong, an expert on mass incidents with access to privileged data, claimed that by 2009, at least 65 percent of mass incidents were related to land problems. A report for the Cato Institute sets the figure even higher: "[i]n the first nine months of 2006, China reported a total of 17,900 cases of "massive rural incidents" in which a total of 385,000 farmers protested against the government. Approximately 80 percent of these in-cidents were related to illegal land-takings."

This shift from agricultural tax to land takings is generally accepted among China scholars. Perhaps due to a lack of data, however, no one has attempted to demonstrate how and when this shift happened on a nationwide scale. In order to do so, we analyze data on administrative litigation, the system through which average Chinese can challenge the actions of local governments in courts. We view administrative cases as a good measure of potential causes of unrest because 1) they are costly in terms of time, money, and effort, 2) they are the most for-mal means of challenging the local state, and 3) no other mode of contention produces publicly available annual statistics disaggregated by grievance type and province. As localities shifted their extraction from taxes and fees to land expropriation, we would expect the number of administrative cases related to taxes will fall and those related to land would rise. Less extraction in the form of taxes means less dissatisfaction with taxes, which means fewer administrative tax cases. Correspondingly, more extraction in the form of land expropriation means more dissatisfaction with land expropriation, which leads to more administrative land cases.

**Data**

To analyze whether the proposed trend was evident at the national level we gathered data on tax and administrative lawsuits from the China Statistical Yearbook. Administrative lawsuits are broken down by type and we have isolated the change over time in land and tax cases in Graph 2. The graph clearly shows that tax administrative lawsuits have declined dramatically over this period while land cases have increased. From 1998-2000 administrative courts heard approximately 2,000 tax cases a year, but this begins to drop in 2000, the year tax-for-fee reforms are launched in Anhui, reaching a plateau of around 300 in 2006-2009. The increase in land cases starts more slowly, but 2006-2009 shows a level of land litigation that is approximately a quarter higher than in 1998-2000. The fact that tax cases fall relatively quickly, and land cases react more slowly, makes sense. While tax litigation would begin to peter out almost immediately once officials dropped onerous taxes and fees, it would take some time for local governments to begin the process of expropriating land and then have peasants file cases against them. The difference in absolute number of land and tax suits results from the fact that peasants' tax disputes often involve only hundreds of renminbi (RMB) as opposed to tens or hundreds of thousands for land cases. Additionally, the loss of land can render a family suddenly destitute in a way that unjust taxation would not.

Official data published by the Chinese government are justifiably treated with skepticism, and data on litigation are no exception. Empirical research has suggested that courts exaggerate the true number of cases to make themselves look more productive and this is primarily true of less-busy courts in poorer areas.[12] For our purposes in this analysis, however, it is extremely unlikely that the relationship we identify between land and tax cases is the product of doctored statistics. From the local courts to the provincial and national governments, no part of the Chinese state has an incentive to provide false evidence of this negative correlation between land and tax cases. Indeed, it is difficult to imagine a scenario in which statistics on administrative litigation relating to land were manipulated upward at the same time that numbers for tax cases were falsified downward.

While this summary data is only suggestive, it does provide prima facie evidence of the shift from agricultural tax to land appropriation. To further determine whether representative empirical support exists for our hypothesis, we also examined data on administrative cases at the provincial level. Unfortunately, such data is published only occasionally or not at all for most provinces. The data used here was found in provincial statistical yearbooks or provincial legal yearbooks. After an exhaustive search through these sources, we used every province for which data was available for 2001-2007 to compile a data set consisting of a reasonably representative subset of five provinces plus a sixth case we created by using the national data minus those five provinces. These provinces run the gamut from rich coastal provinces (Guangdong) to poor inland ones (Anhui). It includes an agriculturally important province, Henan, and a provincial level municipality with relatively little farmland, Tianjin. Below is Graph 3, which shows the land versus tax administrative case frequency comparison of these select cases from 2001-2007. While our choice of years was limited by the available data, this period seems suitable as it begins one year before nationwide tax-for-fee reforms and ends one year after the phasing out of the agricultural tax was complete.

*Graph 2: Total numbers of Administrative Land, Tax and Health Cases 1998-2010*

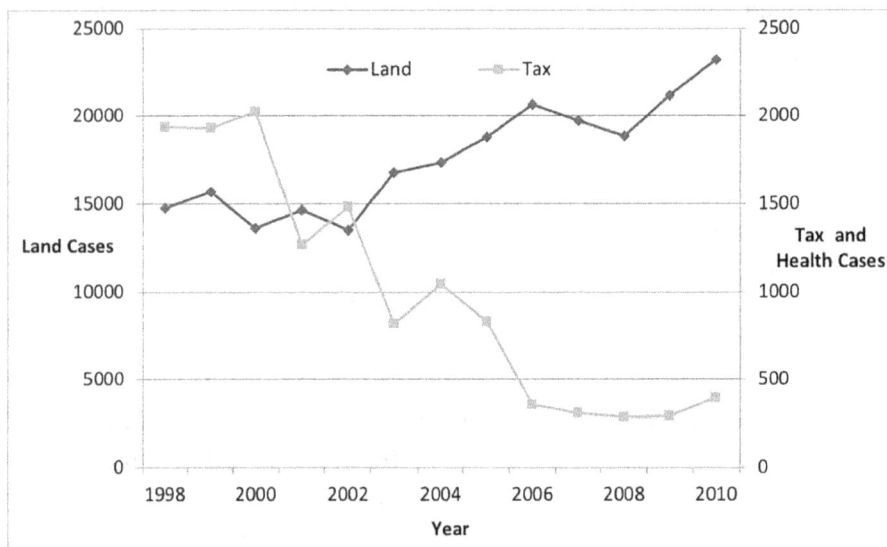

*Source: China Statistical Yearbook (中国统计年鉴) various years.*

The provincial data displays a more differentiated experience than is suggested by the national level graph, but still follows the basic contour of our argument. In most provinces, tax cases peaked around 2003 and then declined dramatically afterward, suggesting that the rural tax-for-fee reforms were successful at reducing excessive taxation. The spikes in tax cases visible between 2002 and 2004 in all six cases (though small in Hebei) suggest that the new regulations initially provided a basis for additional litigation resisting newly illegal taxes, but quickly diminished as officials began to reduce taxes and fees to comply with the reforms.

The pattern in the number of land cases is less settled but in all instances land cases went up after 2003, suggesting an inverse relationship with tax cases. Tianjin, Guangdong, and the national data minus the five provinces more or less followed the pattern displayed in the national data. We see the largest absolute number and decline in tax cases and rise in land cases in Henan, which makes sense considering it is one of the provinces mentioned by Bernstein[13] as a hotbed for tax-related protest. While Anhui was also one of the key sites of tax unrest, the tax-for-fee reforms there were initiated before our data set begins, so it is not surprising that the number of tax cases would already be low. Overall, while untidy, the provincial data lends support to the shift from tax-based to land-based extraction.

Elsewhere, we also conducted a simple panel regression using the provincial data that, for reasons of space, are omitted here but are available on the authors' website. While results should be interpreted with some caution, given the highly limited nature of the data set, they are supportive of our hypothesis and robust. The overall picture, including the existent literature and summary data, strongly suggests that during tax-for-fee reforms and the phasing out of the agricultural tax, land cases increased significantly while tax cases fell dramatically. This is as we predicted, given the spending pressures on local officials and the limited sources of revenue available to them due to the tax-for-fee reforms.

## Conclusion

Previous qualitative research demonstrated that because of the abolition of rural taxation, local cadres began to use a strategy of land expropriation to fund government expenditures. Here we test and confirm this theory at the national and provincial levels by showing the link between a decline in administrative litigation over tax issues and a rise in land cases. This analysis suggests that unrest in rural China is an ongoing problem, deeply rooted in the structure of the modern Chinese state and closely related to China's inadequate fiscal transfer system. This supports the idea that eliminating fees and taxes without sufficient funding simply pushed local governments into increased land seizures that, if anything, created even greater unrest. In the short term, tax reforms may have made the central government look good at the expense of local governments. Ultimately, however, the central government will be forced to deal with the underlying causes of unrest and local government debt or face a serious challenge to its legitimacy and stability.

The systematic underfunding of rural governments not only leads to officials appropriating and repurposing land from rural residents, it is also a major cause of

*Graph 3:[14] Administrative Tax and Law Cases for 6 Cases 2001-2007[15]*

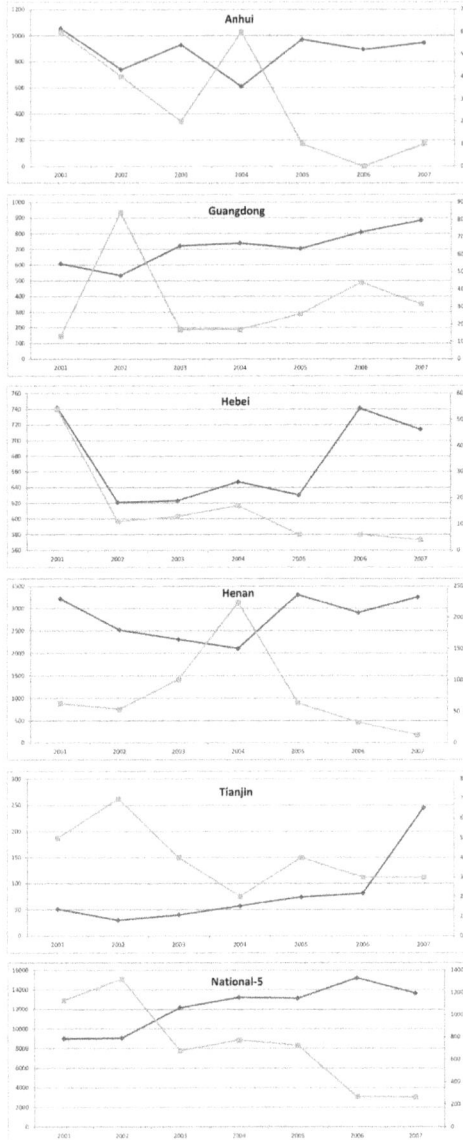

the huge, rapidly increasing, and unsustainable debts of local governments. This debt crisis will likely intensify as local governments run out of farm land to appropriate and sell. Furthermore, underfunded rural localities exacerbate inequality as they fail to stimulate development or even invest in their population through basic services such as education and healthcare. This, in combination with losing their land, pushes more rural residents into the floating population of more than 250 million underserved Chinese in urban areas, a potential source of unrest on a regime-threatening scale.

It is possible that as rising prices in cities push development into rural areas and China continues to urbanize, the CPC's US$200 billion internal security budget will be enough to keep control despite the problems resulting from under-funded rural governments. But if Beijing really wants to tackle rising inequality, ballooning local government debt, and the unrest these can engender, its safest bet would be to increase cash transfers from China's booming coast and cities to its struggling rural areas. If it does not, the historical pattern demonstrated here will surely repeat itself as officials continue to face the unsolvable dilemma created by the central government.

## Notes

1  *We use the term "peasant" here with reservation, though we do so for good reasons: First, it is a common translation for the relevant Chinese term: 农民. Second, the translation "farmer" is somewhat misleading as contemporary peasants are not choosing the profession of farming, but are rather tied to their land through their hukou registration and non-transferable land alloca-tions. Third, it helps situate TFR in China's long history of rural taxation.*

2  *Thomas P. Bernstein and Xiaobo Lü, "Taxation Without Representation: Peasants, the Central and the Local States in Reform China," The China Quarterly 163 (2000): 742–763; Andrew Wedeman, "Stealing from the Farmers: Institutional Corruption and the 1992 IOU Crisis," The China Quarterly no. 152 (1997): 805–831.*

3  *Bernstein and Lü, "Taxation Without Representation."*

4  *John James Kennedy, "From the Tax-for-Fee Reform to the Abolition of Agricultural Taxes: The Impact on Township Governments in North-west China," The China Quarterly 189 (2007): 43–59, doi:10.1017/S0305741006000798.*

5  *Sources: Data for 1993-2005 Albert Keidel, "China's Social Unrest: The Story Behind the Sto-ries" (Carnegie Endowment for International Peace, 2006), 3., 2006 Edward Wong, "Chinese Question Police Absence in Ethnic Riots," The New York Times, July 18, 2009, sec. Interna-tional / Asia Pacific, http://www.nytimes.com/2009/07/18/world/asia/18xinjiang.html., 2008 Ian Johnson, "China Sees Protest Surge By Workers," Wall Street Journal, July 10, 2009, sec. Law, http://online.wsj.com/article/SB124713050245617293.html., 2010 Barbara Demick, "Protests in China over Local Grievances Surge, and Get a Hearing," Los Angeles Times, Octo-ber 8, 2011, http://articles.latimes.com/2011/oct/08/world/la-fg-china-protests-20111009.*

6  *These same power dynamics also permit extraction for the (sometimes sole) purpose of corrup-tion, though local governments are still under significant pressure to increase provision of public goods from both local residents and higher-level officials.*

7  *J.C. Oi and S. Zhao, "Fiscal Crisis in China's Townships: Causes and Consequences," in In Grassroots Political Reform in Contemporary China, ed. Elizabeth J. Perry and Merle Gold-man (Cambridge, MA: Harvard University Press, 2007), 90–91.*

8  *Ray Yep, "Can Tax-for-Fee Reform Reduce Rural Tension in China? The Process, Progress and Limitations," The China Quarterly, no. 177 (2004): 42–70.*

9  *Keliang Zhu et al., "The Rural Land Question in China: Analysis and Recommendations Based on a Seventeen-Province Survey," New York University Journal of International Law and Politics 38 (2005): 761–839.*

10  *Hiroki Takeuchi, "Survival Strategies of Township Governments in Rural China: From Preda-tory Taxation to Land Trade," China Quarterly 22, no. 83 (2013): 4.*

11  *Zhu et al., "Rural Land Question in China," 781–83.*

12  *Xin He, "Why Did They Not Take on the Disputes? Law, Power and Politics in the Decision-Making of Chinese Courts," International Journal of Law in Context 3 (2007): 203–25.*

13    *"Unrest in Rural China: A 2003 Assessment," UC Irvine: Center for the Study of Democracy, 2004, 2.*

14    *Land cases are on the left y-axis and tax cases on the right y-axis of each graph.*

15    安徽省统计局 *Anhui Province Statistical Bureau, ed., Anhui Statistical Yearbook* 安徽统计年鉴 *Various Years (Statistical Press* 统计出版社, *Various Years);* 广东省高级人民法院编 *Guangdong High Court, Guangdong Court Yearbook* 广东法院年鉴 *Various Years (Guangdong: Guangdong People's Press* 广东人民出版社, *Various Years); Hebei Legal System Year Book Editorial Committee, Hebei Legal System Year Book* 河北法制年鉴 *Various Years (China Legal Publishing House* 中国法制出版社, *Various Years);* 中国统计年鉴编委会 *China Statistical Yearbook Editorial Committee, ed., China Statistical Yearbook* 中国统计年鉴 *Various Years (Statistical Press* 统计出版社, *Various Years).*

*Dr. John Wagner Givens is assistant professor of political science and international relations at Kennesaw State University, and an Associate of the China Research Center. Dr. Andrew W. MacDonald is assistant professor of political science at Duke Kunshan University.*

# The Rise of China: A Major Choice for the World

*Fei-Ling Wang*
*Vol. 17, No. 1*
*2018*

Students of international relations have long pondered the question of world political order and its changes. It is generally believed that either a shift of the distribution and concentration of power in the international system (power transition) or a reordering of the units in the system (change of the ordering principles and norms) would constitute a systemic change that will fundamentally alter world politics and reshape nations' behavior and redirect human civilization. Some also suggested that we are not entirely slaves of the past, and our present and future are ours to make and change. Thus ideas, knowledge, and choices all matter. It is therefore critically important to detect, analyze, and cope with a systemic change of world politics for the sake of peace and prosperity. The world has seen quite a few power transfers and even attempts to establish new orders over the recent centuries. Costly world wars (hot and cold ones) have been fought in the 20th century alone. It has been mercifully rare for the world to be presented with a weighty choice about both the power redistribution and unit-reordering in the international system — systemic change in its fullest possible degree.

The rise of China, or more specifically the empowerment of the People's Republic of China (PRC) state, is presenting the world with such a double-barreled, historic situation: a shifting power distribution and a profound choice about how the nations are ordered in the system. The systemic change implied by the new Chinese power is poised to surpass that associated with the long Cold War. On the one hand, the rapidly ascending power of the PRC state promises a great power redistribution that will make Beijing an alternative (even exclusive) power center for the region and then the whole world. Chinese leaders have already openly claimed that they are leading a revolutionary change in the world order, upending the Westphalia Peace established "more than four hundred years ago." On the other hand, and more profoundly, as I argue in my new book (The China Order: Centralia, World Empire, and the Nature of Chinese Power, Albany, NY: SUNY Press, 2017), rising Chinese power presents the world with a choice about the ordering principle of world politics. Therefore, it is no exaggeration to say that the future and fortune of human civilization rests heavily on how the rise of China is managed.

Despite significant scholarship on the subject, the nature and the meaning of the rise of China remain tentative, uncertain, and disputed. I contend that a key problem is that our existing understanding of the Chinese worldview and the nature of the rising Chinese power is insufficient, often inaccurate, and even misleading. I then propose that a careful rereading of the Chinese history in fact offers a rather straightforward, simple, and clear picture about the implications of the rising Chinese power, which may actually disappoint many "overly complicated analyses and overzealous advocates that frequently misinform and misguide." (The China Order p. 5)

My rereading of the Chinese history has yielded evidence suggesting a holistic answer to questions about the nature of the rising Chinese power through analyzing the China Order—an ideation and tradition of governance and world order that give China and the PRC their key characters. "The China Order, the Chinese world empire order, is based on a Confucian-Legalism imperial state, the Qin-Han (秦汉) polity, authoritarian often totalitarian in nature, that justifies and defends its rule with the Mandate of Heaven to unite, order, and govern the whole known world, the tianxia (天下 all under heaven). It denotes a worldwide Qin-Han polity, a Qin-Han world order." (The China Order p. 5)

Unlike many other world empires or attempted world empires (from the Egyptian pharaohs, the Inca, to the world Fascist and Communist movements), the China Order was practiced effectively for many centuries and united the whole known world in Eastern Eurasia from the third century B.C. to the mid-nineteenth century, albeit with frequent pretentions of unity and several, impermanent intervals of disunion. There was only one major pause of the China Order in the Chinese World: the Song Era (10th through 13th centuries), with rich, significant but underexplored lessons. The Qin-Han world empire political system of the China Order has also rejuvenated itself a number of times in the Chinese world. It has been highly attractive and even addictive to the ruling elites (Han Chinese or Non-Han Chinese alike) inside and even outside of the PRC as a deeply internalized part of the millennia-old Chinese culture and worldview. To many in China, the China Order is not just a viable, but also a superior world order, an ideology and a political system representing peculiar socioeconomic norms and culture values. The China Order has fundamentally shaped the Chinese World distinct from that in the post-Rome Mediterranean–European World under a de facto and later de jure world order of divided world polity with international competition — the Westphalia System. It explains the great West-East divergence between Europe and China. The China Order is a world order that is structurally and normatively incompatible with the Westphalia world system.

Since 1949, the Chinese Communist Party (CCP) has reincarnated the Qin-Han polity in the PRC and has sought political legitimacy and security through reordering the world in its image, like the previous imperial rulers. After some pauses and withdrawals after Mao Zedong's fiascoes, including an attempt to launch world revolution, today's CCP has been selectively accepting the West-phalia system with the aim to return to the China Order another day. As the CCP becomes ever more wealthy and confident, there is a significant revival of the China Order ideas in the PRC under the general banner of "the China Dream" and the mission "to construct a human community of common destiny." The rise of the PRC, therefore, "with a modified but tenacious Qin-Han polity in charge that predictably seeks a new tianxia world order, represents a clear and consequential choice about political governance and world order for the humankind." (The China Order p. 4)

Historically and comparatively, the Qin-Han polity and the China Order underperform for the Chinese people. The record of the Qin-Han polity has been the same in the PRC, which has been a suboptimal giant with inferior governance and barely average record of socioeconomic development. Yet, today, "the PRC has an increasingly unobstructed and selectively unilateral access to foreign markets, resources, and especially technology so it enriches and strengthens rapidly without being itself efficient and innovative. An inherently suboptimal giant plagued by an inferior governance, the PRC state nonetheless still rises to be very formidable and competitive in international relations." (The China Order p. 216) Thanks to its extraordinarily strong extraction capability, the PRC state is already a rich and mighty player—"moving in to the center of the world stage," claimed Beijing officially. The rise of the PRC is thus ushering in a new round of power redistribution in the international system on a massive scale, together with its ideal of reordering the nations.

To the peoples of Eastern Eurasia, the Qin-Han polity was grossly suboptimal and even disastrous in its record of governance, economic development, and technological innovation. The best of the glorious Chinese civilization was the periods when there was an absence of the China Order: the pre-Qin Era, the Song Era, and the time since the late-19th century, contrary to the much-distorted official Chinese narratives and claims. To the peoples of the world, a revival of the China Order would mean largely the same fate the peoples had in the Chinese World after the third century BCE.

As the logic of the China Order would predict, rising Chinese power will not stop short of reordering the world unless and until the very Qin-Han polity is transformed and/or the ever richer and more powerful PRC is checked. How to manage the rising Chinese power and how to make the grand choice for the world order will determine the future and fortune of the United States, the world, and for the Chinese people themselves.

The window for an effective, peaceful choice is still open, and there is evidence to trust the Chinese people to make the right choice together with the other nations, provided that they are given the full information and freedom to reread their history and to choose. The great people of China are fully capable of controlling their destiny and steering a great course in history that is different from the China Order, and in so doing make the world and China a better place. Hopefully, the effort to analyze the China Order through rereading the Chinese history may just be a small step in that direction.

---

*Dr. Fei-Ling Wang is Professor of international affairs at the Georgia Institute of Technology and an Associate of the China Research Center. He is the author of The China Order: Centralia, World Empire, and the Nature of Chinese Power, (Albany, NY: SUNY Press, 2017), on which this article is based.*

# Sino-Ethiopian Relations from Meles Zenawi to Abiy Ahmed: The Political Economy of a Strategic Partnership

*Daniel Kibsgaard*
*Vol. 19, No.2*
*2020*

## Introduction

Ethiopia has emerged as one of China's closest political and economic partners in China's wider engagement in Africa. In exchange for infrastructure development and support in its ambitions for industrialization, Ethiopia offers business contracts for Chinese firms and has been a loyal supporter of Beijing in international forums. Although a close strategic partnership between the countries was established after the 2005 elections, Prime Minister Abiy Ahmed's reform agenda appears to be drawing him back to Western actors. Far from representing a shift in alliances, this move is consistent with Ethiopia's historic pattern of balancing external powers against each other to reaffirm its own independence.

It is too early to say how the COVID-19 pandemic will impact this relationship, but Chinese humanitarian aid is unlikely to appease African states' desire for comprehensive debt relief. Beijing has stated it will help resolve debt difficulties, but on a bilateral basis. This most likely will not include write-offs and may ultimately serve to increase Ethiopia's as well as the broader continent's dependence on China.

## China in Ethiopia

Ethiopia has been a key destination for China's expanding construction and telecommunications companies. Under the framework of "resources for development," Beijing typically mobilizes its vast financial reserves to invest broadly in infrastructure projects across Africa in order to receive natural resources in return. However, with its growing populations, Africa has increasingly provided an opportunity for China's burgeoning firms to find new markets as declining infrastructure contracts in China are forcing firms abroad. Furthermore, Africa acts as a "testing ground" for Chinese companies, while the expansion of Chinese businesses abroad also provides opportunities for better paid work and offsets pressure on the domestic labor market.

China is particularly attracted to Ethiopia because of the diplomatic clout Ethiopia holds in Africa. This is due not only to the various multinational institutions based in Addis Ababa such as the African Union (A.U.), but also the symbolism of Ethiopia as one of the only African states not to have been colonized. As President Hu Jintao stated in 2004, "Ethiopia could play a pivotal role in enabling China to consolidate its cooperation with other African countries." Historically, African states have been instrumental in securing China's United Nations Security Council seat and strengthening China's position in international relations. Cooperation with China demands recognition of its One-China policy and there is an implicit expectation of diplomatic support when China is criticized internationally. This is reflected in the A.U.'s support of China's position in the South China Sea dispute. However, China's presence would not be possible without Ethiopia's own enthusiastic embrace of Beijing.

### Ethiopia's Realignment to China

With the brief exception of Italian occupation 1936-1941, Ethiopia takes pride in its longstanding independence. This has been a challenging project historically, which Ethiopia achieved by playing off rival powers against each other to strengthen its own position. Meles Zenawi, whose Ethiopian People's Revolutionary Democratic Front (EPRDF) overthrew the communist Derg regime in 1991 and who stayed in power until his death in 2012, demonstrated the continuity of this longstanding policy. He successfully ushered in the post-Cold War era by strategically realigning to China as a way to leverage against U.S. hegemony.

Although the U.S. helped the EPRDF come to power in 1991, Meles did not wish to remain within the American sphere of influence. Meles was fundamentally at odds with the neoliberal economic paradigm promoted by the U.S. Arguing that the proposals from the IMF and World Bank would not solve the problem of endemic poverty in Ethiopia, Meles once wrote that "development is a political process first and a socioeconomic process second." He believed in state monopolies over key sectors of the economy, a heavily regulated private sector, non-interference of foreign direct investment (FDI) in the state's policies, and a top-down approach to development. This statist emphasis on sovereignty in its economic development was inspired by Meles's Marxism, and his admiration of East Asia's rapid economic growth.

Meles consequently felt that Ethiopia's economic growth would be secured by collaboration with China. While South Korea and Taiwan were his favored examples, China's rise represented a serious political challenge to American development hegemony and the concomitant loan conditionality that Meles had tried to resist. This began with Meles's visit to China in October 1995 and Chinese President Jiang Zemin's reciprocal visit to Ethiopia in May 1996. Ethiopia was closely involved in the first Forum on China-Africa Cooperation (FOCAC) in 2000 and was the first African country to host the meeting in 2003.

However, Sino-Ethiopian relations only seriously intensified following Meles's violent suppression of protests over the disputed 2005 election results and resulting Western criticism of the crackdown. When the European Commission suspended general budget support and the World Bank froze new lending programs, Meles was pushed closer to China. At the 2006 FOCAC summit in Beijing, Meles stated that "China was always at the side of Africans, which created mutual trust between us. China also deserves credit for never interfering in the political affairs of the continent." Meles seemingly ignored or overlooked the fact that only a few years earlier, China sold more than $1 billion in arms to both sides during the Ethiopia-Eritrea War (1998-2000), bypassing the U.N. embargo. Furthermore, as a member of the U.N. Human Rights Council, Ethiopia helped defeat all motions criticizing China in 2007. Crucially, party-to-party relations were significantly expanded and in 2010, a Memorandum of Understanding was signed between the EPRDF and the CCP. Economic ties also increased rapidly. According to a 2012 World Bank survey, Chinese FDI increased "from virtually zero" in 2004 to $74 million annually in 2009. During this time, the EPRDF reestablished a single-party state, securing 99.6 percent of seats in Parliament in 2010, and 100 percent in 2015.

Ethiopia's realignment appeared all but complete when the foreign ministers of Ethiopia and China published an article in 2014 which expressed the aim to "upgrade our cooperation to a fully-fledged strategic partnership." However, this strategic partnership was primarily focused on the party-to-party relationship between the EPRDF and the CCP which contributed to the development of a ruling-party oriented capitalism in Ethiopia. This is illustrated by EFFORT, an endowment run by EPRDF officials that owns more than 60 companies in major industries, and routinely receives preferential treatment when entering joint ventures with Chinese firms.

Ethiopia consequently saw the consolidation of political power and economic assets by the former revolutionary leadership, as inequalities and dissatisfaction widened. China thus became enmeshed in the EPRDF regime at the expense of Ethiopia's private-sector and democratic institutions. It should nonetheless be noted that Addis Ababa used its alliance with Washington in the Global War on

Terror to strengthen Ethiopia's authoritarian turn by justifying draconian anti-terror legislation that severely curtailed freedom of speech. Before delving into the more recent political ramifications of this partnership, an overview of China's impact on Ethiopia's infrastructure and industrialization development will be provided.

**Infrastructure**

Ethiopian and Chinese officials typically depict their economic relations as "win-win," most notably with regard to the vast investment in infrastructure. For example, the completion of the Chinese-funded Addis Ababa–Djibouti Railway in 2018 reduced a week-long journey to a 12-hour ride, facilitating goods transport and cutting costs for 90 percent of Ethiopia's external trade. Even though the railway has been beset by major issues, such as a lack of supporting infrastructure and insufficient revenue, it still strengthens Ethiopia's prospects for economic growth.

While these infrastructure projects are benefiting Ethiopia in important ways, they are designed to serve Chinese interests first. China's infrastructure projects are largely funded by concessional loans which have low interest, a five-year grace period and a grant component of more than 35 percent, making them extremely attractive. Whereas these loans do not contain any political conditionality, they are heavily tied to stipulations requiring the use of Chinese companies, labor (especially at the managerial level), and materials. This, in combination with political ties, low bidding prices, and the ability to outcompete Ethiopian firms, explains the success of Chinese firms in Ethiopia.

This success is most visible in road construction, where the Chinese share of the total in Ethiopia in 2011 was between 70 and 80 percent. Although the majority of the permanent Chinese-employed workforce in Ethiopia is in fact Ethiopian, they are normally employed in low-skilled jobs, which prevents transfer of expertise and creates resentment. Furthermore, the equipment used to build roads is often outdated, stopping effective transfer of technology. This, in combination with the low bidding prices offered by Chinese firms, results in poor-quality construction.

Additionally, a significant proportion of road projects create losses. In some cases, Chinese contractors lose 40 percent of the contract price. This is only made possible because Chinese state-owned enterprises (SOEs) are backed by company savings and state bank loans, meaning that the Chinese taxpayer is effectively footing the bill for Ethiopia's infrastructure development. This demonstrates how China's SOEs act as instruments of Chinese foreign policy in that they are helping establish Beijing's diplomatic foothold in Ethiopia.

China has also been heavily involved in constructing Ethiopia's telecommunications. In 2006, China's ZTE was granted a monopoly over the market as the Ethiopian government seemed to ignore its own procurement rules requiring competitive bidding. Government control and poor quality have resulted in some of the lowest fixed-line and internet access rates in Africa. Monopoly profits are in turn used to fund Chinese infrastructure projects, creating a circular flow of money. Moreover, Ethiopia is dependent on China for after sales. This dependency only seems to be intensifying as a $1.6 billion agreement was signed in 2013 with Huawei and ZTE to upgrade existing infrastructure.

Activists have claimed that Chinese authorities have provided the Ethiopian government with technologies that can be used for political repression, such as surveillance cameras and satellite jamming equipment. Moreover, a 2018 Le Monde Afrique report claimed that China had bugged the African Union headquarters in Addis Ababa. In addition to hiding microphones in desks and walls, China had allegedly been transferring confidential data to a server in Shanghai between 2012 and 2017. Although both the African Union and the Chinese government denied the accusations, observers say the incident demonstrates the lack of leverage African states have over China and warn against relying too heavily on China for their development. The A.U. now uses its own servers, and information no longer passes through Ethio Telecom, Ethiopia's state-run operator built by China's ZTE. This incident strengthened the U.S. government's long-held belief that China uses its telecommunications firms, Huawei and ZTE, to spy on foreign governments and citizens.

The greater concern for Ethiopians is how Chinese loans have placed an enormous debt burden on the country, causing economic volatility. Ethiopia is the second-largest recipient of Chinese loans in Africa with more than $13.7 billion provided between 2000 and 2017. Government debt currently stands at 59 percent of GDP, with some 50 percent owed to China while foreign exchange is drained as imports outrank exports by as much as 400 percent. This unsustainable situation reveals the persistent structural weakness of the Ethiopian economy and has fueled public outrage in recent years. A Chinese Foreign Ministry spokesperson recently stated that China is open to restructuring loans to African countries, but the long-term health of the economy will depend on whether the government's efforts to industrialize succeed.

## Industrialization

In response to its chronic foreign exchange shortage, which predates its partnership with China, Ethiopia hopes to spur its industrialization by encouraging its comparative advantage in the leather industry and by emulating the successful East Asian industrial parks. China has played a mixed role in both efforts but with mostly positive results for industrialization prospects.

Despite initial fears that cheap Chinese imports would displace local manu-facturers, the Ethiopian footwear industry responded by becoming more com-petitive and implementing effective industrial policies. Chinese footwear began flooding the Ethiopian market in the early 2000s, after economic liberalization in the 1990s opened a once-closed market, leading to fears of deindustrialization. However, a 2007 study of small and medium footwear enterprises by Tegegne Gebre-Eghziaber showed that while Chinese imports had been highly disruptive, the Ethiopian footwear industry had responded by either undercutting these im-ports or focusing on better quality. After several years of adjustment, 82 percent of the firms Gebre-Egziabher spoke to told him that they were now competitive against Chinese imports and that the leather sector in Ethiopia was booming. Furthermore, while Chinese imports were initially attractive for their cheap price, they declined in popularity after being revealed to have poor quality.

The Ethiopian government also intervened to protect the footwear industry. It listed a number of areas of investment reserved for domestic investors only, including leather hides and skins. Furthermore, in November 2011, the export of semi-finished skins destined for footwear production was banned to further encourage domestic industry. In response to the poor quality of many Chinese products, the government established the Joint Committee on Quality Control, which demands Chinese exports be given a certificate by an inspector agency.

In addition to defending its leather industry, Ethiopia has embarked on an ambitious policy of opening industrial parks to attract foreign manufacturers and benefit from the spillover effects including skills and technology transfer. While China has been the most avid investor, many local firms do not benefit from subcontracting as happened in East Asia. This is seen in the fact that in 2011, 61 percent of total material inputs and supplies used in factories were imported. This is because many goods could be imported at a cheaper price from China than they could be sourced locally. This nonetheless contradicts a fundamental goal of FDI, which is to boost local competitiveness through active interaction with ad-vanced foreign businesses. Whereas Ethiopian firms would like to see more joint ventures, Chinese firms have largely been unwilling, further hindering manage-rial skill and tech transfer. There have also been reports of rampant labor abuse and exploitative wages. Average wages at Chinese firms are nonetheless above the Ethiopian average.

China has responded to these criticisms and is increasingly encouraging spill-over benefits. The Huajin International Light Industry City was built in coopera-tion with the Ethiopian government in 2017 and aims to serve as an Ethiopian supply chain cluster. To counteract the issue of China's employment practices, Huajin has selected graduates from Ethiopian universities to receive training in China to become the future managers of its Ethiopian factories. This builds on previous efforts, most notably when China built Africa's largest vocational train-ing school in Addis Ababa in 2008. In addition, many of the issues associated with low spillover from Chinese firms have more to do with underlying condi-tions than discriminatory practices. This suggests that as expanding infrastructure development cuts costs and more Ethiopians receive qualified training, Ethiopian ownership of its industrialization will increase. A $1.8 billion deal signed in 2018 with the State Grid Corporation of China to secure power lines to cities, 16 in-dustrial parks, and the Addis-Djibouti railway is a step in the right direction.

Progress is slow, however, as Ethiopia failed to reach its targeted 15-fold in-crease in textile and leather exports in 2015. Combined, they still only account for a fraction of total exports. Ethiopia's traditional dependency on agriculture has not changed and Chinese investments have not significantly helped agricultural development. Nonetheless, Ethiopia has benefitted from this investment and the prospect of increased Ethiopian ownership bodes well for the country's economic growth. Unfortunately, the global economic stillstand induced by COVID-19 will undoubtedly impact this development.

**The Abiy Era**

Despite all the advances in the Ethiopian economy that the strategic partner-ship with China enabled, it also contributed to growing political and economic instability which came to a breaking point when Prime Minister Abiy Ahmed came to power in April 2018. His predecessor, Hailemariam Desalegn, was forced to resign two months prior after years of protests eroded his legitimacy and that of the EPRDF. Although protests began over corrupt land deals, they quickly turned into a wider uprising against corruption, repression and ethnic discrimination. Between 2015 and 2017, more than 1,000 protesters were killed and 21,000 were arrested in a predominantly Oromo revolt against the Tigray-dominated regime.

In response, Abiy, who is Oromo, has enacted wide-ranging political reforms to appease protesters and mend ethnic relations. Since coming to power, the young prime minister has released thousands of prisoners, moved toward democ-ratization, and even brokered a peace agreement with Eritrea for which he was awarded the 2019 Nobel Peace Prize. In November 2019, Abiy dismantled the EPRDF and created a pan-Ethiopian coalition called the Prosperity Party (PP), which includes formerly marginalized ethnic groups. This move threw into ques-tion the future of Ethiopia's strategic partnership with China as it was increasingly based on party-to-party relations between the EPRDF and CCP.

While China has not expressed concerns regarding this political develop-ment, it has greatly reduced its willingness to invest in the country. Less than two months after Abiy came to power in April 2018, China announced it was scaling back its investments in Ethiopia. Beijing also expressed frustration after major investments, such as the Addis-Djibouti Railway, failed to generate sufficient revenues. Abiy was seemingly able to win back China's confidence when he renegotiated the repayment period for some loans from 10 to 30 years at the September 2018 FOCAC in Beijing.

China's move does, however, come in response to years of growing economic volatility. Despite averaging 10 percent GDP growth since the early 2000s, Ethiopia's economic situation is deteriorating as foreign exchange dries up and its trade deficit grows. In December 2016, the Ethiopian parliament demanded to ascertain the country's external debt repayment capacity before ratifying new concessional loan agreements with China due to rising Chinese interest rates and shorter repayment periods. In addition, the IMF raised its debt distress rating to "moderate" in 2017 and then to "high" in 2018.

In response to decreasing Chinese willingness to extend new loans, Abiy appealed to Western donors who were more than happy to step in. Western actors are throwing their support behind the new Prime Minister who is hailed for his pro-democracy and pro-market reform agenda. In December 2019, the IMF and World Bank pledged over $5 billion to the country to cover about 60 percent of the total financial need for Abiy's three-year Homegrown Economic Reform Program. The United Arab Emirates also entered the fray with a $3 billion aid and investment package in 2018 revealing interest from Gulf States as well. Far from signaling the end of Chinese involvement in Ethiopia, these recent developments demonstrate Ethiopia's rising importance in international politics and its increasing ability to find the best deal to further its own development.

That said, the COVID-19 pandemic complicates this picture. While Ethiopia has not yet registered a large number of confirmed cases which would confirm a widespread outbreak, the country and Africa broadly are struggling to face the global crisis. Although China is doing commendable work in fighting the virus (e.g. cooperating with Ethiopian Airlines to distribute much-needed medical supplies to 12 African countries), humanitarian aid will not substitute for debt relief. African debt to China stands at $143 billion with $8 billion due this year, creating an untenable situation for countries like Ethiopia that could lose up to 10 percent of GDP with the world economy brought to a standstill. African leaders such as Ghana's finance minister therefore believe China is not doing enough and are calling for a moratorium on all external debt as well as debt write-offs. Prime Minister Abiy recently published an article on Project Syndicate in which he called on "developed countries (including China)" to help Africa and match their rhetoric with action.

However, observers do not expect China to go far beyond its support for multilateral efforts such as the World Bank's $160 billion emergency economic program of which Ethiopia is an initial project country. Instead, China will continue to review its bilateral loans on a case by case basis and is unlikely to stray far from its historical approach of suspending loan payments, restructuring debt, and debt/equity swaps. Beijing has only forgiven five percent of its loans to Africa, but these were largely zero-interest and with its own economy to worry about it will not start now unless other states do so as well.

After already having much of its debt restructured in recent years, Ethiopia may be forced to hand over greater ownership of infrastructure projects such as dams and the Addis-Djibouti Railway. Although this is not necessarily a bad thing and can provide much needed foreign exchange, the greater cost could be political. With Chinese loans already being so dependent on diplomatic support for Beijing's policies, Prime Minister Abiy may yet be forced to align closer to China, which could impact his own domestic reform program. On the other hand, the crisis presents an opportunity for African states to leverage their unity in multilateral negotiations with China and break with Beijing's insistence on bilateralism. China's Foreign Ministry has stated that it will help resolve African governments' debt difficulties but in the absence of American leadership and with Europe preoccupied at home, China is better placed to resolve the issue on its own terms.

## Conclusion

Ethiopia gained much in terms of infrastructure and industrialization from its 15 years of close cooperation with China. However, Ethiopia's unsustainable debt levels force it to reduce its dependency on Chinese loans for its growth, just as Beijing does not want to overexpose itself to Addis Ababa's volatility. Meanwhile, Abiy's pro-democracy and pro-market reforms have resulted in renewed Western engagement. Combined, these developments have halted further intensification of Sino-Ethiopian relations and reasserted Ethiopia's historic ability to balance external powers against each other in its own interest. Yet in the absence of sufficient multilateral mobilization and uncertain Chinese debt relief, COVID-19 may seriously challenge this foreign policy dictum.

## References

Adem, Seifudein, 'China in Ethiopia: Diplomacy and Economics of Sino-optimism', *African Studies Review* 55, (2012), pp. 143-160.

Aglionby, John, Feng, Emily and Yang, Yuan, 'African Union accuses China of hacking headquarters', *Financial Times*, (29 January 2018).

Allo, Awol K., 'Why Abiy Ahmed's Prosperity Party could be bad news for Ethiopia,' *Aljazeera*, (5 December 2019).

Anberbir, Yohannes, 'MPs raise concerns on external debt repayment capacity', *The Reporter*, (17 December 2016).

Associated Press, 'Chinese firm featured in government-backed propaganda film accused of labor rights abuses', *South China Morning Post*, (2 May 2018).

Bekele, Kaleyesus, 'Ethiopian dispatches Covid-19 supplies to Africa,' *The Reporter*, (25 April 2020).

Brautigam, Deborah, 'Chinese Debt Relief: Fact and Fiction,' *The Diplomat*, (15 April 2020).

Brautigam, Deborah, *The Dragon's Gift: The Real Story of China in Africa*, (Oxford, 2009).

Cabestan, Jean-Pierre, 'China and Ethiopia: Authoritarian affinities and economic cooperation', *China Perspectives 2012/4*, (2012), pp. 53-62.

Clapham, Christopher, *The Horn of Africa: State Formation and Decay*, (London, 2017).

De Waal, Alex, 'The Theory and Practice of Meles Zenawi', *African Affairs 112*, (2012), pp. 148-156.

Driessen, Miriam, 'The African Bill: Chinese struggles with development assistance', *Anthropology Today 31*, (2015), pp. 3-7.

'Ethiopia', Human Rights Watch, (January 2018).

Fikade, Birhanu, 'Economists forecast 10% hit to GDP,' *The Reporter*, (11 April 2020).

'Freedom on the Net 2012: Ethiopia', Freedom House, (2012).

Gebre-Eghziaber, Tegegne, 'Impacts of Chinese imports and coping strategies of local producers: the case of small-scale footwear enterprises in Ethiopia', *Journal of Modern African Studies 45*, (2007), pp. 647-679.

Geda, Alemayehu and Meskel, Atenafu G., 'Impact of China-Africa Investment Relations: Case Study of Ethiopia', *African Economic Research Consortium Collaborative Research on the Impact of China on Africa*, (2010).

Gedamu, Yohannes, 'Why Abiy Ahmed's Prosperity Party is good news for Ethiopia,' *Aljazeera*, (18 December 2019).

Tedros Adhanom Ghebreyesus and Wang Yi, 'Ethiopia-China relations: an excellent model for South-South cooperation', *Federal Democratic Republic of Ethiopia Ministry of Foreign Affairs*, (1 January 2014).

Hackenesch, Christine, 'European Good Governance Policies Meet China in Africa: Insights from Angola and Ethiopia', *German Development Institute Working Paper*, (2011).

Hess, Steve and Aidoo, Richard, 'Beyond the Rhetoric: Noninterference in China's African Policy', *African and Asian Studies 9*, (2010), pp. 356-383.

Jobson, Elissa, 'Chinese firm steps up investment in Ethiopia with 'shoe city'', *The Guardian*, (30 April 2013).

Kiruga, Morris, 'Ethiopia's China Challenge,' *The Africa Report*, (27 March 2019).

Lefort, René, 'The Ethiopian Economy: The Developmental State vs. The Free Market', in Gérard Prunier and Éloi Ficquet (eds.), *Understanding Contemporary Ethiopia*, (London, 2015), pp. 357-394.

Li, Hangwei and Musiitwa, Jacqueline, "Coronavirus diplomacy': China's opportune time to aid Africa,' *The Africa Report*, (24 April 2020).

Maasho, Aaron, 'China denies report it hacked African Union headquarters', *Reuters*, (29 January 2018).

Marshall, Monty G. and Elzinga-Marshall, Gabrielle, 'Global Report 2017: Conflict, Governance and State Fragility', *Center for Systemic Peace*, (27 August 2017).

Mengesha, Simegnish Yekoye, 'Silencing Dissent', *Journal of Democracy 27*, (2016), pp. 89-94.

Nicolas, Françoise, 'Chinese Investors in Ethiopia: The Perfect Match?', *French Institute of International Relations*, (2017).

'Out of reach', Economist, (24 August 2013).

Rota, Matt, 'Ethiopia plays Europe off China in bid to boost investment,' *Politico*, (3 February 2020).

Runge, Maxelle, 'Two African countries, two strategic Chinese aid packages, two different outcomes', *Master's Thesis Leiden University*, (15 July 2016).

Thakur, Monika, 'Building on Progress? Chinese Engagement in Ethiopia', *South African Institute of International Affairs Occasional Working Paper 38*, (2009).

Tronvoll, Kjetil, 'The Ethiopian 2010 federal and regional elections: Re-establishing the one-party state', *African Affairs 110*, (2011), pp. 121-136.

Sands, Gary, 'Ethiopia's Broadband Network – A Chinese Trojan Horse?', *Foreign Policy Association*, (6 September 2013).

Seyoum, Mibratu, Wu, Renshui and Yang, Li, 'Technology spillovers from Chinese outward direct investment: The case of Ethiopia', *China Economic Review 33*, (2015), pp. 35-49.

Sun, Yun, 'China and Africa's debt: Yes to relief, no to blanket forgiveness,' *Brookings*, (20 April

2020).

Sun, Yun, 'China in Africa: Implications for U.S. Competition and Diplomacy', in John P. Banks et al., *Top Five Reasons Why Africa Should be Priority for the United States*, (2013), pp. 6-7.

Venkataraman, Manickam and Gofie, Solomon M, 'The dynamics of China-Ethiopia trade relations: economic capacity, balance of trade & trade regimes', *Bandung: Journal of the Global South 2*, (2015), pp. 1-17.

The World Bank, 'Chinese FDI in Ethiopia: A World Bank Survey', (2012).

'World Bank, IMF pledge over 5 bln USD financial support to Ethiopia's economic reform,' *Xinhua*, (13 December 2019).

Yewondwossen, Muluken, 'Ethiopia minimizes foreign long term loans', *Capital*, (20 March 2017).

Meles Zenawi, 'States and Markets', in Akbar Noman et al. (eds.), *Good Growth and Governance in Africa: Rethinking Development Strategies*, (Oxford, 2011).

Zewde, Getahun, 'Post 2006 Ethio-China Trade Relations: Challenges and Prospects', *Asian Research Journal of Arts & Social Sciences 3*, (2017), pp. 1-11.

Ziso, Edson, 'Good Growth and Governance in Africa: Rethinking Development Strategies', Doctoral Thesis University of Adelaide, (2017).

---

*Daniel Kibsgaard holds a master's degree in the Theory and History of International Relations from the London School of Economics and Political Science.*

# Review: China and India: Comparisons of Soft Power

*John Garver*
*Vol. 17, No.1*
*2018*

*Review of Parama Sinha Palit, Analyzing China's Soft Power Strategy and Comparative Indian Initiatives (Los Angeles, London, New Delhi: SAGE, 2017).*

Because India is situated at the very geographic center of the South Asia-Indian Ocean region, Indian civilizational influences have washed repeatedly over that vast region. Indian patriots are keenly aware of this history, and it is easy to assume that Indian influence in the region is somehow natural or inevitable. That may indeed be the case, but the breadth and vigor of China's efforts to make itself and its policies attractive to the publics and governments of the region suggests that Indian soft power faces a new and very strong competitor.

Dr. Parama Sonha Palit's book, Analyzing China's Soft Power Strategy and Comparative Indian Initiatives, offers an interesting and solid study of an important but under-researched aspect of China's rise in Asia: the scope and character of China's exercise of soft power. After extracting from the secondary literature a working definition of soft power (the attractiveness of a country) and exploring the evolution of Chinese scholarly thinking about soft power with Chinese characteristics, Palit examines China's pursuit of soft power in several geographic regions, starting with South Asia. The overarching purpose of China's soft power activities in the region, Palit concludes, is to establish the image of China as a benign power. Palit turns to a survey of the various mechanisms China uses to advance this soft power goal. The list is long.

**Diplomacy:** China's leaders travel frequently and strategically, explaining China's policies and inveigling foreign support for those policies, assisted by a large and growing cadre of well-trained young diplomats assigned to regional capitals. China participates effectively in multilateral organizations, including a few that it effectively controls (e.g. the Shanghai Cooperative Organization), and is frequently able to block activities adverse to China's policy interests.

**Information:** Agencies of the Chinese government (including the Information Office of the State Council) issue a substantial and growing volume of documents outlining and defending China's policies. An array of attractive magazines – often targeting specific foreign audiences and explaining China's views – are supported and guided by the government. The Xinhua News Agency provides global coverage educating China's people about foreign events, and educating foreign audiences about China's own policy perspectives. China Central Television (CCTV) offers an attractive view of China and presentation of China's view of world affairs. Party and state organs guide almost all these information activities.

**Economic:** The huge size and rapid growth of China's economy, plus China's success in lifting hundreds of millions of its citizens out of poverty, hold considerable attraction for foreign firms and governments. Foreign governments seek trade and investment with China. Beijing occasionally uses foreign hopes of expanded economic cooperation in a carrot-and-stick fashion to influence foreign policies in other, non-economic, areas of interest to Beijing. China also provides loans or grants to countries it views as strategic. Foreign governments sometimes find Chinese assistance more attractive than loans by Western countries that carry transparency stipulations. Repayment obligations derived from Chinese loans give Beijing further leverage. Multiple lavishly funded infrastructure projects linked to China often are attractive to countries in the region.

**Cultural Diplomacy:** Confucius Institutes serve as gateways to interest in China's civilizational heritage. Presentation of China as an ancient, glorious but non-Western civilization appeals to non-Western countries perhaps resentful of histories of Western domination. The nonviolent, harmony-seeking nature of China's traditional Confucian civilization is juxtaposed with the violent, conflict-ridden and exploitative nature of Western civilization.

**Higher Education:** China recognizes U.S. leadership in higher education as a major component of the great influence of the United States in the world. Beijing is striving to turn China into a leading global provider of higher education through dispensing of fellowships, recruitment of prominent foreign faculty, linkups with leading non-Chinese universities, and establishment of English language-based programs to attract foreign students. The objective is to educate coming generations of foreign leaders, giving them in the process an understanding of China's view of the world.

Supplying higher education to bright and ambitious young men and women from South Asian countries will probably be a key factor influencing the relative status of India, China and other countries in future decades. Palit offers an interesting discussion of China's "aggressive marketing" of Chinese university study to South Asian youth – initiatives that include participating in exhibitions, offering scholarships for students and faculty, or establishing programs using English as the language of instruction. When Xi Jinping visited India in 2014, for example, he announced plans to offer 10,000 scholarships for South Asian students and faculty. Tertiary education in China also has the distinct competitive advantage of being much cheaper than study at American, European or Japanese universities. Palit notes that large numbers of Bangladeshi and Sri Lankan students are studying medicine in China.

One of the most intriguing questions raised by Palit's study is whether China might actually become the dominant purveyor of soft power in the South Asian region. This is not a concern raised by Palit herself. Although the book title promises to examine "comparative Indian initiatives," there is no systematic effort to compare India's activity in each of the areas deployed by China and enumerated above. Chapter 9 addresses "Indian Soft Power: Strategies and Approaches," but does not compare Chinese and Indian efforts in, for example, trade with and investment in South Asian countries, the scope of the two rivals' respective information operations in key South Asian countries, the frequency and level of leadership exchange visits, or the number of South Asian students who receive tertiary education in India and China. It would be interesting to know how India compares with China as a provider of tertiary education to youth in key South Asian countries. This could be a major variable influencing the reputation and status – the soft power – of India and China in the region over a longer period. Palit acknowledges this by discussing the Chinese side of the equation, but comparison with India's role is absent. It is widely understood that Indian universities have educated large numbers of youth from across South Asia.

Is China now surpassing and supplanting India in this crucial regard?

A comparison of the reciprocal exchange of high-level Chinese and Indian leaders with various South Asian countries would also be interesting. Palit examines the coming and going of China's leaders, and explains how such visits help create a positive, benign image of China. Data comparing visits by Chinese and

Indian leaders to South Asian countries is readily available – for example on the websites of the foreign ministries of various countries – but none is provided by Palit. Similarly, one searches in vain for comparison of the information operations of China and India in South Asian countries. In such economic areas as trade and investment, comparisons of Indian and Chinese roles with South Asian countries (e.g. trade with India and China as percent of various South Asian countries' total trade) would be useful. Palit's presentation of data suggests that China is about to surpass India, or perhaps already has, in soft power in South Asia. India is only "beginning to articulate soft power… in a more forceful fashion that any time in the past." (Italics added.) India's soft power effort has been "less pronounced in scale in the past than similar Chinese efforts." It is "likely" that under Prime Minister Narendra Modi, India's soft power effort will "undergo some fundamental change." India's soft power efforts labor under considerable burdens, Palit says. India's stress on its history of cultural influences in the region is "somewhat risky" in that it "might give rise to fear of cultural colonization by India… India's ability to command respect is considerably diminished by the resentment it meets in the region."

India, like almost every country in the world, is pondering its response to the remarkable rise of China as a leading power. The question is more portentous for India because it has long dominated the geography of South Asia as well as the maritime flanks constituting the Indian Ocean. Repeated waves of Indian cultural influences did indeed wash over India's home region and the broader world. And China was kept far away by burdensome geography and technological backwardness. Now those barriers are vanishing. China is becoming a major power, perhaps the major power, in the region. A robust literature has emerged already on the swift development of Chinese naval power across the Indian Ocean, on Beijing's ambitious One Belt, One Road infrastructure-building efforts, on China's rise as the leading economic partner for most of the countries of the region, and on China's push for deeper partnership with countries from Myanmar to Bangladesh, Nepal, Pakistan, Iran and Djibouti. Despite omissions about India's efforts to counter China's soft power rise in the region, Palit's study adds an important component to the observation of the evolving rivalry between these two ambitious and proud powers.

---

*Dr. John Garver is Professor Emeritus of International Affairs in the Sam Nunn School of International Affairs at Georgia Institute of Technology and an Associate of the China Research Center.*

# About the Editors

**Penelope B. Prime:** Beginning with her first visit to China in 1976, Dr. Prime has more than four decades of experience studying the dynamic Chinese economy. After majoring in Chinese studies and studying Mandarin as an undergraduate, she earned a Ph.D. in economics at the University of Michigan. She is Founding Director of the China Research Center and Managing Editor of China Currents. Dr. Prime was Clinical Professor in the Institute of International Business, J. Mack Robinson College of Business, Georgia State University from 2012 to 2020; professor at Mercer University, 2006 to 2012, earning tenure; and professor at Kennesaw State University, 1991 to 2006, earning tenure. Between 1987 and 2009 she co-developed and led an eleven-week, study abroad with Carleton College to Asia and China. This seminar occurred eight times, involving 40 students each time. She has also taught at Emory University and Duke Kunshan University as a visiting professor. Dr. Prime's research focuses on China's economy and business environment, including China's foreign trade and investment, domestic market reforms, and provincial and local-level development.

**James R. Schiffman:** Dr. Schiffman is an Associate Professor in the Communication Department at Georgia College & State University in Milledgeville, Georgia. Previously, he served as Chief Copy Editor at CNN International, where he was involved in editorial decision making, network style, hiring, and training. Prior to joining CNN, Dr. Schiffman was a staff correspondent for The Wall Street Journal in Atlanta and The Asian Wall Street Journal in Hong Kong, Seoul, and Beijing. As a correspondent in Beijing between 1986 and 1988, Dr. Schiffman reported extensively on Chinese economic reforms, the role of foreign investment, and Chinese politics and culture at a time of rapid change and turmoil. Dr. Schiffman speaks Mandarin Chinese, and lectures occasionally to academic and community groups. He earned a Ph.D. in Communication at Georgia State University in May 2012 and is the editor of China Currents.